The Role of Finance in
the Transition to Socialism

The Role of Finance in the Transition to Socialism

Stephany Griffith—Jones

Allanheld, Osmun Publishers
Frances Pinter (Publishers) Ltd

In memory of my father, with whom I would
have so much enjoyed discussing this study.

To my mother, for her constant encouragement
and support in my work.

Published in Great Britain in 1981 by
Frances Pinter (Publishers) Limited
5 Dryden Street, London WC2E 9NW
ISBN 0 86187 201 0

Published in the United States of America in 1981
by Allanheld, Osmun & Co. Publishers Inc.
(A Division of Littlefield, Adams & Company)
81 Adams Drive, Totowa, New Jersey 07512
ISBN 0-86598-069-1

Library of Congress Cataloging in Publication Data

Griffith-Jones, Stephany.
    The role of finance in the transition to socialism.

    Includes bibliographical references.
    1. Finance--Communist countries--Case studies.
2. Finance--Soviet Union. 3. Finance--Czechoslovakia.
4. Finance--Chile. I. Title.
HG171.G74 1982   336'.09   81-12844
ISBN 0-86598-069-1   AACR2

81 82 83 84/ 10 9 8 7 6 5 4 3 2 1

Printed in the United States of America

CONTENTS

ACKNOWLEDGEMENTS

The need to study systematically the role of finance in the transition to socialism began to crystallize while I was working at the Central Bank of Chile during 1970-72. I am grateful to many of my colleagues there, and in the Ministries of Finance and Economics, with whom I discussed some of the issues treated in this study, although at the time our concern was not academic but geared towards policy-making and its economic and political implications. I am particularly grateful to Jaime Barrios, then General Manager of the Central Bank, with whom I had the opportunity of discussing the practical and theoretical issues which arose during decision-making on monetary and credit policy. These discussions - as well as our disagreements - sparked off my wish to study other historical experiences. The deep shock caused by Jaime's death in September, 1973, seemed initially to make such a study meaningless; after a short period however, it became even more important than before the coup to study these issues in relation both to the Chilean and other experiences.

I am particularly grateful to Professors Michael Ellman and Charles Feinstein, who gave such generous support to my work, offering both an in-depth discussion of the issues involved and useful suggestions about the structure of the study itself. They both surpassed by far their formal obligations as Supervisors; I am extremely grateful to them for this.

I am also grateful for very valuable comments to the following people, who offered them either after reading sections of my first draft or during discussions at seminars I gave in Cambridge, Oxford and at the Institute of Development Studies: Wladimir Brus, Ricardo Ffrench-Davis, Edgardo Floto, Carlos Fortin, Keith Griffin, Michael Kuzcinski, Roberto Pizarro, Robert Rowthorne, Osvaldo Sunkel and David Vines. Special thanks must go to Professor Jaroslav Krejci, who gave me such detailed comments on the draft of the chapter on Czechoslovakia, and to my friends, in particular Barbara Stallings and Gabriel Palma, for their encouragement of my work. I am also greatly indebted to Professors Valpy Fitzgerald and Alec Nove for their very valuable comments, as well as to Gordon White for his useful suggestions during the final revision. The final responsibility, as always, is mine alone.

My work on this study was financed by the British Council and the World University Service; I thank both institutions for their support. I am also grateful to the Institute of Development Studies at Sussex University, which allowed me limited but crucial time to finish this investigation.

I thank Ann Segrave for her help with polishing the English and copy-editing the final version. I thank Rosalind Woodhouse, Joy Goddard and Pat Tugwell for helping to type the final version.

S.G-J.

PREFACE

This is a work with important implications. Since the Second World War, in all parts of the world, the left-wing has struggled against the naivities of 'monetarism'. This has reinforced a deep-rooted preference for thinking in 'structural' rather than 'financial' terms. They could draw on a dictum of the Left Keynesians; what is physically possible is surely financially possible.

That attitude has in fact a fundamental rationale. But is has nonetheless in practice proved disastrous. It leads to an almost total neglect of finance. Has the manifesto of any left-wing party seeking power ever made specific references to the monetary policy it will pursue? Which socialist government on first gaining office has bothered much about the financial implications of its policy decisions?

A pattern is visible in the life history of socialist regimes. Grasping the levers of state power generates euphoria in the leadership. Now at last they can raise wages, subsidize food prices, launch housing schemes, increase social services, build schools and hospitals, etc., etc.

There is of course very good justification for such measures. Objectively, no doubt, they are all essential. Moreover, they are expected by the working classes and the left-wing intelligentsia that has helped the government to power. To refrain from carrying them out may cost important political support, especially in the trade unions. But a terrible price has to be paid. Typically the economic situation deteriorates rapidly, leading eventually to political crisis and often a reversal of the social gains.

As Stephany Griffith-Jones shows, it is precisely a socialist government, not a conservative one, that most needs deliberate and strict financial policy, especially on the budget and the rate of interest. This is not merely because monetary stability is required for controls to operate efficiently and for the price mechanism to work in the sectors which cannot be controlled, at least for some years. Inflation jeopardizes the balance of payments just at a time when opponents outside and inside the country may be trying to deprive it of foreign exchange, causing shortages of fuel, industrial inputs, food, etc., and further aggravating inflation. So what happens financially can be of immense physical significance, and make structural change difficult if not impossible.

Socialist governments are naturally much plotted against. There are always high-ranking officers and foreign government officials only too willing to engineer the downfall of a government of this hue, if need be by violence. They are to 'blame' for what happens, of course, but - and this is something that has to be faced - a socialist government which lets inflation gather force plays into their hands and sets itself up for a coup.

Those socialist governments which have survived, because of special circumstances, the traumas of birth and infantile irresponsibility, have grown up to be extremely careful about their financial health, guarding their foreign exchange reserves with scrupulous care and imposing financial balance not merely in their own accounts but throughout the range of public institutions. From financial irresponsibility - and partly because of its effects - they swing to the opposite extreme, a crude version of monetarism, accompanied sometimes by severe political repression.

The three case histories in this book illustrate this pattern in a way invaluable for socialists who are in office or who hope to gain power in the future - if they will only take heed.

The Soviet experience immediately after the revolution of 1917, seems surprisingly familiar. In the period known as 'War Communism', as Stephany shows, the inherited supply problems and price inflation were aggravated by a romantic desire to play down the importance of money or even abolish it. Only the exhaustion of the capitalist powers at the end of the war, plus the size and geographical remoteness of the Soviet Union, protected the revolutionary state from effective foreign intervention (such as toppled Bela Kun in Hungary shortly afterwards).

Yet although ideological inertia permitted persistence in policies that were clearly failing, they had to be abandoned eventually. After 1922 the direction was completely reversed. The New Economic Policy would in many respects have gratified the most doctrinaire staff member of the IMF. To balance the budget, taxes were increased; part of social expenditure was made the responsibility of state and local authorities; and government administrative staff were reduced by more than 50 per cent. The increase in the money supply was halted and a currency reform introduced gold backing. Wages were frozen, ensuring a sharp fall in their real value and the consequent strikes were repressed, often with violence; trade unions were brought under government control. Moreover, tax and price policies were manipulated to provide 'incentives' to peasants and traders. (This seemingly excessive generosity reflected a rather simplistic 'class analysis' emphasizing the need to gain the support of the peasantry and petit bourgeoisie). The rise in production was accelerated, inflation slowed down and foreign payments were brought back into balance. The regime survived - but, not surprisingly, the result of such a drastic stabilization policy was a rapid increase in inequality and unemployment. To repress the resistance that these generated was one of the 'objective' justifications for the Stalinist terror.

In Czechoslovakia after the Second World War, the government, at first a coalition, confronted the problems of post-war chaos with a very similar naivete, its leaders declaring that the job of financial policy was simply to mobilize money for whatever investment was physically possible. Among many gems of official wisdom quoted by the author, one stands out; in a planned economy a Czech socialist proclaimed; 'there can be no inflation unless the authorities wish it'!

While the government did adopt some measures to reduce excess demand, credits to the public sector grew rapidly. Price controls were partly ineffective and black markets flourished for many years after the war had ended. (This was in fact used by the Communist Party as a reason, not for better financial policy, but for further nationalization.) The consequent economic problems, together with a deterioration in relations between the socialist and capitalist blocs, contributed to the overthrow of the coalition by the Communists in 1948. There was a shift towards financial orthodoxy which was facilitated by Communist control of the trade unions, but it was accompanied by (and not unrelated to) increasing political repression, which became severe in the 1950s.

In parts of the world further from the reach of the Red Army, socialist governments cannot be saved from the consequences of financial irresponsibility; on the contrary, internal and external enemies can combine to exploit these with every prospect of success. A prime example is the third case study in the book, the Allende administration in Chile. As the author (herself an official in that regime) recognizes, it is difficult to criticize that administration without seeming to exonerate the power-hungry generals, who overthrew it with US support. However, analyzing its mistakes may - on top of the Soviet and Czech experiences - help others to avoid repeating them.

The author points to many simplistic errors made by government economists in the analysis of Chile's problems. Since they found spare capacity in 1970 in both labour and capital, Ministers believed in, indeed promised, an acceleration in economic growth. Moreover since inflation was due to structural problems, the structural reforms they planned would be accompanied by a slowing down in price inflation.

However, there were considerable organizational problems about actually mobilizing the surplus capacity and carrying out the reforms. Moreover, the fiscal deficit climbed rapidly. Revenue was falling short of what was needed (partly because of insufficient government strength in Congress to legislate higher taxes, partly due to the fall in the price of copper). Yet the government was unable to curb expenditure, and public sector wages showed very big increases. (In Chile the trade unions could not be so easily converted into state instruments as in the Soviet Union and Czechoslovakia.) Since prices were controlled, the results were enormous deficits in the (growing) group of public corporations. Interest rates were held down to negative levels in real terms.

The consequent rapid acceleration in price inflation to more than 500 per cent a year aggravated the outflow of private capital and created black markets, especially in foreign currencies. Not merely was the government unable to control demand, it did not have the power to introduce rationing either, except on an informal basis. In its last months, industrial production declined because of a shortage of raw materials and spare parts and because of big strikes, stimulated by the opposition. Housewives faced growing shortages, queues, etc., and many joined public demonstrations of protest.

The stage was set in 1973 for a reversal of policy here too - but accompanied in this case by a counter-revolution. The geographical position of Chile, and the major investments there by US copper companies, made it much more vulnerable. Moreover, the government coalition, 'Popular Unity', was really somewhat misnamed - its popular base was never secure, and it consisted of a group of competing parties each with their own trade union base and their own formula for socialism, blaming the others for 'reactionary' tendencies.

Here too the pendulum has swung right back, with 'monetarist' policies imposed by the junta and opposition to them brutally repressed - in this case under a 'Right-wing' banner.

There have been in fact several experiences in other parts of the world which confirm the lessons that follow directly from Stephany's analysis. In Cuba post-revolutionary euphoria led in the 1960s to a contempt for financial policies and accountancy, indeed even for money itself, more profound even than in the Soviet Union in 1917-20. Massive Soviet aid prevented the collapse of the regime, but in 1970 social troubles of a seriousness which we cannot judge from outside forced a complete reversal of policy. The regime was able to carry this through itself, and there is now here too a new insistence on monetary incentives, balanced books, limits to supply of money etc. A degree of unemployment has appeared - and political controls have been tightened up.

In Portugal, after the quasi-revolution of 1974, successive governments repeated the same pattern. Government expenditure increased rapidly and although the economic consequences were cushioned at first by a big stock of gold, the severe external disequilibrium forced in due course the adoption of restrictive financial policies and recourse to the IMF. The political pendulum swung gradually further to the Right, with predictable consequences so far as social policy and unemployment are concerned.

Michael Manley's government in Jamaica also let the financial situation get out of hand, partly because one of the two trade union organizations is controlled by the then opposition. Simultaneously, pro-Cuban rhetoric and measures against the bauxite companies led to a net flight of capital. The withdrawal of IMF support was hardly a surprise, and the deteriorating economic situation and increasing violence set the stage for an election which swept the government out of office and brought about a complete reversal of policy.

Mildly socialist governments seem to show mild tendencies to financial irresponsibility with correspondingly less drastic consequences. Is it far-fetched to see certain parallels even in recent British history? The Labour government of 1974-79 could hardly be called socialist but it attempted to shield the working class from the consequences of the post-colonial economic decline, at the cost of budgetary discipline. Policy was already starting to swing in its closing years; the Chancellor, Dennis Healey, obtained from the IMF both financial and political support, but wages policy collapsed and here too the government was replaced by one dedicated to financial respectability, at the cost of rapidly rising unemployment, and civil liberties are under somewhat greater pressure. Yet the Labour Party still seems unable to draw up a credible incomes policy, let alone a financial strategy, particularly important in a country so much part of the transnational capitalist economy.

How many more political disasters, one wonders, over how many decades have to take place before the Left draws the lessons in this book? In the first place, commitments to wage increases, heavy investment in social infrastructure, etc., help a party gain power, but they greatly complicate its life once it has succeeded. The experience documented here shows that big gains of this kind cannot be made in the early years of socialist governments. These only take power at a time of national crisis, which leaves a legacy of financial disequilibrium. The civil service, inherited from the earlier regime, is unlikely to be willing, or even able, to implement far-reaching reforms. The structural changes that are attempted, such as land reforms and nationalization, cause - in the first instance at least - disorganization and declines in output. Capitalists, especially the transnational corporations, cut investment and export capital.

A Left-wing political leader hoping to achieve power ought to ensure, especially after the experience of Chile, Jamaica, etc., that a proper financial policy is worked out in advance to cover this period of dis-organization. Honesty, indeed mere prudence, also requires that even while in opposition socialist leaders should tell the public of the problems that can be expected. This might jeopardize the chance of victory, but we can now see that the victory may well otherwise prove hollow and short lived.

The theorists and ideologues of the Left could also well turn from grand models of the world system and spare some attention for the following question: what financial guidelines would meet the needs of socialist governments, especially in countries dependent on import oil and exporting primary products that are subject to wild price fluctuations and harvest vicissitudes? When there are no agreed rules, all the finance minister in a Left-wing government can do is to nag his colleagues not to spend quite so much - or go to the other extreme and become plus Friedmanite que Milton!

Financial guidelines are even more urgently needed now that the chronic foreign exchange surplus of oil-exporting countries is reflected in a chronic deficit in the rest of the world, a situation that can be expected to continue, on and off, for at least a decade (until alternative cheap sources of energy have been developed on a very large scale). Any socialist government taking office will almost certainly inherit a state of near-bankruptcy with low liquid external assets, heavy debts, and a trade deficit.

Sooner or later such governments seek help. The Soviet Union has barely enough capacity to support a handful of clients (Cuba, Ethiopia, Afghanistan, South Vietnam etc.) There are of course many sources in the capitalist world - private and governmental - but rarely will any of them provide much capital until the International Monetary Fund has approved the financial policy.

Left-wing governments make just criticisms of the Fund's political bias, in insisting on the dismantling of controls (except of course controls of wages), which is not required by its Charter. But these complaints are somewhat naive. What can one expect from an institution controlled by the major capitalist governments, which gain from other economies being 'open'? There is no secret about this control; they have the big majority of the voting power in its directorate.

In any case, the need for a strict financial policy does not arise, fundamentally, because of the prejudices of the IMF (useful though this may be as a whipping boy), nor even because of the strength of the capitalist powers. It arises out of the objective situation, especially the inconsistency between the aspirations of a socialist government's supporters, which will have been stimulated by 'consciousness raising', and the inevitable drop in living standards, at least in the short run, for the reasons outlined in this book. This is one of the typical internal contradictions in a new socialist state, and leads to the usual accelerating inflation, dwindling foreign exchange reserves, difficulties in financing essential imports, etc. etc. Indeed much of what the Fund imposes in 'conditionality' governments would have to carry out anyway, even if it did not exist. To my knowledge Finance ministers, including socialists, who are at the end of their tether, and more so their officials, often secretly welcome powerful outside pressure on their cabinet colleagues to behave at least in ways more consistent with financial equilibrium.

Every Left-wing leader should buy this book and distribute it to those who may become Ministers. If it is widely circulated, the 1980s could prove a less disastrous decade for the Left.

Dudley Seers
February 13, 1981

Institute of Development Studies
University of Sussex

1 Introduction

'To transform victory into power, and power into construction of socialism'.

Mapu slogan,   Chile, 1971

The subject of this work is the study and evaluation of financial policy during the _preliminary_ transition to socialism. Surprisingly, very little analysis of this issue has been carried out, even though it is of great importance.

The crucial significance of the problem struck me while working at the Central Bank of Chile, during the Allende Government; at times the issue of money was so enormous that the printing presses could not keep up with it! Two questions seemed to demand an answer. Did the monetary and financial policies pursued at this stage contribute to the achievement of Popular Unity's political and economic goals? If not, were alternative short-term and financial policies, more conducive to the achievement of the Government's goals, feasible? This study attempts to answer such questions for Chile's frustrated transition to socialism and for two other countries with successful passages to socialism. It is hoped that the description and analysis herein may be of some use in future experiences of preliminary transition to socialism.

In this study, I do not deal with the whole period of transition to socialism, but only with its initial stage. During this crucial first period, there is intense political struggle for control of the State; the main aim of the revolutionary forces is to consolidate their power. In one of his earlier works, Bettleheim[1] characterises with precision this initial or preliminary stage of the transition as:

> the period of initial instability, of the period preceding what Marx calls the social stability of the mode of production. The initial stage is that in which the fate of the new social formation has not yet been sealed, or in which this fate is still uncertain.

Preobrazhensky[2] characterises this period in the Soviet case as one in which the main tasks of the economy and the State were 'to hold out, to feed the people somehow, and to conquer'. In a completely different context – an attempt at a parliamentary transition to socialism in Chile – the aim of this first stage was described by one of the Popular Unity parties as 'to transform victory into power'.

It is difficult to establish the general characteristics of this initial stage of transition to socialism for different historical experiences; as for example Bettleheim[3] has pointed out:

> the stages of transition of each economy can be qualitatively different from the apparently analogous stages passed through by countries which have preceded it on the same road.

This is not merely for reasons internal to each country, such as its level of development and its class structure, but also because of transformations in the international economic system and the particular country's links with it. Several features can be seen, however, to characterise the experience of preliminary transition, particularly in those countries which will be examined in detail below. The first is that the period is dominated by acute struggle for political power, whether this struggle is armed or parliamentary. A second characteristic is that the revolutionary forces make use of that part of the state power which they have gained to carry out structural economic transformations, i.e. nationalisation of the means of production; this is perceived as essential, both for increasing further the

power of the revolutionary forces and laying the base for socialist planning
and management. A third characteristic of this period are the particular
difficulties inherent in economic management. Socialist planning is still
inevitably weak and fragmented. In the Marxist tradition, this is often
described by drawing a distinction between 'nationalisation' (a juridical or
a political act which can be carried out rapidly) and 'socialisation' (which
requires the state to develop the capacity to account for and allocate
effectively the means of productions and their products); this latter
capacity requires not only nationalisation but also a period of historical
experience. At the same time, many of the links between units of production
characteristic of capitalist production are being destroyed, often at a
faster rate than they are replaced by effective planning[4]. We shall
return to these problems later.

A fourth characteristic of this pre-transition stage is that relatively
little net capital accumulation is being carried out. A great deal of
resources are absorbed by the struggle for power, especially if it is an
armed one. The emphasis in the State's economic management is mainly on
dealing with pressing short-term problems, and not on laying the base for
future socialist growth. Accumulation by the private sector is necessarily
very small, given the uncertainty surrounding both the current political
situation and the possibility of achieving socialism.   Preobrazhensky[5]
explains clearly the need to postpone the accumulation effort during this
stage in the Soviet case:

> We do not know what will be the cost of the conquest
> of power by the proletariat in other countries, but in
> our   country   this   conquest   cost   so   dear   that
> accumulation on a production basis could not begin at
> once... The period of War Communism confronted the
> State   not   with   the   problem   of   accumulation   and
> expanded reproduction under conditions of a new system
> of property, but with the task of military victory, on
> the one hand, and on the other, the task of feeding
> that commune of poor people, fighting against the
> whole capitalist world.

As in the Soviet experience, in most other cases of power struggle for
establishing socialism, the main effort is centred on using existing spare
capacity or reconstructing that which has recently been destroyed.   A
substantive effort of net capital accumulation will almost inevitably follow
- and not be simultaneous with - this initial stage. For this reason, I
shall not lay much stress here on the important issue of socialist capital
accumulation, although I shall look at some aspects of the debates about
this topic - such as the transfer of surplus to the State - which have
relevance for the preliminary transition.

In this study, I concentrate on the period I call the 'preliminary
transition' or 'pre-transition' and that Soviet historians[6] name 'the
period of social revolution' (distinguishing it from the next stage which
they call socialist industrialization). I do not deal here with this period
of socialist accumulation, or with either the stable functioning of a state
socialist economy, or less that nebulous final outcome of socialism,
Communism.

As this study deals with a period which attempts to establish the pre-
conditions for socialism, it seems essential to define, albeit extremely
briefly, its meaning.

A country will be considered as socialist, or state socialist, if it has
state ownership of the main means of production and distribution, a planning
system which is the main regulator of the economy, and a state controlled by

a party or parties espousing Marxist ideology. There is a vast and important debate on the definition of socialism, to which I shall not refer as it is beyond the scope of this work; I shall only, in the concluding chapter, attempt to extract some implications from the study of the preliminary transition for future progress towards socialism. It seems important to stress that even though I concentrate here on the design of economic policies which contribute to socialism, this does not imply that I believe that existent socialist or state socialist countries necessarily belong to a "more advanced mode of production" than the capitalist one in every aspect; in particular, it seems essential to point out the critical problems of the political systems in state socialist countries, given the authoritarian character of the decision-making process in them[7].

In much of the Marxist literature, the role of money and finance in both the preliminary and the long-term transition to socialism is either underestimated or discussed at a very abstract level. As will be seen later, an important part of the discussions have - in different periods and countries - focussed on debates between supporters of the 'liquidationist tradition'[8] and those who grudgingly defend or accept the role of money at least in the first stages of the transition to socialism. The abstract nature of the debate seems to have implied that the concrete issues of how to use monetary and specific financial policies to achieve the goals of that particular stage were hardly tackled. (Some of Preobrazhensky's contributions are quite an important exception.) Furthermore, the emphasis on the need to abolish money as a socialist target - either in the near or the distant future - has often adversely influenced policy-making, particularly in the preliminary transition. The ideological preference for a particular mechanism, i.e. the desire to reduce the role of money rapidly, has contributed in many cases to the adoption of measures incompatible with the main political and economic targets. This is discussed in some detail in the case studies outlined in Chapters 3 to 6.

The argument presented here - that discussions on the role of money and finance within the framework of Marxist economics have to some extent obscured the real issues faced by countries beginning the transition to socialism - has important parallels with similar views on the negative influence of Marxist economics in defining a proper role for prices in the socialist economies sustained by Nove[9] and on the inadequate nature of Marxist-Leninist theory for interpreting the problems of socialist planning sustained by Ellman[10].

Marx and Engels themselves deliberately refrained from conjecture about a future socialist society or from drawing up concrete proposals for the building of socialism. Their references to the subject are very fragmentary, appearing either in the course of analysing capitalism or expounded in argument[11].

It was Marx's and Engels' followers who began to design programmes of action, often by simplifying and vulgarising Marxist theory so as to adapt it to the needs of party propaganda. Towards the end of the last century, the possibilities of a socialist revolution seemed to have been lost in a distant future. This led to the ossification of details about a future Utopian society into party dogma. The German Social Democrats included as axioms in their 1891 programme that a socialist economy excludes market relations and that the corresponding reduction in the role of money and finance are indispensable features of the transition to socialism[12]. These views influenced not only early Bolshevik thinking but also socialist thinking in other countries for many decades. Marxist movements in capitalist countries, preoccupied with their daily struggle, had little time to think about the socialism of the future. When they did, they tended to accept a view of socialism diametrically opposed to the capitalist system; opposition to capitalism was extended to opposition to mercantile and monetary relations.

In the next chapter (in sections 2.IV and 2.V), the Bolsheviks' debates on the role of commodities and money in the transition to socialism and its influence on their economic policies during the period of War Communism are examined in some detail. I shall refer here, however, to the most complete and influential work representing the 'liquidationist' tendency written during that period, Bukharin's <u>The Economics of the Transition Period</u>[13]. In this work, the necessary 'naturalisation' of economic relations during the transition to socialism follows from the interpretation of commodity and money relations as categories of capitalist economy alone. In the main chapter of this work, Bukharin[14] argues that in the transition period, the postulate of equilibrium is invalid because the system is unable to arrive at equilibrium; as a consequence the collapse of the money system can be expected.

> Money represents that real social tie, those knots, in which the entire developed commodity system of production is entangled. It is conceivable that in the transition period, in the process of the annihilation of the commodity system as such, a process of 'self-negation' of money occurs. It is expressed first in so-called 'money devaluation', second, in the fact that the distribution of money symbols becomes dependent on the distribution of products, and vice versa. Money ceases to be a universal equivalent and becomes a conventional - and thereby highly important - symbol of the circulation of products.

Bukharin clearly attaches a negative ideological connotation to the surviving commodity relations; thus, he perceives[15] 'the struggle against or for the commodity market as a hidden struggle around the models of production' (capitalism vs communism).

It should be noted, however, that even Bukharin in some passages hints that the functions of money are being abolished, not only because this is ideologically desirable, but also because of the dramatic shortage of goods, which inevitably implies a fall in the demand for money[16].

A good example of a 'liquidationist' view in the Third World which influenced policy-making in the preliminary transition during the Cuban experience can be found in the writings of Ernesto Guevara, who directed the Cuban Central Bank after the 1969 Revolution, as well as occupying other key economic posts in Cuba. In one of his most important articles, 'On the Budgetary System of Financing'[17], first published in 1964, Guevara wrote:

> The characteristics of the period of transition are those of a society which is eliminating its old ties in order to rapidly enter a new era. The tendency should be, in our opinion, to eliminate the old categories as vigorously as possible. These include the market, money and consequently the motive force of material incentives, or rather, the conditions which bring the categories into being.

Two main lines of explanation have been presented by Marxist thinkers to justify the survival of money and commodity relations, particularly in the initial stages of the transition to socialism. The first was pioneered by Preobrazhensky[18] and further developed by Stalin[19]; it attributed the

survival of commodity and money relations in the Soviet Union to the
co-existence of State property with other forms of property, such as private
producers and collective farms.   According to this explanation, money
relations would wither away as the importance of the state sector grew.

There is a second line of thinking which considers this explanation as
partially correct, but inadequate. It stresses that even today in the state
socialist countries there cannot be 'effective social direction' by the
planning authorities over nationalised means of production.   This view has
been developed by many authors[20]; this point is rather clearly brought out
for example in some of Bettleheim's earlier writings[21].   Bettleheim
stresses that given the limits of effective planning, it is necessary to
allow for relatively autonomous economic units within the state sectors
which will have relative freedom of manoeuvre and can take economic
decisions.   Furthermore, the relative autonomy of these units will require
these units to have[22] 'powers of disposal and rights of usage, powers to
alienate and acquire,' Bettleheim concludes that:

> If this analysis is accepted, then one is led to
> consider likewise that money plays within the state
> sector of the socialist economy, not merely the role
> of a unit of account but also a real economic role.
> And this role is, to make it possible, to a certain
> extent, for the different economic subjects to get rid
> of their products, or to provide themselves with
> products, on the basis of their own initiatives...
>
> In the socialist economy of today, money thus plays
> not merely an accounting role but also a real one.
> There are, for this reason, in the planned economies
> of today, side by side, a material plan and a
> financial plan.

Bettleheim[23] deduces further implications from the fact that even in the
most advanced socialist countries it is still impossible to 'carry out an
effective allotment of the means of production, or of products in general,
in advance, and that there is need for socialist trade and state commercial
organisations.' He accepts that the disappearance of commodity and money
relations when the 'objective conditions' for it are not yet given can lead
to inefficiency and 'the squandering of resources'; in such a case, it would
also have the contrary effect to that desired ideologically because: 'while
giving oneself the illusion of planning 'more closely' one would be merely
planning less well;' similarly, the attempt to 'deny' money and prices,
would 'lead to the opposite of the desired aim - notably to the development
of a black market.'

Bettleheim thus makes important points against the 'liquidationist'
tradition; as we shall see, the grounds he gives for continuing to use money
relations during the transition to socialism are particularly relevant
during the initial stage which we study here.   Furthermore, he perceives
correctly the danger and costs of eliminating monetary relations, when the
'objective conditions' are not yet ripe.   His analysis on this subject
however presents two serious problems.   Firstly, Bettleheim accepts the
survival of money and commodity categories during the transition rather
grudgingly, particularly in his later works on the subject[24]; he hopes for
a quick disappearance of these relations 'in the fairly near future'[25],
due mainly to political conditions such as 'effective participation of the
masses in the formulation and operationalising of plans' achieved 'through a
process of struggle'.   In his extremely abstract and rather naive
discussions on the subject, Bettleheim repeats - in relation to mature
socialist economies - many of the arguments which he correctly criticised in
the 'liquidationists' analysis of early socialism.   This aspect of

Bettleheim's work, however, is outside the scope of this study[26].
Secondly, even though Bettleheim repeatedly states the need to study
concretely the use of monetary relations in different stages of socialism,
he explicitly recognises that this goes beyond his task.   There is on the
whole relatively little analysis in his work of specific financial policies
(i.e. prices, monetary, taxation) – a serious limitation for policy-makers
actually involved in the process of transition in a specific country.

Some of Preobrazhensky's contributions differ fundamentally from those of
writers like Bettleheim, who have concentrated on rather abstract
discussions about whether to use monetary and financial relations in the
transition.   In his major work, The New Economics, (op.cit.) Preobrazhensky
evaluates the contribution of specific financial policies to the achievement
of what he perceives as the crucial aim in the period he studies: an
increase in primitive socialist accumulation.

Although I deal here with a previous period (the preliminary transition),
which poses rather different economic problems, some of Preobrazhensky's
analysis, as well as his more concrete approach, is of relevance here.
Preobrazhensky discusses in detail the use of financial and economic levers
to increase the surplus transferred from non-socialist forms to the
socialist state, and to minimise the inverse flow; drawing a parallel with
the capitalist state, he stresses that the task of the socialist state
consists not 'in taking from petit-bourgeois producers less than capitalism
took, but in taking more'. Amongst the financial mechanisms he discusses to
achieve this aim are taxation, price policy and money issue.   Amongst the
main methods of primitive socialist accumulation, Preobrazhensky[27]
attributes 'a very great, a directly decisive role in peasant countries such
as the Soviet Union to... taxation of non-socialist forms'.   Secondly, he
stresses the importance of the role of money issue as a 'source of state
revenue, which more correctly should be grouped with taxes, but is
externally and formally not as a rule so grouped in theoretical economic
writing'[28].   However, Preobrazhensky does not discuss the important fact
that money issue as a source of taxation has a declining yield to the state.
Thirdly, Preobrazhensky emphasizes the importance of pricing policy 'not
only for socialist accumulation, but also for the normal course of
production, even in its unexpanded state'. He defines as not only desirable
and possible, but as[29] 'also inevitable under our conditions a price
policy consciously calculated so as to alienate a certain part of the
surplus product of private economy in all its forms'[30].   He correctly
stresses that state ownership of large scale industry increases enormously
the potential for using price policy as another form of taxation of private
economy.   Emphasis is placed on the advantages of an appropriate price
policy over other forms of taxation; the most important advantage perceived
in the Soviet case was extreme facility of collection, which implies no
cost.   In other contexts, such as the parliamentary experiences of
transition examined below, price policy in State enterprises offers an
additional advantage over other forms of taxation: it does not require
legislative approval. Preobrazhensky only mentions but does not discuss the
possible political difficulties of the price policy he suggests; he
discusses equivalent exchange with the peasants as utopian and says that the
negative effects of higher prices on the working class can be compensated by
higher wages.   As will be seen, these political aspects rather briefly
dismissed by Preobrazhensky were of great importance both in the Soviet and
other cases.

There are several reasons why an appropriate financial policy is
particularly important during the preliminary transition to socialism. Some
of them can be deduced from the discussion in the Marxist literature on the
role of money in the general transition to socialism, outlined above.
Others spring from the specific characteristics of the pre-transition to
socialism.

Particularly during the preliminary transition, important sections of the economy are not nationalised. Links both within the non-state sector, and between it and the state sector will be mainly based on market relations. This will require a financial policy that will allow those market links to function effectively; a minimum of stability will be required so that money performs its role as unit of exchange adequately. Furthermore, within the state sector itself effective physical planning of production and distribution is necessarily still very weak and fragmented during this initial stage[31]. It is therefore essential to use the mechanisms inherited from the capitalist system, i.e. market links, to help perform many of the functions of production and distribution within the state sector. This implies the need for money as a relatively stable unit of exchange also within the state sector.

A second factor to be considered is that the value of money has to remain relatively stable so that an effective system of planning and control can begin to operate. If inflation is too high, money becomes unsuitable as a unit of account; financial planning and control of the growing state sector becomes practially meaningless. A minimum of financial stability is even more essential during the pre-transition, when effective planning is carried out mainly in monetary terms[32]. Furthermore, the problems and disruptions resulting from large financial disequilibria would distract planners from essential tasks, such as the development of an effective planning apparatus.

There is a third function which financial policy must help undertake during this phase. The political leadership should make explicit choices on the distribution of resources between different social groups and economic sectors, given the contry's existing constraints. The role to be played by financial policy will be particularly crucial while there is no effective physical planning and resource allocation and while the power struggle has not been resolved; as a result, strong pressures towards higher consumption by different social groups or classes will often be accompanied by the wish or need to increase expenditure in certain sectors; i.e. defence. The projection of financial disequilibria - both internal and external - could show the political leadership the need to make urgent choices. If such choices are not made in time, the country begins to live 'above its means'. The resulting high levels of inflation and decline in foreign exchange reserves would threaten any government attempting the already difficult tasks of the pre-transition, in the face of both internal and external opposition.

Yet another important function of financial policy in countries attempting to begin a transition to socialism is to preserve or accumulate a prudent level of foreign exchange reserves, permitting a much larger degree of autonomy from foreign pressures. Such countries should expect antagonism to their project from capitalist governments and financial institutions, which may lead to the curtailment of foreign credits and aid. Furthermore, the country may face large private capital outflows, and financial flows from socialist contries may be insufficient to offset the net loss of external flows. A high level of foreign exchange reserves will act as a protective cushion against probable net capital outflows (or reduction in net capital inflows) as well as for unexpected changes in the international environment, such as a deterioration in the country's terms of trade. If a country attempting to initiate a transition to socialism exhausts its foreign exchange reserves, it will face a particularly difficult situation. It will be extremely difficult to obtain additional external finance from private banks or international financial institutions; to obtain finance from such sources - at a time when a country's bargaining position is weak - it will probably have to accept conditions incompatible with its socialist aims.

Financial policies have another important role to play in the pre-transition: to strengthen the state sector, both absolutely and

relatively to the private sector[33].   As Preobrazhensky pointed out,
financial policies in areas such as taxation and pricing of state
enterprises can play a crucial role here.

The criteria which will be applied here to evaluate the 'correctness' of
general and specific financial policies during the preliminary transition
phase will include their contribution - or otherwise - to the achievement of
the political strategy pursued by the revolutionary forces.   Given the
intensity of the power struggle and the difficulties facing economic
management during the preliminary transition, the need to define such
'correct' policies is particularly great.

These criteria differ radically from those governing an orthodox evaluation
of economic policies, i.e. achievement of growth or inflation level targets.
They also differ from a purely ideological evaluation of the economic
policies or mechanisms chosen, so common in Marxist literature, i.e. were
the market and monetary relations abandoned with too much or too little
speed.

The need to define financial policies conducive to political goals implies
that such policies are oriented to avoiding serious financial disequilibria,
that would lead to hyper-inflation and/or depletion of foreign exchange
reserves.   As discussed above (and illustrated below for the case studies),
hyper-inflation and depletion of foreign exchange reserves, which threaten
the viability of any economy or political regime, are particularly damaging
during the preliminary transition to socialism.

The link between short-term and financial policies with political targets
requires an understanding of the general political and economic situation
within which each concrete preliminary transition develops.   This necessary
but complex task is made more difficult because of the 'under-development'
of economic and political inter-disciplinary analysis, particularly crucial
for periods of rapid change in society[34].

In each case, it is necessary to analyse the power of the revolutionary
nucleus (mainly the revolutionary party or parties) over the state and
society, as well as the role of the state in the economy.   The potential
opposition to the revolutionary forces also needs to be examined; given both
their general importance, and their particular significance in the cases
studied, the role of the armed forces and police, the 'middle groups' and
the international context will be mainly stressed here.   Within this
context, the particular 'road to Socialism' chosen can be better understood
and analysed.

It is also necessary to examine for each case whether there is a viable
alternative in the short-term to the market, both politically and
technically.   As mentioned above, market relations are particularly
necessary at this stage to link the state and private sectors; severe
disruption or elimination of the market would inevitably alienate the small
producers, as their economic activity is so closely linked to the market;
furthermore, market links play a particularly crucial role - even within the
state sector - while there is no effective alternative mechanism for
production and distribution.   This latter point as particularly relevant for
Chile under Allende, when there was practically no effective planning, and
very little concrete idea of how it should be carried out.

Also on the economic front, the problem of food supply is of strategic
significance; for this reason its implications for inflation and Balance of
Payments will be examined in more detail both later in this Introduction and
in the case studies.   The significance of agriculture will be naturally

greater in the poorest countries, where a larger proportion of consumption goes on foodstuffs and a larger proportion of employment is in the countryside. In this respect, there is a sharp difference between, for example, the USSR and Chile; in the USSR in 1922, agriculture employed 74 per cent of the active population, whereas in Chile in 1970 this figure was only 12.4 per cent.

A similar methodology will be followed for each of the case studies. I shall first examine the political and economic framework, including an understanding of the main political and economic aims of the revolutionary forces. I shall describe in some detail the causes of financial and monetary disequilibria, as well as the main factors underlying them. I shall then describe the financial and monetary policies pursued, as well as their effects. This will be followed by an evaluation of the policies pursued. The criteria for evaluation in each of the case studies will be whether, given the existing conditions and constraints, the revolutionary forces had a coherent strategy for using financial policies to further their political and economic aims.

The cases studies will be the Soviet Union during the period 1917-25 (Chapters 2 and 3), Czechoslovakia, 1945-48 (Chapter 4) and Chile, 1971-73 (Chapter 5). The conclusions from the case studies can be found in Chapter 6. The Soviet chapters rely on material available in English. The Czechoslovak chapter relies largely on Czech sources (as the literature in English on economic and financial matters during this period is very scarce); this was possible due to my knowledge of the language. The Chilean chapter relies basically on Chilean primary sources, using also some material gathered when I was working in the Central Bank of Chile. Naturally, I have used the understanding gained from my experience and involvement during the Allende Government, both as citizen and Government official.

Although I shall return to these subjects in later chapters, it seems useful to pinpoint some of the fundamental political differences between the experiences studied. The Soviet revolution had particular characteristics because it was the first country to become socialist; it helped overthrow a declining autocratic regime by means of a violent revolution, at a time when the country was deeply affected by its involvement in the First World War. The triumphant revolutionary party (the Bolsheviks) relied mainly on the use of force to sustain power.

Of crucial importance for the survival and triumph of the Bolshevik Revolution was the Red Army, which successfully defeated armed internal and external opposition. The Secret police also played an increasingly repressive role during this period. Force was used against particular social groups; thus, the requisitions of grain from the peasants during the Civil War were often accompanied by force. As shall be seen, this changed after 1921 when the emphasis was on conciliating the peasantry.

The Bolsheviks rapidly emerged as the sole party in control of the state apparatus and with a dominant influence on society. By 1918, the activities of all other parties were seriously restricted; by 1921, they had in practice been banned. In fact by 1921, as Lenin himself recognized, the party and the state apparatus had become fused into one. The Bolshevik Revolution not only implied a clean break with the Tsarist regime; it also led to complete control of the state apparatus by the Bolsheviks.

The Bolshevik party increasingly conditioned or determined the activities of other organizations within society. Trade unions, cooperatives, youth organizations, the press, became one way 'transmission belts' for Party

directives.   Political activity in the broader sense, which was genuinely
autonomous of the Bolshevik Party, decreased.

During the period studied here, the Bolshevik Revolution faced an extremely
unfavourable international situation.   Many countries were its enemies,
willing initially even to send troops to help overthrow the Revolution; no
country was its ally.

As shall be seen in detail in Chapters 2 and 3, during the 1917-25 period
economic   and   financial   policies   changed   dramatically;   however,   they
corresponded broadly to the changing political aims and constraints of the
Bolsheviks in each period.

In Czechoslovakia, the struggle for power occurred as the country emerged
after the Second World War.   Although it had an important pre-war democratic
tradition, its political structures had been partly disrupted by the Nazi
occupation.   After the War, a National Front coalition government was formed
which involved all legally recognized parties and which had complete control
over   all   the   state   apparatus;   this   coincided   with   the   banning   of
collaborationist parties and the expulsion of collaborationist elements from
the Government, Army and the police.   Thus, the forces most strongly opposed
to socialism were neutralized thanks to specific historical cicumstances.

The Communist Party emerged victorious from democratic elections though not
with an overall majority.   There was also extensive electoral support for
the Socialist party, important sectors within which supported Communist
policies.

As shall be seen in Chapter 4, the Communist strategy varied during this
period, but stressed the non-violent and constitutional nature of the
process (in this sense if differed sharply from the Soviet experience); the
Communist Party, however, emphasized the significance of institutional
changes which favoured it (most crucially within the armed forces and
police).   Since 1945, the main task defined and successfully carried out by
the Communist Party was to control political and state institutions.   By
contrast,   economic   questions   such   as   nationalisation   were   considered
secondary.

At the Communist Party's insistence, very close links - both technical and
ideological - were established after 1945 between the Czechoslovak and
Soviet Army.   These measures reduced even further the danger of a right-wing
coup, as well as making more explicit Czechoslovakia's place within the
Soviet sphere of influence.   As shall be seen in Chapter 4, this had a
determining influence on the final outcome of the power struggle in
February, 1948.

Internal political factors and their use by the Communist Party also played
an important role.   As well as exerting control over the armed forces and
police, the Communist party achieved a dominant influence over the radio.
Widespread   support   for   the   Communist   Party   amongst   the   workers   was
channelled through tightly organized and centralized mass organizations, the
main one being the trade unions.   This was accompanied by the increasing
inability of the right-wing parties to counter the Communists' initiatives,
particularly at a mass level.

As the Communists stressed, the power struggle between 1945 and 1948 was
carried out within the framework of the 1920 Constitution[35].   Within the
existing national and international context, the forces supporting state
socialism were in a strong position, and the Communists' effective use of
institutional changes within the existing framework helped their cause.   As
shall be seen below, economic policy played a secondary, but very important
role in their struggle for power.   In particular, financial policies were

very effectively used to achieve political targets.

The Chilean Popular Unity experience emerged in a country with a strong democratic tradition, particularly within Latin America, at a time when there were no major disruptions or conflicts in the country. The previous government to that of Allende was a fairly progressive reformist one. As will be discussed in more detail in Chapter 5, Popular Unity consisted of a coalition of several parties, with important tactical and even strategic differences amongst them; as a result, there was no clear political direction. In contrast to the two previous cases, Popular Unity controlled only part of the state apparatus, the Executive, which it had won through elections; it was in minority in Congress.

In spite of internal differences, Popular Unity – and the President himself – were basically committed to a democratic road to socialism[36].

Furthermore, the strategy de facto chosen by Popular Unity (see Chapter 5) was based on using the existing institutional framework to achieve economic as well as ideological changes; it was believed this would later allow institutional changes in the political sphere. As in Czechoslovakia, a non-violent and constitutional road was chosen; however, much less emphasis was placed by the revolutionary forces in Chile on institutional changes, i.e. within the Army, plebiscite to change Congress. As a result, Popular Unity not only had much less initial political hegemony over the state and society than the socialist forces in Czechoslovakia, but this did not increase significantly during the process.

Given the path chosen, Popular Unity's ability to sustain or increase its power within the state and society was constrained by several important elements[37]. As later developments showed, the most crucial one was ensuring that the armed forces maintained their constitutional tradition, and did not interfere in the political process. In contrast to the other two cases studied, the Left had much less room to manoeuvre in this area. A particularly serious problem was the influence of the anti-socialist ideology of 'national security' in which the armed forces were trained, largely under American influence. However, most Chilean analysts today agree that one of the fundamental weaknesses of Popular Unity strategy was its lack of a coherent policy towards the armed forces. The problem of obtaining the support – or at least the neutrality – of the 'middle groups' implied further difficulties, discussed in Chapter 5. However, it is essential to stress here the negative effect which large-scale disruptions of the market and severe financial disequilibria had on the political attitude of these groups towards the government. Popular Unity's limited control of the state apparatus (particularly in Congress) allowed the Opposition parties to obstruct the Government's actions. (This differs from the Czechoslovak case where all legal parties participated in the National Front Government.) Last but not least, the international context was on the whole unfavourable to Popular Unity. Chile was clearly within the American sphere of influence, with an economy partly dependent on the US. As a consequence, the United States' opposition to the Allende regime had many harmful effects, particularly economic (see Chapter 5 and abundant bibliography on this). Support for Popular Unity from the Socialist bloc was significant but limited, both economically and politically. Again here, a crucial difference from the Czechoslovak experience emerges.

Finally, institutions outside the state (such as trade unions, communal organizations, the press) were autonomous from the government and the Popular Unity; many of them were controlled by the opposition parties. This ensured the genuinely pluralistic character of the Chilean road (which would have made it a great political achievement, had it been sustained); however, it made the power struggle even more difficult for the government. For example, the autonomy of the trade unions (in spite of their electoral

support for the Left) made it impossible to implement an incomes policy.
Although the Government's respect for freedom of the press was praiseworthy,
it was unfortunately not accompanied by moves to improve Popular Unity's own
media in the ideological struggle with the Opposition.

Given the political context and constraints, as well as the strategy
adopted, economic policy in Chile should have played a more crucial and
complex role than in the other two countries. As shall be seen in Chapter
5, short-term and financial policies did not play this role very
successfully. It was particularly important in the Chilean experience to
ensure a normal economic evolution and avoid serious disequilibria. This
was important not only to help win elections but also to maintain the
support of the 'middle groups', and above all, to avoid the intervention of
the armed forces. In this respect, it must be remembered that one of the
main reasons given by the armed forces for the coup was 'to save the country
from economic chaos'. Undoubtedly, it was not the main reason, but
certainly it helped provide a good rationalization[38]. Obviously, one of
the main targets of any revolutionary movement must be to avoid helping to
justify a right-wing coup!

As can be seen from the above discussion, there were fundamental differences
in the political evolution of the three cases to be studied. In the Soviet
case, although no international support was forthcoming, the opposition
shown by other countries proved rather piecemeal and had ultimately little
impact on the outcome of the Civil War. Furthermore, during the stage of
War Communism, the main target of the Bolsheviks necessarily was to achieve
military victory over the armed opposition, at a time when the economy was
so seriously disrupted. The Red Army was forged especially for this purpose
by the Bolsheviks and played a key role in the survival and consolidation of
Soviet power. Besides the crucial military sphere (where the struggle was
essentially concentrated), the Bolsheviks, very soon after the October
Revolution, had emerged as the sole party in control of the state. The
country they controlled was one with an autocratic tradition.

Political developments in the Czechoslovak and Chilean experience were very
different from those of the Soviet Revolution. Both of the former are small
countries, where external pressures have a much more determinating influence
on political developments (this is particularly true in the Czechoslovak
experience). In both cases, the Left began with a more limited control of
state institutions than in the Soviet experience. Both were countries with
an important democratic tradition, in which a significant 'shift to the
left' occurred amongst its population; in both cases, this shift was
reflected in an increasing electoral support for the Marxist parties, as
well as for non-Marxist parties which shared many of the former's commitment
for structural changes.

However, there were crucial differences between the Popular Front in
Czechoslovakia and Popular Unity in Chile. One of them was the
international position of both countries. As a result of agreements reached
by the Big Three at the end of the Second World War (mainly at Yalta and
Teheran), it was accepted that Czechoslovakia would be placed in the Soviet
sphere of influence. In the wake of these agreements it was the Soviet Red
Army that liberated Czechoslovakia from the Germans. The Soviet Union was
very keen to ensure this, given Czechoslovakia's great strategic and
economic importance. On the contrary, Chile was and had been for a long
time a country clearly in the American sphere of influence; the interest
which the Soviet Union had in, the influence it exerted on, and the support
it granted to the Popular Unity government in Chile was much smaller than in
the Czechoslovak experience. The geographical accident that Chile is one of
the contries of the globe furthest from the Soviet Union (as well as from
China) may have had more than trivial importance.

A second crucial distinction between the Czechoslovak and Chilean experience was the attitude of the Armed Forces. As a result of the Soviet liberation of Czechoslovakia and at the insistence of the Czechoslovak Communist Party, increasingly close links were developed between the Czechoslovak and the Soviet Armed Forces after 1945. Czechoslovak officers were sent to Soviet military schools, for technical and ideological training; officers who had collaborated with the Nazis had been purged in 1945; the Soviet Union equipped important sections of the Czechoslovak Army; it was even reported that several months before the Communist take-over in February 1948, steps were being taken to integrate Czechoslovakia within the military plans of the Soviet Union. All these measures not only reduced the possibility of a right-wing military coup, but also meant that Czechoslovak military leaders tended to adopt a standpoint similar to that of their Soviet colleagues.

The position of the Chilean Armed Forces was radically different to that in Czechoslovakia. As seen above, Chilean officers were educated (many of them by American officers) in the doctrine of 'national security' which included an important anti-socialist element. As a result of this and other factors, hardly any Chilean officers supported socialism. The initial support given by large sections of the Armed Forces to the Popular Unity government was based on their respect for a democratically elected government, which acted within the laws and the constitution. This sector which was gradually weakened co-existed with an increasingly growing group within the Armed Forces which opposed socialism in general and the Popular Unity government in particular. Increased political tension, as well as the growing economic problems further strengthened the anti-socialist group, till it became strong enough to carry out the coup that violently overthrew the Allende government in September 1973.

Thus, in the Chilean experience during the Allende government the political initiative was increasingly in the hands of the right. Given both the important constraints it faced (such as the character of the Armed Forces) and the disagreements within the coalition, no significant initiative was taken by the Left to increase its share of state power. In the Popular Front Czechoslovak experience, the international and national context was very favourable for the forces supporting state socialism, and particularly for the Communist Party; this favourable context made it easier for the Communists to maintain the initiative for increasing drastically their share of state power and helped to make such initiatives successful. Unfortunately, the fact that the Czechoslovak revolution was to such a great extent directed from above and abroad introduced lasting distortions into the type of socialism adopted.

Before beginning the case studies, it seems necessary to discuss the approach used in them on the transmission mechanisms involved in inflation. The explanation of the causes of inflation will be carried out at two levels. First, the evolution of monetary expansion and budget deficits (the immediate mechanisms which lead to financial disequilibria) will be described; then, the main underlying factors - both economic and political - which contribute towards explaining the evolution of these financial variables will be studied. This corresponds to a perception of inflation which combines different strands of existing theoretical analysis; it assumes that monetary expansion is to a great extent caused by 'structural', 'cost-push' or 'extraordinary' pressures, but that it is undoubtedly inflationary in effect[39].

Analysis of the sources of inflationary pressures has always been of concern to economists. Instead of attempting to review or summarize the vast literature[40], I shall attempt to extract those elements which seem most relevant within the context of a preliminary transition to socialism, particularly to the countries studied here.

In the literature on inflation in industralized countries, the two extreme interpretations are the monetarist and cost-push theories. The monetarist interpretation stresses that the rate of inflation is determined by excess aggregate demand; the main mechanism which causes an expansion of aggregate demand is growth of the money supply. This position is best summarized by Friedman's statement that 'Inflation is at any time and in any place a monetary phenomenon'[41]. In its more sophisticated versions, the monetarist school incorporates the role of price expectations; furthermore, these versions attribute excessive monetary growth not just to government irresponsibility but also to the pursuit of other economic and political objectives, incompatible with a more restrictive monetary policy. Thus Parkin[42] says: 'In general, then, it seems that we can explain the behaviour of monetary growth in terms of our attempts, both through the public sector and privately, to consume too much.'

In their policy recommendations, monetarists are even more simplistic than in their diagnosis. Since inflation is the result of past and present attempts by governments to over-utilize the productive capacity of the economy through the issue of money, it can only be reduced by cutting the rate of monetary expansion.

At the other end of the spectrum are the cost-push interpretations of inflation, often linked to a 'class struggle' analysis of society. Prices are not determined at 'equilibrium' level by free competition in the market, but are to a great extent 'administered prices': their level is determined by the bargaining position of large enterprises and powerful trade unions. Therefore, the cost-push school stresses the need for a study of the institutional framework within which wages and prices are determined, as well as the sociological and political forces that condition this framework. Implicit in this interpretation is a view of inflation as basically linked to a debate and a struggle about shares in the national product. It is interesting to note that very diverse ideological sources adhere to this type of interpretation. Thus, an OECD report written in 1972[43] notes that 'inflation is not only a symptom of unresolved tensions within the economy ... it is also the mechanism by which efforts to alter the distribution of income or expenditure which are not accepted by those concerned are partially frustrated'. A Marxist adherent to the cost-push or conflict theory of inflation, Devine[44], makes a diagnosis of inflation close to that of the OECD:

> The expansion of the money supply is essentially a
> symptom, rather than a cause, of inflation. It is
> either the result of the State seeking to make
> expenditures that socio-political pressures make
> necessary and that these same pressures prevent from
> being financed by taxation or by borrowing from the
> private sector; or it is the result of the State being
> obliged to accommodate pressures elsewhere in the
> economy for fear of the socio-political consequences
> that would follow if it did not.

This type of analysis, while acknowledging a fairly high degree of statistical association between the price level and the money stock, maintains that the direction of causation is the reverse to that of the monetarist view. Thus, the supply of money accommodates itself to the level of money income, which varies mainly as a result of pressures on wages. The central bank increases the money supply 'passively' so as to finance a higher level of prices without increasing unemployment. As in this view monetary policy does not play an active role in provoking inflation, it is not very effective for controlling inflation; the main policy instrument is incomes policy.

The debate between cut-push and monetarist interpretations has remained
largely unresolved. As Trevithick[45], for example, points out in a recent
work, the 'difficulty of distinguishing between cost and demand influences
would appear to be insuperable.' Empirical evidence cannot 'show' in what
direction the causal relation between the money supply and the price level
runs.

It seems worthwhile to note that the dichotomy between cost-push and demand
pull interpretations of inflation has been somewhat exaggerated in the
debates. This is particularly true for countries - such as those undergoing
a preliminary transition to socialism - where the state sector is an
important part of the economy; in such cases, wages, fiscal and monetary
policy are very closely linked. Thus, a large increase in public sector
real wages - whether in the central government or state enterprises - will
lead to growing public sector deficit and larger increases in the money
supply. However, the effective implementation of a restrictive monetary
policy will necessarily imply lower increases (or larger decreases) of real
wages for public employees. Incomes policy for the state sector and
monetary policy interact so closely that a clear-cut causal link between
them cannot always be established. In policy terms, the choice of one or
the other (or both) should to a large extent depend on feasibility of
implementation, both political and institutional.

There are other interpretations of inflation: of relevance in developing
countries - and mainly in Latin America - is the structuralist school or
approach. I shall look at this school in some detail in Chapter 5; however,
its main characteristics will be briefly outlined here[46]. This approach
views inflation as generated in the course of the attempt to develop in the
face of structural rigidities; these rigidities are perceived as fundamental
facets of the economic, institutional and socio-political structure of the
country which inhibit expansion. The major bottlenecks considered are food
output, foreign exchange, rigid tax structure and low rate of capital
formation.

An important distinction, initially developed by Sunkel[47], is made between
inflationary pressures and propagation mechanisms. Inflationary pressures
are the structural features described above, as well as exogenous factors,
such as rising import prices. Propagation mechanisms are those which pass
on the inflationary impulse and may contribute to its cumulative character;
however, they are not the real causes of inflation; they consist of the
various ways through which different groups defend their real relative
income or expenditure: the workers by wage readjustment, private enterprise
by price increases and the public sector through an increase in nominal
fiscal expenditure. These propagation mechanisms are perceived as the
result of the political inability of society to solve in some final way two
major struggles of economic interest. The first concerns income
distribution among different social groups involved in the economic process;
the second is related to the distribution of the productive resources of the
community between the public and private sectors of the economy.

As we can see, some followers of the 'structuralist' school have common
elements with the 'cost push' diagnosis of inflation. Like the latter, its
interpretation and its policy prescriptions are opposed to those of the
monetarist school; similarly, as in the previous debate, there is no
theoretical or empirical basis for settling the dispute between monetarists
and structuralists unambiguously (see Fitzgerald, op.cit. and Thorpe,
op.cit.).

As regards policy suggestions, the structuralists concentrate mainly on the
long-term. There is a large gap in their thinking at the level of

short-term policy-making; as shall be discussed further in Chapter 5, the
structuralists tend to lack a coherent and practicable alternative for
short-term economic management, particularly in conditions of
disequilibrium[48]. Furthermore, insufficient emphasis is placed by the
structuralists on the need not only to balance total supply and demand in
the short-term through prices and money supply, but also to balance the
traded and non-traded sectors within the economy[49].

From the brief survey above, it becomes evident that no clear-cut framework
can be extracted from the debates on inflation in the economic literature.
Therefore, it is necessary to rely heavily on personal reading of the
evidence in each particular country and period of time. It will be agreed
here that as monetary expansion is inflationary in effect, it is in fact the
immediate 'cause' of inflation, (or the main 'propagation mechanism' of
inflationary pressures, if one uses structuralist terminology). The main
determinants of monetary policy, barely analysed by the monetarist school,
are very often sociological/political pressures, structural problems in the
economy, or extraordinary circumstances, such as a war or civil war. As we
shall see, these pressures and problems tend to be exacerbated in the stage
of preliminary transition to socialism.

The statement that monetary policy is basically determined by underlying
economic and political forces needs to be qualified. The monetary mechanism
plays a much larger role in inflation than is implied in much of the more
simplistic 'structuralist' or 'cost-push' analysis; as Thorpe[50] points
out, there is a dangerous tendency in that approach 'to conceive of
inflation as a totally non-monetary phenomenon, and hence perhaps to
underplay the dangers of deficit financing.' Given the underlying pressures
and forces, there is a certain 'degree of autonomy' for monetary policy in
most situations.

The use of some elements of monetarist thinking may seem surprising in a
study on the preliminary transition to socialism, given that most
monetarists are such firm adherents of the free-market mechanism and the
private sector, such great enemies of socialism and of government intervention and such enthusiastic supporters of stabilisation policies whose
effects on employment and income distribution are often so damaging for the
working class. However, it is clearly possible to reject or even oppose
many of the ideological positions which most adherents of monetarism share
and accept the proposition that strict control over growth in the money
supply is necessary if inflation is to be conquered. One can even believe
in the socialization of the means of production and yet support policies to
control the growth of the money supply. As Cobham[51] puts it, 'it is not
your monetarism or your anti-monetarism, but what you do with it, that is
determined by your politics'.

Until now, no distinction has been made here between different policies
(fiscal v. monetary) leading to an expansion of aggregate demand. In fact,
it has been only recently realized that even for developed countries, the
largely semantic debate between monetarists and Keynesians on the relative
importance of monetary v. fiscal policy on the determination of the overall
pressure of demand has concealed the considerable amount of common ground
that unites both approaches. The origins of this confusion can be traced to
the widespread practice of treating monetary and fiscal policy as
independent instruments; there is, however, a very high degree of
interdependence between both policies. In the countries studied here, the
distinction between fiscal and monetary policy is even less significant than
in the industrialized countries today, due to the virtual non-existence of a
capital market in these countries, where the Government could finance its
deficit. There was thus very little scope for investment in financial
intermediaries or Treasury bills by the private sector. As a consequence,
the demand for money was primarily for transactions; where the asset motive

existed, it was usually satisfied by investment in real as opposed to
financial assets.   This implied that an increase in budget deficit was
basically financed by monetary expansion; the impact of this expansion was
more certain and immediate than in countries with sophisticated capital
markets through which an important part of the budget is financed.   The
effect of the budget deficit is therefore felt not on interest rates, but
directly in increased expenditure on goods, services and assets, with
consequences for inflation and the external account.

In the case studies, I shall start with an identity; although simplified, it
should provide a useful framework to begin analysing the causes of monetary
expansion[52].

> Change in money supply $\equiv$
>
> Public sector borrowing requirement
>
> + Net Bank lending to private sector
>
> + Net foreign exchange operations
>
> − Sales of public sector bonds to private sector

As discussed, in the cases studied sales of public bonds to the private
sector will play a rather small role.

A particularly crucial role will be played in the preliminary transition to
socialism by the public sector borrowing requirement, given the large and
increasing size of the public sector and the heavy social and political
pressures on it.

Many of the trends and elements which lead to a large state sector deficit
during the preliminary transition to socialism already existed − though
often on a smaller scale − in the capitalist or mixed economy functioning
previously in that country.   The general trends are well illustrated for
Latin American countries after the Second World War by Fitzgerald[53].   On
the one hand, there is a clear tendency for the fiscal deficit as a
percentage of Gross Domestic Product to grow, because government expenditure
increases at a quicker pace than that of taxation; pressures for expanding
'development', social welfare and defence expenditure are combined with
difficulties in increasing taxation (particularly direct) at sufficient
speed.   State enterprises suffer a chronic tendency towards losses or low
profits, the latter almost always insufficient to finance their capital
investment.   As a result, governments have to rely on internal borrowing
(which as seen above is severely limited), borrowing abroad (which has heavy
costs in terms of increased dependency as well as future debt servicing)
and/or increased monetary expansion.

Many of these trends and forces will be aggravated during a process of
preliminary transition to socialism.   The traditional difficulties
encountered in increasing direct taxation will probably be exacerbated,
particularly if the socialist forces have only partial control over the
state apparatus.   If the wealthy resist paying high taxes to finance a
capitalist or mixed economy state, they will be even more reluctant to
finance a state attempting a transition to socialism! Pressures for real
salary and wage increases for state workers and employees, often contained
by previous governments, may become explosive as a result of the partial
victory of the Socialist forces.   Government expenditure on welfare will
probably expand for similar reasons.   Defence expenditure may increase, if
the process is threatened from abroad.   The losses or low profits of a
rapidly growing state enterprise will most probably grow, as a result mainly
of the price and wages policies pursued.

A second source of monetary expansion is net bank lending to the private sector. This could be expected to play a relatively minor role as source of expansion; in fact, given the decline in the size of the private sector, a fall in this item could be feasible. However, as shall be seen, particularly in the Chilean case, significant expansion of this item occurred, largely linked, in Chile, to the perceived need to obtain political support from the 'middle groups' by giving economic concessions to 'small and medium entrepreneurs'.

As seen above, the 'conflict' or 'structuralist' approaches emphasize that inflation reflects struggles between different classes or groups (as well as between the public and private sector) for an increased share of the national income. The intensity of the power struggle in a society during the preliminary transition to socialism will inevitably make this conflict sharper, and this will be felt through pressures exerted on the rapidly growing (in size and importance) state sector.

The dominant inflationary pressures and mechanisms vary according to the different experiences of preliminary transition to socialism, as we shall see in much more detail in the following chapters. Thus, in the Soviet case during the period 1917-20, as in any country suffering the effects of civil and external war, inflation was largely due to large budget deficits caused by expanded defence expenditure, combined with a sharp decline in economic activity. The possibility of reducing defence expenditure was one of the important factors which allowed stabilization during the first phase of New Economic Policy. Control of the trade unions by the Communist Party helped 'regulate' the wages increase, and prevented a wage/price spiral which would have made stabilization more difficult. During 1945-48, in Czechoslovakia, inflationary pressures arose partly from increased government expenditure linked to post-war reconstruction and re-structuring: workers' incomes grew more than the government planned, but for reasons discussed in Chapter 4, there was no incomes explosion. In Chile during the Allende Government no effective political mechanisms existed to control wage increases in either the public or private sector; real wages and salaries rose rapidly as price controls were initially very effective; government expenditure also grew due to higher welfare spending and new public works projects to increase employment. The resulting budget deficit grew rapidly, and this lead to rapid monetary growth. As shall be seen in Chapter 5, the initial impulse towards inflation in the Chilean experience was demand generated, as the expansion of aggregate demand could no longer be satisfied by increased output and/or imports. As price controls became less effective, pressures for wage increases accelerated; the wage/price spiral accelerated, as did price expectations[54].

When examining inflation in specific cases of preliminary transition to socialism, it is also crucial to look at the evolution of supply; this means analysing the distinction between different production sectors, as well as incorporating the external sector. A useful starting point, particularly for developing countries, is a modified version of Kalecki's analysis on 'financing economic development'[55]. It is worth noting that Kalecki in this article formalized the Latin American 'structuralist' approach in terms more useful for projection and planning. In his analysis, Kalecki defines as the main 'financial' problem of development that of adequate supply of necessities (mainly agricultural), given that the growth of national income is constrained by the increase in the supply of necessities. Kalecki also stresses the potential role which a surplus in foreign trade and/or foreign credit may play to increase the supply of wage goods. Taxation is perceived as restraining consumption of non-essential goods by the higher income groups.

Kalecki, like the Latin American structuralists, sees the increase in production of wage goods, especially of staple food, as limited by

institutional factors, such as feudal land ownership. In the preliminary
transition to socialism, the food supply constraint is crucial; however, the
restrictions on food produced (and the proportion of it marketed) arise
mainly not from the inherited system of land tenure; on the contrary, they
arise from the revolutionary process itself, including the effects of
agrarian reform. Constraints on staple food marketed is often accompanied
by increased demand for such necessities in the cities, as real wages and
salaries rise.

In experiences of preliminary transition to socialism, increased demand for
staple food in the cities is often confronted with an inelastic or declining
supply of such goods. The result is either inflation, increase in food
imports, scarcities, food rationing, or combinations of these alternatives.

As will be seen below, in the Soviet case, the main problem was reduced food
supply to the cities, and not increased demand; restricted food availability
resulted mainly from the disruption caused by the civil war and from the
nature of the 1917 agrarian revolution. In contrast, during Popular Unity's
experience in Chile, the basic cause was increased food demand mainly from
the poorer strata, due to a rise in their real incomes. In fact, food
production rose in 1971 but declined after 1972, mainly as a result of the
acceleration of agrarian reform. However, as food imports rose sharply, the
total per capita supply of food grew rapidly between 1970 and 1972[56]. In
spite of this, in Chile, excessive demand for food created serious problems:
black markets, scarcities and rising food prices in the cities. In the
Czechoslovak experience, demand and supply factors had relatively equal
importance; as shall be seen, the disequilibria were moderated by the
existence of a rationing system and the availability of foreign credit and
aid for food imports.

Putting this discussion in a broader context, it is possible to detect two
fundamental causes for large disequilibria between demand and supply (both
aggregate and in specific sectors) during a preliminary transition to
socialism; this analysis is of greater relevance in experiences carried out
within the existing institutional framework, such as the Chilean experience.

These two basic factors are: (a) a trend towards expansion and change in
composition of aggregate demand, to which existent supply could most
probably not respond under any circumstances and (b) specific constraints to
the supply response caused by the structural transformations[57].

As discussed above, in such cases aggregate demand tends to increase sharply
as the money supply grows to finance large deficits in the fiscal sector and
the state enterprises. These financial flows reflect not only a process of
redistribution of nominal income — from the wealthier groups of the
population to the poorer ones — but also an expansion of total nominal
income available for consumption. The latter tends to occur partly because
the surplus available for redistribution, particularly within the specific
political context and the existent class alliance, is insufficient to
compensate for the increased income granted to the poorer strata. The
problem is often not visualized clearly in advance by left-wing politicians,
who over-estimate the surplus, mainly from 'the rich', effectively available
for redistribution[58]. Furthermore, the propensity to save will probably
be lower amongst the poorer strata.

Large disequilibria will probably result in all sectors and at an aggregate
level; they will probably be largest in wage goods. The increase of
aggregate demand will tend to concentrate particularly on necessities, of
which agricultural goods are an important proportion, (as the lower income
groups have a higher propensity to consume these goods than the wealthier
groups). In the short-term, the ability to expand internal supply will be
constrained by existing investment; only marginal increases or shifts in

production are feasible, without additional constraint. Supply problems will be aggravated by the inevitable disruptions caused by changes in property and management. In the case of food supply, disrupted production is often compounded by a lower proportion of food marketed, as a more egalitarian land redistribution increases the new owners' consumption levels.

Supply of necessities can for a time be increased - as in the Chilean experience - by imports (or in other cases, by a reduction in exports). At the same time, nationalization of the export sector may curtail the inflow of foreign exchange to the country in the short term.

If these disequilibria occur on a large scale, they lead to a depletion of foreign exchange reserves and/or the need for increased foreign credits, as well as high inflation and/or scarcities. They reflect the inevitable fact that unless total supply increases indefinitely (either as a result of national production growth or massive net inflows of foreign finance), large increases in real government deficits and consumption by certain groups must ex-post somehow be balanced not only by a reduction in investment, but also by reduced consumption by other groups.

Financial and short-term economic policies are clearly not mere 'technical problems,' to be discussed as secondary during the preliminary transition to socialism, or to be used mainly so as to gain short-term political support from different groups in society. A consistent policy for the short-term (with approximate orders of magnitude) will help the revolutionary forces to face the power struggle from a stronger position. An optimum short-term economic policy in such a context will thus be defined not merely by the creative design of adequate specific policies within the existing political constraints (i.e. prices, taxation), but through the political leadership setting a proper framework by defining targets on such crucial matters as levels and speed of income redistribution, pace of structural reforms, probable levels of foreign credits and aid, minimum net foreign exchange reserves, maximum levels of politically acceptable inflation and the feasibility of alternative distribution mechanisms, such as rationing.

It can be concluded that the problems of finance play a very important role in the preliminary transition to socialism. A broader understanding of these issues can be reached if they are related to the changing nature of the state's economic role, as well as the changing control which a socialist government is able to exert over the state apparatus.

During the preliminary transition there is a large expansion of the state's participation in the economy, as well as its role. The growth of the state sector is not necessarily accompanied by an increase of the surplus which it is able to capture from the private sector. On the contrary, there are important reasons and trends which may lead in the short-term to a decline in the surplus captured by the state, and often to an increase in the state sector deficit (see discussion above, and Chapters 2 to 5).

Therefore although the expansion of the state sector leads to a potential increase of the surplus it could capture, the real surplus captured may in fact be severely reduced, the acute struggle for political power (whether it be peaceful or armed) will be almost inevitably reflected in pressures by different social groups and classes to increase their consumption, as well as on the government to increase its expenditure. At the same time, although the expansion of the state sector provides the potential base on which effective planning can be built, in the short-term there may be great difficulties (both technical and political) to carry it out. This may be particularly serious because in this phase the economic links previously existing between economic units are being disrupted.

The growth in the public sector deficit in an economy attempting a transition to socialism can hardly be financed by internal borrowing; net external finance can also be expected to be limited, particularly from capitalist countries and institutions. The main source of finance will probably be an increase in the money supply.

The resulting expansion and change in the composition of aggregate demand may be so large that existent supply would not be able to respond under any circumstances. In preliminary transition to socialism, the supply response may be further inhibited by the short-term effects of structural transformations (i.e. of Agrarian Reform on food supply). The serious problems resulting from the gap between demand and supply (both aggregate and sectoral) have already been discussed above, and will be illustrated in the Chapters below.

The ability of a government attempting to initiate a transition to socialism to limit their disequilibria and/or to minimize their negative effects will depend not only on its understanding of the issues and its technical handling of them but also on the extent of its political control over the state apparatus at any particular time. Its control may naturally change in the course of time allowing new policy instruments to be used if its share of state power increases.

Some instruments for extracting more surplus from the private sector, such as increased prices of state enterprises may be applicable even with a limited control of the state apparatus. Other apparently orthodox measures such as large increases in direct taxation may however require a far greater control of the state. Unorthodox measures for controlling financial disequilibria while attempting to ensure equity (such as rationing or monetary reform) would require probably an even larger share of state power.

We shall return to these issues at a more concrete level in the chapters which follow.

Notes

1   Charles Bettleheim, The Transition to Socialist Economy, Harvester
     Press, London, 1975, p.26.

2   E. Preobrazhensky, The New Economics, Oxford University Press, 1965,
     p.117.

3   Op.cit. p.18.

4   Preobrazhensky was one of the first to deal perceptively with this
     type of problem (see in particular The New Economy, op.cit. pp.127 and
     178). He points out that in these initial stages, the socialist form
     has not yet developed all its advantages but it has lost some of the
     advantages of the capitalist economy.

5   The New Economics, op.cit. p.116.

6   See D. Lane, The end of inequality?   Stratification under State
     Socialism, Penguin Books, London, 1971.

7   A brief but suggestive discussion of these issues can be found in
     Chapter 10 of M. Ellman, Socialist Planning, Cambridge University
     Press, 1979.

8   The 'liquidationist tradition' refers to the view that economics, its
     laws and concepts (i.e. commodity, price, money) relate only to
     economies based upon private property in the means of production. For
     a brief discussion of this theme, see Chapter 12 of A. Nove, The
     Soviet Economic System, George Allen and Unwin, 1977.

9   Op.cit. Chapter 12.

10   Op.cit.

11   Even though very fragmentary, there seems to be some support –
     particularly in Engels' works – for the view that even in the
     beginnings of socialism there would be little role for commodities and
     money. (See, for example, F. Engels, Anti-Duhring, London, 1936.)

12   The 1891 German Social Democratic programme is described by its
     author, Karel Kautsky, in Das Erfuhrter Programme, Dietz-Vorwats,
     Berlin, 1922.

13   Published in English by Bergman Publishers, Pluto Press, New York,
     1971. This book is of particular interest to the economic historian
     as it includes Lenin's marginal notes, thus allowing a comparison
     between Lenin's views and those of Bukharin.

14   Op.cit. pp.143 and 146.

15   Op.cit. p.94.

16   See in particular footnote 119, p.197, op.cit. where Bukharin replies
     to the question 'Can we use the rouble as a unit of measure?' ...What
     do these numbers signify when many objects cannot be attained at all
     in additional quantities, i.e. when the money quantity becomes
     absolutely meaningless?'

17   Article in Venceremos, The Speeches and Writings of Ernesto Che
     Guevara (edited and introduced by J. Gerassi), Macmillan Company, New
     York, 1968.

18   The New Economics, op.cit. pp.215-216.

19   J. Stalin, Economic Problems of Socialism in the USSR, Macmillan
      London, 1952.

20   Such views were already expressed in the Soviet Union in 1921 (see,
      for example, perceptive comments on the insufficient development of a
      'conscious social regulator' expressed by Olminsky in his review of
      Bukharin's book, quoted in L. Szamuely, First Models of the Socialist
      Economic Systems, Akademiai Kiado, Budapest, 1974). There is now an
      extensive literature on the problems and limitations of planning based
      on the historical experience of socialist countries. For discussions
      of these issues see, for example, Ellman, op.cit. as well as the
      bibliography there.

21   C. Bettleheim, The Transition to the Socialist Economy, op.cit.
      particularly Chapters 2, 3 and 5.

22   Op.cit. in (21), pp.109-110.

23   Op.cit. p.136.

24   See C. Bettleheim, Economic Calculation and Forms of Property,
      Routledge, London, 1976 and Bettleheim's articles from Monthly Review,
      collected in P. Sweezy and C. Bettleheim, On the Transition to
      Socialism, Monthly Review Press, 1971.

25   C. Bettleheim, The Transition to Socialist Economy, op.cit. p.174.

26   For a detailed critique of this aspect of Bettleheim's work see A.
      Nove, "Market socialism and its critics", Soviet Studies, July 1972.

27   The New Economics, op.cit. pp.88-89.

28   Preobrazhensky together with other Bolshevik writers (i.e. Yurovsky)
      seem to have been amongst the first who clearly interpreted money
      issue as a form of taxation. Keynes had done so however, in a
      somewhat earlier work, (The Tract on Monetary Reform, Macmillan,
      London, 1923).

29   Op.cit. p.110.

30   In previous pages, he discussed the negative effects on state
      enterprises of a price policy which does not even cover their costs.
      The transformation of this price policy into a system would
      undoubtedly mean 'a gradual dissipation of large-scale state
      industry'.

31   As we discussed, even in the most advanced state socialist countries,
      the planning system still has very serious limitations; according to
      Bettleheim, this leads to the need in those countries to use market
      and money relations. This argument is naturally much more valid
      during the preliminary transition, with a very incipient planning
      system.

32   The elements for the financial plan are largely inherited from the
      capitalist state. Material plans are either non-existent or
      fragmentary and rather ineffective. See chapters 2 to 5.

33   The extent to which this goal is pursued would have to be decided by
      the political leadership.

34   As Hirschman (A Bias for Hope, Yale University Press, New Haven,
      1971), points out, 'both economists and political scientists continue
      to use models with primitive links between economics and politics in
      which the phenomena belonging to an external discipline are introduced
      as a sort of prerequisite ...'.

35   After February 1948, the situation changed rapidly, as Czechoslovakia
      reflected increasingly the Soviet political system under Stalin.   The
      Communist party assumed the role of 'universal caretaker'.

36   Allende repeated often that Chile faced 'the need to find a new way of
      constructing socialist society ... Chile is tody the first nation on
      earth to pursue this second model of transition to Socialism', Speech
      in G. Martner (ed.), El pensamiento económico del gobierno de Allende,
      Editorial Universitaria, p.113, Santiago.   There were, however, some
      relatively small sectors within Popular Unity – as well as to the left
      of it – which believed in the 'armed road'.

37   It is impossible to analyse these factors in detail here.   For good
      ex-post analysis, from different perspectives, see for example, S.
      Bitar, Transición, Socialismo y democracia, la experiencia chilena,
      Siglo XXI.

38   See literature quoted in 37 for more detailed treatment of this
      crucial subject.

39   This follows a very similar type of analysis to that put forward by
      E.V.K. Fitzgerald in 'The Fiscal Crisis of the Latin American State',
      J.F.J. Toye, (ed.), Taxation and Economic Development, Frank Cass,
      London, 1978.

40   For a recent review of inflation theory in developed countries see,
      for example, J.A. Trevithick and C. Muluey, The Economics of
      Inflation, Martin Robertson, 1975, and D. Laidler and M. Parkin,
      'Inflation, a survey', Economic Journal, Dec. 1975; also of relevance
      here is D. Cobham, 'The Politics of the Economics of Inflation',
      Lloyds Bank Review, April 1978.

41   Milton Friedman, Dollars and Deficits, Prentice Hall, 1968.

42   Michael Parkin, 'On inflation', Lloyds Bank Review, July 1975.

43   Expenditure trends in OECD countries 1960–80, OECD, Paris, July 1972.

44   Pat Devine, 'Inflation and Marxist Theory', Marxism Today, March 1974.

45   J.A. Trevithick, Inflation, Penguin Books, 1980.

46   There is no need to chronicle the emergence of this school or record
      its major contributions and shortcomings as this has been well done
      elsewhere.   For good sympathetic surveys with ample bibliography see
      D. Seers, 'Inflation and Growth in Latin America' in ECLA, Economic
      Bulletin for Latin America, February 1962 and R. Thorpe 'Inflation and
      Financing of Economic Development' in K. Griffin, (ed.), Financing
      Development in Latin America, Macmillan, 1971.   For a flavour of the
      debates at the time, see Baer and Kerstenetzky, (eds.), Inflation and
      Growth in Latin America, Yale University Press, 1964.

47   Osvaldo Sunkel, 'La inflación chilena: un enfoque heterodojo',
      Trimestre Económico, Oct–Dec. 1958.   This article is widely considered
      to be the first comprehensive statement of the 'structuralist' inter-
      pretation of inflation.

48   See also 'Introduction' to R. Thorpe and L. Whitehead (eds.),
      Inflation and Stabilisation in Latin America, Macmillan, 1979.

49   This point is made in the first section of Fitzgerald's article on
      'Stabilisation Policy in Mexico: the Fiscal Deficit and Macroeconomic
      Equilibrium, 1960-77' in op.cit. in 48.

50   Thorpe, op.cit. Also, see Introduction to R. Thorpe and L. Whitehead
      (eds.), op.cit.

51   Op.cit. above.

52   Money is defined here to include fixed term deposits and savings
      accounts.

53   See E.V.K. Fitzgerald, 'The Fiscal Crisis of the Latin American
      State', op.cit.   For a discussion of advanced capitalist countries,
      see J. O'Connor, The Fiscal Crisis of the State, St. Martin's Press,
      New York, 1973.

54   H. Kalecki, 'A model of hyper-inflation', The Manchester School of
      Economic and Social Studies, vol. XXX, Sept.1962.

55   M. Kalecki, 'Problems of financing economic development in a mixed
      economy', Selected Essays On The Economic Growth Of The Socialist And
      Mixed Economy; Cambridge University Press, 1972.

56   S. Barraclough, y J. Fernandez, Diagnóstico de la Reforma Agraria
      Chilena, Siglo XXI, Mexico, 1974.

57   In cases of armed struggle, there are additional important constraints
      on supply, (see Chapter 2) whereas the expansion of demand for
      consumption will be more moderate.

58   For an interesting discussion of these trends in Chile's Popular Unity
      experience, and the lessons to be extracted from them, see S.G. Kolm,
      La transition socialiste, Les Editions du Cerf, Paris, 1977. For a
      quantitative evaluation of the Chilean case, see S. Bitar, op.cit.
      also A. Foxley and O. Muñoz, 'Income Redistribution, Economic Growth
      and Social Structure: the case of Chile', Oxford Bulletin of Economics
      and Statistics, February 1974.

2

THE ROLE OF FINANCIAL POLICY IN THE SOVIET UNION: 1917-21

This chapter begins with an account of the general political and economic framework, starting with a brief description of the Russian economy during World War I. The objectives of the Bolsheviks at the time of the Revolution are then described, as well as the general economic conditions prevailing in the period 1917-21. The causes of financial and monetary disequilibria during this period are then examined. The financial variables are briefly described; the economic factors and policies implicit in these variables are then discussed in more detail.

The effects of financial and monetary policies, such as inflation and the decrease in the real value of money issue are discussed, followed by the problems caused by the moneyless economy, as well as the effects on income distribution.

After examining the evolution of the Bolsheviks' own thinking about money and finance during the period, more recent interpretations about the influence they had on financial developments during the period are briefly examined. The empirical evidence compiled and analyzed in this study supports the view that hyper-inflation and the moneyless economy were basically unavoidable.

I.   Political and economic framework

1.   Brief description of the Russian economy during the First World War

a)   General aspects

During World War I, national production fell sharply. A high and rapidly increasing proportion of it was channelled into the war effort.

TABLE 2.I

NATIONAL PRODUCT AND ITS COMPONENTS

(billion gold rubles)

Years	National Product	Military Expenditure
1914-15	15.8	4.3
1915-16	13.9	5.7
1916-17	12.2	7.1

Source: P.I. Lyashchenko, History of the National Economy of Russia to 1917, Octagon Books, New York, 1970

While all economic sectors were affected by the war, the hardest hit was agriculture. Massive mobilization of peasants into the army, confiscation of horses and cattle, interruption of supplies of fertilizers, funds and machinery, provoked a shrinkage both in area cultivated and in yield[1].

Even more serious was the fall in the proportion of the crop which peasants were willing to market. As nearly all industrial production was converted to the war effort, the supply of goods to the villages dried up. Peasants lost interest in selling grain, especially after the value of currency began to fall quickly. By the winter of 1916-17, the large cities were hungry.

The Tsarist Government had already in 1916, adopted measures for controlling the grain trade, to the extent of imposing compulsory purchase of a proportion of farm produce at official prices. The Provisional Government went further: it declared the grain trade to be a state monopoly and

prohibited all private trade in grain outside the villages. However, this
latter measure was weakly enforced, and private trade continued.

b)   Financial aspects

Normal methods of raising revenue were incapable of financing the increase
in state expenditure caused by the war. An additional problem for fiscal
policy was the introduction of prohibition at the outbreak of war (the
profits accruing to the state from the vodka monopoly plus excises on other
liquors accounted for approximately 20 per cent of total tax revenues); due
to the effects of war, customs decreased as did revenue from the railways.
Increases in indirect taxation accounted for a great part of the additional
revenue obtained.

The increase in taxation barely covered the increase in civilian expenditure
(see Table 2.II), leaving a deficit roughly equivalent to the level of total
war expenditure, which rose sharply.

TABLE 2.II

REVENUE, EXPENDITURE AND DEFICIT OF STATE BUDGET, 1914-1917

(million rubles each year)

	1914	1915	1916	1917
Total 'normal' revenue[a]	2,961	3,001	4,345	5,039
Total expenditure	4,859	11,562	18,101	27,607
'Normal' expenditure[b]	3,204	2,839	3,151	4,445
'War' expenditure	1,655	8,724	14,948	23,160
Deficit	1,898	8,561	13,756	22,568
Deficit as % of total expenditure	39.1	74.0	76.0	81.7

Sources: R.W. Davies, Development of the Soviet Budgetary System,
           Cambridge University Press, 1958.

           L. Yurovsky, Currency Problems and Policy of the Soviet Union,
           London, 1925.

           S.S. Katzenellenbaum, Russian Currency and Banking 1914-28,
           London, 1925.

(a)   Total 'normal' revenue includes revenue from taxation.

(b)   Total 'normal' expenditure includes both 'ordinary' expenditures and
      'extraordinary' expenditure not for war purposes.

The tremendous growth in military expenditure had to be financed by internal
and external loans, and by increasing currency in circulation. A
substantial part of the deficit, also, was financed by note issue (see Table
2.III), which led to a rapid increase in the quantity of money.

TABLE 2.III

EVOLUTION OF FINANCIAL VARIABLES (1914-17) [a]

	1914	1915	1916	1917
Ratio of Note Issue to Deficit	67%	31%	25%	73%
Percentage Increase of the Volume of Money	77%	91%	61%	180%
Real Yield of Issue in Paper Money (million 1914 rubles)	1,397[b]	2,068	1,768	2,500

(a)   Sources: Yurovsky, op.cit.
                  Katzenellenbaum, op.cit.

(b)   Data refers to second half of 1914.

As can be seen from Table 2.III, the real yield of paper issue declined from 1916 when prices began to increase more rapidly than money supply (see Table 2.IV).

TABLE 2.IV

INCREASE IN MONEY CIRCULATION AND LEVEL OF PRICES

Periods	Money circulation[a]	Level of Prices[b]
1 July 1914-1 Jan. 1915	92%	1%
1 Jan. 1915-1 Jan. 1916	91%	42%
1 Jan. 1916-1 Mar. 1917	79%	120%
1 Mar. 1917-1 Oct. 1917	71%	135%

Sources: (a) Katzenellenbaum, op.cit. and Davies, op.cit. The complete series for money circulation is found in Katzenellenbaum. Yurovsky, op.cit. -who has isolated data on money circulation, which seem to contradict each other-, gives higher increases in money circulation.

           (b) Bogolepov, 'The Financial System of Pre-War Russia' in Sokolnikov G.S. and Associates, Soviet Policy in Public Finance 1917-28, Oxford University Press, 1934. Yurovsky, op.cit. and Arnold A., Banks, Credit and Money in Soviet Russia, Columbia University Press, 1937. Although the three authors give the same index, according to Bogolepov it is one of wholesale prices, while according to Arnold it is of retail prices.

The initial growth in the purchasing power of the total money supply is explained by an increase in demand for money. This was caused by various factors.

During the early war years, the volume of monetary transactions increased in step with production. Furthermore, as a result of mobilization, many goods formerly consumed by the producers themselves had to be bought by the state to feed peasants enrolled in the army, thus increasing the proportion of goods marketed.

At first, with prices rising only slowly (and future rises underestimated)

peasants hoarded paper notes. Furthermore, after the convertibility of the
credit notes was suspended, gold and silver coins began to be hoarded. The
general disorganization brought by the War, as well as deliberate government
policy, caused a fall in the volume of banking credit to enterprises; also,
the increase in the money supply damped down the volume of credit between
enterprises.

As time passed the factors which had attenuated the influence of the
increase in the money supply on price levels were either exhausted - they
had a 'once-for-all' effect - or, worse still, reversed. Among the former
factors were the hoarding of gold and silver coins, the decrease in credit
and the increase in monetary transactions due to a greater proportion of
commodities marketed. Other factors reversed their direction. The initial
rise in production was replaced by a fall (see Table 2.I), and the
population - particularly the peasantry - began to abandon hoarding as they
realized that the real value of money was falling.

The process therefore was reversed. In the last fifteen months of the
Tsarist Government, prices were rising faster than the quantity of money,
and this tendency strengthened under the Provisional Government. The
Bolsheviks therefore inherited an economy where price rises were
accelerating and where the real yield of note issue was falling. These
tendencies accelerated after the Revolution.

2.   Political and economic objectives

The dominant objective of the Bolsheviks at this stage was the defence and
consolidation of political power. Economic goals were particularly strongly
linked and subordinated to this political aim. They also had to be modified
by political circumstances such as foreign aggression and Civil War.

The political objectives will be examined first. In his well-known April
Theses[2] published in April 1917, Lenin proclaimed that

> The specific feature of the present situation in
> Russia is that the country is passing from the first
> stage of the revolution - which, owing to the
> insufficient class-consciousness and organization of
> the proletariat, placed power in the hands of the
> bourgeoisie - to its second stage, which must place
> power in the hands of the proletariat and the poorest
> sections of the peasants.

The concrete and only possible form of revolutionary government would be the
Soviets of Workers' Deputies. Both these principles were accepted by the
Communist Party's April Conference. The slogan of 'all power to the
Soviets' became clearer throughout Lenin's writings in this period[3]. As
Bukharin and Preobrazhensky[4] point out in 1919, for the Bolsheviks, Soviet
power was the realization of the dictatorship of the proletariat, organized
in these Soviets as the ruling class; with the aid of the peasantry, it
should crush the bourgeoisie's and the landlords' resistance.

The main economic task, as Lenin had pointed out in the April Theses, was to
bring production and distribution under the control of the Soviet of
Workers. It was 'by means of workers' control (over the capitalists) that
all resistance of the capitalists would be made impossible'. Workers'
control, according to Lenin, contained two elements: (a) confiscation of
capitalists' property and (b) accounting, organizing and controlling
proudction and distribution.

Initially, the first type of measure - the 'direct expropriation of the
expropriators' - was in the forefront. In October 1917, the abolition of

landlords' rights to their land and the nationalization without compensation
of all land and forests was decreed. Most of the nationalized land was
distributed amongst the peasantry.

The process of nationalizing industry was a complex one advancing much more
rapidly than initially contemplated in the Bolshevik programme[5]. By 1920,
nationalized industry employed 73 per cent of all hired industrial
workers[6]. In December 1917, large joint-stock banks were nationalized,
followed in 1918 by other banks and credit institutions.

The second economic objective - accounting, organizing and controlling
production and distribution - was described by Lenin in October 1917[7]:

>   workers' control can become the country-wide,
>   all-embracing, omnipresent, most precise and most
>   conscientious accounting of the production and
>   distribution of goods.

In an article written in March-April 1918,[8] Lenin assesses the changes in
the nature of the tasks facing the Bolsheviks.

>   Up to now measures for the direct expropriation of the
>   expropriators were in the forefront. Now the
>   organization of accounting and control in those
>   branches of the economy in which the capitalists have
>   already been expropriated, and in all other branches
>   of the economy, advances to the forefront...

It is this latter element which should be a starting point to:

>   correctly determine the immediate tasks of economic
>   and financial policy in the sphere of nationalization
>   of the banks, monopolisation of foreign trade, the
>   state control of money circulation, the introduction
>   of a property and income tax satisfactory from the
>   proletarian point of view....

However, the more immediate tasks and concrete policy measures which could
be deduced from this general principle were not outlined in any of Lenin's
articles. The economic policies followed in the period of War Communism
seem to have been dictated more by the need to maintain power in the face of
economic adversity and urgent military requirements[9].

3.   General economic conditions

Between 1917 and 1921, two distinct sub-periods can be distinguished: the
first beginning with the October Revolution and ending in the summer of
1918, the second - usually called War Communism - extending till 1921. A
watershed is provided by the outbreak of the Civil War. In the first
sub-period, the government still attempted to maintain relations between
different sectors of the economy on the old basis of 'money and market';
after mid-1918, money and market rapidly lost importance. A general
characteristic of the whole period was the abrupt decline in economic
activity.

The primary problem was that of supplying food to the cities and to the
army. As during World War I, agricultural production declined because of
general devastation, loss of man-power, destruction of livestock and
shortage of implements and fertilizers. Furthermore, the Bolsheviks lost
important parts of their territory (at one time the Soviet Government
controlled less than half of the grain area).

A further problem partly caused by equalization of the size of the unit of production, was that the small peasant holding not only produced less, but also wished to consume a higher proportion of its produce, cutting the marketable surplus. The main difficulty in securing food supplies for the towns was that no adequate return in industrial goods could be offered to the peasants and consequently state purchases of food became less and less effective. As will be discussed below, the alternative of taxing the peasantry was not viable. The Soviet Government could obtain food for the cities only by requisitioning the surplus product in each peasant farm.

Requisitioning was effective in preventing starvation in the cities and the collapse of food suplies to the army. However, it brought a decrease in the real income and consumption of the peasantry. The scale of requisitioning - which appears to have represented over 25 per cent of the peasant's income - was sometimes double that of total payments in pre-war days[10].

Compulsory collections depressed agriculture, not only because of their volume, but also because of the harsh methods applied. The shrinkage of sown area, to a great extent provoked by this policy, was a harder problem to overcome than the withdrawal of grain had been in 1918. In political terms, the compulsory collections threatened the alliance with the peasantry.

The impact of civil war on industry was even more serious. Civil war, as Carr[11] points out, transformed all major industry into a supply organization for the Red Army and made industrial policy an item of military strategy.

Fuel losses were dramatic: at one stage the Soviet Government lost nearly all its coal supply. The fall in imported materials was another serious blow which, added to intensive use of the railways for urgent military purposes and generalized destruction, caused severe transport problems.

Insufficiency of food rations lowered the intensity and efficiency of work in factories and increased absenteeism. One of the most dramatic symptoms of industrial decline was the dispersion of the proletariat, with food shortages and unemployment provoking a massive flight of workers from the cities to the country. The civil war swept many proletarians into the armed forces, and by 1921-22, the number of hired workers in industry was less than half the 1913 total[12]. According to several estimates[13], by 1920 industrial output had fallen to below 15 per cent of the 1913 level.

4. Regulation of the economy by the central authorities

Although in this period the authorities played a dominant role in the functioning of the economy there was no central planning or coordination of State activity. The essence of War Communism was the requisition of agricultural goods and the centrally organised allocation of supplies for industry, the consumer and the army. This implied the increasing replacement of money as a means of exchange by direct allocation of supplies and payment of wages in kind.

A major feature was coercive requisitioning of food from the countryside[14]. To allow this process to take place, state monopoly was imposed (and private trade abolished) for an increasing number of products. Allocation of supplies to nationalized industries as well as distribution of their finished products was carried out by state bodies - at first at fixed prices. Increasingly, exchange took the form of barter. Industrial organizations were paid by the central authorities for their production in kind (foodstuffs and raw materials). Consumer goods were distributed to workers through rationing from 1918, and through wages in kind from 1920.

But the centralization of economic activity did not imply central planning
or coordination of state activity. The institution originally charged with
this task — Vesenkha — failed to accomplish it, because it tried instead to
manage nationalized industry.

Vesenkha attempted to regulate industry through a set of intermediate bodies
called Glavki. As time passed, these institutions increased in power; by
1920 they managed all orders and supplies for their sector. As
nationalization advanced, the Glavki became congested by dealing with a
growing number of medium-sized firms, about which they had little
information. Lack of systematic kowledge about the volume of goods stored,
received and delivered in different enterprises was characteristic, allowing
widespread stealing. Often factories suffered for lack of raw materials,
which were, however, available.

There was a lack of coordination between the different Glavki as well as
amongst other government institutions, which sometimes issued contradictory
instructions. The number of officials concerned with central administration
grew. The ratio of administrative employees to industrial workers doubled
during this period.

An attempt was made to solve the administrative chaos which resulted from so
many decisions passing through a few bottlenecks by means of the 'shock'
system. Enterprises of special importance — usually from a military
viewpoint — were given priority in the supply of fuel, materials and food.
This method often tended to increase rather than to diminish the confusion,
as the priority scale applied was too crude.

II.   Causes of financial and monetary disequilibria

First, the purely financial variables determining the monetary disequilibria
will be briefly examined. Then the economic factors and policies underlying
them will be analyzed.

1.   Magnitudes of financial variables

During the period 1918-1921, the figures of money issued coincide almost
exactly with the figures of deficit in the State Budget because further
issues of paper money became the only financial means of covering the Budget
deficit.

TABLE 2.V

EVOLUTION OF FINANCIAL VARIABLES

Year	Deficit (million rubles)	Deficit as % of Total Expenditure	Issue (million rubles)
1918	31,126	66.6	33,500
1919	166,443	77.3	164,200
1920	1,055,555	86.9	943,600
1921	21,936,916	84.1	16,375.300

Sources: Katzenellenbaum, op.cit.
            Shmelev article, op.cit. in Sokolnikov, op.cit.

The figures given in Table 2.V do not portray reality exactly. Firstly, the
Budget was incomplete: it did not record all of the income which
increasingly accrued in kind to the state (in the form of requisitions as
well as labour and team duties). This limitation refers to the State's
power to extract resources from the economy; it does not, however, impair
the validity of the purely financial figures. The other serious problem is

the splitting of all economic transactions into two categories: some
expressed in fixed prices, others in free-market prices. Transactions by
government institutions and enterprises are expressed in fixed prices.
Wages and salaries of those employed by government and state enterprises are
expressed in free-market prices. As fixed prices fell increasingly behind
free-market prices, and payments in kind grew in importance, the budget
became merely a record of those expenditures by government institutions made
out of currency issues.

These figures have the peculiarity of being neither budget estimates (in the
sense that they were published at the end or after the period to which they
corresponded) nor actual figures - which were never published by the
Commissariat of Finance. An additional problem was that by 1920, many
nationalized enterprises were refusing to carry out book-keeping.

A proof of the limited validity of these budgets was provided by
Golanov[15], when he showed that the transfer expenditures and receipts
within the budget did not balance. Furthermore, these figures are not
comparable from year to year, due to the lack of a precise price index in an
economy ruled by two different sets of prices, with varying importance over
time.

2.   Fiscal and savings policies

In the Sixth Congress of the Communist Party held in July 1917, the
Bolsheviks proposed:

> the reform of the whole tax system by introducing a
> property tax, a tax on the increase in the value of
> property, and a high indirect tax on luxury goods,
> reform of the income tax.

During the first six months after the Revolution, little was done on fiscal
policy. Only a small number of Bolsheviks had any knowledge of financial
matters, and leadership was weaker here than in other policy spheres.

In May 1918, a programme was put forward which again emphasized direct
taxation. Yet it proved impossible for the government to carry out
large-scale direct taxation. Attempts to design a new income tax structure
failed partly because of lack of a suitable apparatus. Furthermore, the
government's economic measures had deprived the propertied class of much of
their income. The peasantry, who had large cash reserves, could not be
taxed without endangering their support for the Revolution. In fact, a
draft decree on a graded tax already approved by the Council of People's
Commissars in 1917 had to be withdrawn following opposition from the peasant
section of the Soviets' Central Executive Committee[16]. At the Congress of
Councils of National Economy in 1918, violent peasant resentment to local
contributions was expressed. The industrial workers - who provided the main
political support of the regime, and whose incomes were very low - could not
be taxed. Subsequent criticisms of Narkomfin (Commissariat of Finance) for
being unoriginal and unimaginative, seem relatively unfair, due to the
circumstances prevailing in that period.

Traditional taxes also yielded little revenue. Customs became insignificant
due to the fall in foreign trade. Excise revenues decreased as production
fell and as exchange of products stopped passing through the market. When
it was decided at the end of 1918 to place increasing reliance on indirect
taxation it was too late to obtain significant resources.

Of greater importance in the first year were taxes and 'contributions'
raised by local Soviets for their own use[17]. The revenue was based on
'contributions' levied on well-to-do citizens. This policy served two

purposes: it relieved the central authorities of financing local authorities
and it had political importance since it weakened the richer groups in the
countryside. It encouraged the Bolsheviks' rural supporters to manage local
affairs, without relying on officials - often hostile to the regime[18].

By the autumn of 1918, normal methods of raising money revenue were
exhausted. The government made a final effort in the form of an
Extraordinary Revolutionary Tax, intended to expropriate the cash resources
of the property-owning groups. Though measures - including acts of violence
- were used to enforce its collection and it was also levied on the middle
peasantry, its yield was substantially lower than expected[19].

This showed how complete had been the success in expropriating the
bourgeoisie, and how limited were the possibilities of future taxation on
their income (unless the middle peasantry were heavily taxed). Further, it
showed the dramatic limitations of the apparatus for assessment and
collection of direct taxation.

The limitations of Budget statistics have already been pointed out. As an
indicator only, the evolution of revenues (in real terms) is shown in Table
2.VI.

TABLE 2.VI

EVOLUTION OF TAX REVENUES

Year	Receipts (Million Gold Rubles)	% of 1913 total
1913	3,431.3	100.0
1918	199.7	5.8
1919	63.1	1.8
1920	19.4	0.6

Source: Shmelev, op.cit. in Sokolnikov, op.cit.

Other sources show an even greater fall.

This drastic decrease in money tax revenues did not imply that the state was
obtaining a decreasing part of the economy's resources: the state obtained
its resources mainly in kind.   In 1920 an attept was made to replace the
money budget by a balance of state income and expenditure in kind, which
implied a different concept of fiscal policy.   This attempt, though perhaps
of some theoretical interest, reached no results relevant for future
developments in the USSR or other socialist countries. As time passed, less
and less attention was given to financial problems (which seemed
insurmountable) and more emphasis was laid on the operation of the economy
in kind.

Money taxes lost their significance by 1920 and several taxes and duties
were abandoned.   In February 1921 a draft decree was prepared for abolishing
all money taxation.   The introduction of NEP prevented this step from being
taken.

Little can be said about the exact evolution of government expenditure, due
to poor statistical data.

It was difficult to limit central government expenditure.   The state was
obliged to maintain a large army and had to create an apparatus for
administering the growing nationalized sector.   The bureaucracy grew also,
because of the Bolsheviks' lack of experience and their wish to control the
state machinery.

The initial institutional attempts at controlling Central Government expenditure were not very successful[20]. The greatest problem, which turned attempts at centralised budgetary control into unreal paper work was increasing inflation.

Initially, it had been hoped that profits from nationalized enterprises would be a source of budget revenue. But on the contrary, nationalized enterprises became an increasing burden for the state budget. Their high losses had several causes, one being the rapid fall in industrial production. Another factor was galloping inflation in the 'free market', accompanied by fixed prices for goods sold by nationalized enterprises. Sales revenue could not equal money wages expenditure, which rose to meet increasing free-market prices[21]. Furthermore, employment and overhead costs fell less than output. The relative constancy of industrial employment was largely determined by the political impossibility of further reducing the industrial labour force – which provided the base for the Bolshevik Party.

Institutional and organizational factors played an important – though secondary – role in explaining the high levels of overhead costs and employment. The excessive reliance on administrative methods created several problems. The increasing entanglement of the planning apparatus caused a rapid growth in the proportion of subsidiary workers and employees to directly productive workers. The limited role played by the financial authorities implied a disregard for costs.

Initially loans and grants were made to nationalized enterprises via the state bank. The committee set up to examine applications for credits did not take its job seriously, nor was it properly coordinated with Vesenkha[22].

By the second half of 1918, Vesenkha obtained exclusive control over financing of industry (the Treasury automatically issued all grants which Vesenkha approved). The National Bank played no role. This institutional set-up had further adverse consequences. Vesenkha, in charge of physical planning and administration under the civil war, was interested in stimulating production without trying to limit costs. Vesenkha officers' expertise and interest in financial problems was obviously limited. Those enterprises who had profits reinvested them, and only losses were carried to the budget[23]. These problems created both excessive financial demands and inefficiency in the use of scarce physical resources.

As will be seen in Section III-3, financial control of nationalized enterprises lost all meaning as inflation grew and as money transactions lost importance. A budget deficit can be financed by an increase in saving (either foreign or internal). The Soviet Government could not hope to obtain foreign loans, mainly because of the hostility of foreign governments[24]. Encouragement of private savings – through placement of bonds – was also impossible, because of high inflation. Repudiation of previous domestic loans and the nature of the Bolshevik programme made this even less feasible.

3.   Increase in money circulation

Budget deficits were mainly financed by currency issue. Money in circulation increased approximately 120 times[25]. Annual increases of money in circulation are shown in Table 2.VII.

III.   Effects of financial and monetary policy

It is impossible to isolate completely the effects of one phenomenon (such as financial disequilibrium) from the rest of the economy. For analytical reasons, certain phenomena will be treated as being determined or conditioned essentially by the financial disequilibrium.

1.   Inflation

As shown in Table 2.VII, prices rose at an incredible speed. During most of the period 1918-21, prices were doubling every three or four months.

TABLE 2.VII

EVOLUTION OF MONEY AND PRICES, 1918-21

Year	% increase in money in circulation (over preceding years)[a]	%increase of free-market prices (over preceding years)[b]	Ratio of fixed prices to free-market prices (1917=100)[c]
1918	122	690	0.33
1919	267	1,376	0.10
1920	419	635	0.013
1921	1,400	1,616	fixed prices become gratuitous

(a)   Arnold, op.cit. based on Nashe Denishnoe Sbornik Materialou po Istorii. Deneznezhnogo Ofrascheniao. 1914-25, ed. by L. Yurovsky. Moscow. Commissariat of Finance.

Other sources give practically the same data.

(b)   Arnold, op.cit. based on the All-Union Budget Index of the Bureau of Labour Statistics. Other sources give slightly different increases.

(c)   Shmelev, op.cit. in Sokolnikov, op.cit. the index for the free-market prices does not correspond exactly to that of column two.

Prices rose much faster than the volume of currency (a tendency which began in 1916). As noted above, in the period between the Revolution and the end of War Communism, the quantity of money increased 120 fold; but during the same period price levels increased over 7,900 fold. This implies that the rate of inflation during this period was 65 times faster than the rate at which the volume of currency increased. As shown in Table 2.VII, the faster rate of increase in prices as opposed to currency is particularly marked in 1918 and 1919. There are several reasons which explain the rapid fall in the demand for money. In the first place, output declined drastically. During those years, there was a large contraction of territory under Soviet authority and a much smaller proportion of production went to the market. This implied that money was used in a smaller proportion of transactions in the economy. Finally, accelerated inflation led to a desire to abandon hoarding, particularly on the part of the peasantry.

A second important aspect is that two distinct sets of prices ruled throughout the economy. By 1919, nearly every consumer good was supposed to be sold at a fixed price. However, the majority of the food consumed by the urban population was bought in the 'free market' at prices increasingly divergent from these fixed prices[26]. As part of wages came to be paid in kind these products were sold on the 'free-market'. Often public institutions and nationalized industries sold on the 'free-market', although this practice was prohibited.

Although fixed prices were regularly increased, they diverged more and more from the 'free' prices at which the same commodities were exchanged on the

illegal but tolerated black market.   By 1920 distribution at fixed prices
virtually implied free distribution, which was finally introduced.

2.   Decrease in real value of money issue

Initially inflation enables a government to obtain command of resources by
financing with money issue the purchase of goods which it requires.

The private sector in the Soviet case (mainly the peasantry), when it
detects this phenomenon tries to reduce cash balances, thus increasing
money's velocity of circulation, which in turn accelerates inflation.   For
the government to acquire the same quantity of resources it has to increase
progressively its rate of currency issue.   This leads to a fall in the real
value of aggregate money in circulation and of money issue.

The Tsarist government, unable to finance the war through taxes, used note
issue as an important source of revenue.   This method initially allowed the
state to command a high level of resources.   However, from 1916 prices grew
quicker than money in circulation, and to obtain the same level of resources
issues were drastically increased.   As shown in Table 2.VIII, in 1917 the
resources obtained by the government through note issue increased (through a
quicker growth rate of money issue).   Rapidly increasing inflation after
1918 implied that the resources which the government could obtain through
currency issue fell sharply.   Not only taxation, but also the printing of
money was unable to provide the Soviet Government with the resources it
needed.

TABLE 2.VIII

REAL YIELD TO THE STATE FROM MONEY ISSUE

Year	Real yield (million 1914 rubles)
1914 (second half)	1,397
1915	2,068
1916	1,768
1917	2,500
1918	525
1919	386
1920	186
1921	146

Source: Same as Table 2.III.   The 1918-1921 period coincides almost
            exactly with Arnold, op.cit.   .

The yield from note issues fell from 81 per cent of total state revenues in
1918-19 to 27 per cent in 1920-21, while the yields accruing from
confiscations, levies, taxes in kind, etc. increased from 19 per cent to 73
per cent over the same period[27].

3.   The moneyless economy

The government could not obtain the resources it needed through the market
mechanism, even with the help of the printing press.   This was not merely an
effect of financial disequilibrium.   The underlying fact was that the civil
war made it even more crucial to safeguard food supplies to the army and the
towns, while sales of manufactured goods to the peasantry became impossible
as the army claimed all that a declining industry could produce.   The chief
instrument for obtaining the required supplies could no longer be trade and
exchange, but the extra-economic method of removing surpluses by
requisitioning.

In the field of financial planning and control, inflation was extremely damaging. The depreciating ruble was not only an inefficient medium of exchange, but also a completely unsuitable unit of account, (thus making impossible the accounting and control which Lenin had emphasized so much). This created serious technical difficulties for the operation of the budget, making it impossible to forecast government income. Appropriations granted in the budget quickly diminished in value (although at different rates, as relative prices changed rapidly). Revising budget appropriations - several times during the year - adversely affected financial discipline: it was impossible for the financial authorities to distinguish between expenditure revisions due to inflation and those due to lowered efficiency.

A related aspect was the problem of book-keeping. Recognizing the nominal value of transactions at fixed prices, government institutions and enterprises began to refuse to keep accounts between themselves - whether in money or other units. A considerable share of the transactions within the nationalized portion of the economy was never recorded. This made any control - not only financial but also physical - by the planning authorities virtually impossible[28]. By the end of 1920, the abolition of payments by the population for basic goods and sources had become widespread. The same occurred with payments between state institutions and enterprises, and debts between state enterprises were cancelled.

4.   Income distribution

As pointed out by Kalecki[29], normally wage and salary earners tend to suffer from hyperinflation, as the adjustment of wages lags behind price increases; profits - mainly of big business - increase. However, the Soviet case was different for two reasons. Big business was nearly completely nationalized at an early stage, and could not benefit from hyperinflation. As inflation increased, workers' incomes were protected by rationing and payments in kind. Thus the main negative effects of hyperinflation on income distribution occurring in a capitalist country were avoided because of the massive expropriation of the means of production and the physical distribution of goods - in this case of transition to socialism.

Several factors make it difficult to estimate the evolution of wages and their participation in national income. Workers were paid in kind, through a system which was not uniform through time, and differed for various regions. Rapid inflation and the two markedly different price systems add to measurement difficulties. An additional problem was that established rations or wages in kind could often not be paid, due to lack of supplies. General disorganization of statistics and accounting add yet another problem.

It seems easier to determine the effects of inflation on other groups' incomes. Hyperinflation complemented the redistribution of wealth and income caused by expropriations. Cash in the hands of the propertied class lost its value. Rents were fixed at low levels, and due to rapid inflation had a purely nominal value. These were obviously desirable effects from the Bolshevik viewpoint, since they weakened the propertied class and their economic force to resist the revolution[30].

Peasants who had hoarded money also lost income due to inflation, reducing their willingness to exchange their products for money. As will be discussed in the chapter on NEP, this threatened the very survival of the Soviet economy.

The final effect of inflation on peasant incomes depended on the ratio between industrial and agricultural prices. However, as time passed, it was neither inflation nor relative prices, but direct requisitioning which determined the peasantry's income level.

A group which obviously benefited from inflation and scarcity were those who operated on the black market (later called the Nepmen). Their enrichment through speculation, which the government was practically unable to control, was a further symptom of generalized disruption. It undoubtedly had a demoralizing effect on the working class.

IV   Evolution of the Bolsheviks' attitude towards money and finance

Opinions were split among the Bolsheviks about the role which money and finance should play during this period[31]. A small group - more important in the early years - thought financial orthodoxy convenient and compatible with Marxist thought. Thus, Sokolnikov, the first Commissar of Finance, said - referring to the abolition of money - "never, nowhere, not in a single Marxist work written before the October Revolution can one find it printed out that that is the way to attain Socialism"[32]. It is interesting to note that Lenin himself was very cautious about the abolition of money. As late as November 1920, he stated that "It is economically incorrect to dispense with money (or its substitutes) before the peasantry is furnished with things and before the uses of money are eliminated".

As inflation spread, and as the economy increasingly had to be managed on an administrative basis which replaced 'market and money' relations, those who supported the view that the abolition of money was desirable from the viewpoint of Marxist ideology became increasingly influential. Perhaps the most representative book in the 'liquidationist' tradition published in the period was Bukharin's The Economics of the Transition Period[33]. In it, he advocated the necessary naturalization of economic relations in the transition period. He then went on to say,

> Understandably, in the period of transition, in the process of destroying the commodity system as such, also the process of money's 'self-denial' will take place. This finds its expression in the so-called 'depreciation of money'.

The justification of this view was based on two arguments. The first stated that depreciation of the ruble was used or tolerated by the Soviet Government, because destroying the bourgeois monetary system helped to ruin the bourgeoisie[34]. As has been discussed, inflation did help decrease the wealth of the propertied classes, but it was not very important in achieving this objective. Excessive money printing threatened to disrupt the economy, and therefore weakened Bolshevik power. Had hyperinflation been deliberate, it would not have been an efficient instrument for achieving the political aims of this stage.

The second line of argument was that the depreciation of the ruble would lead to the moneyless communist order of the future. It was said that restricting the role of money would save the Bolsheviks much 'unnecessary work'. This argument had a serious bias in that it implied that the inflation policy adopted should have a purely long-term ideological aim, independent of the crucial short-term power struggle.

As inflation grew and money played a smaller role within the economy, the defenders of the role of money and finance were placed in a difficult position. Thus, Kristinskii[35], the Commissar of Finance in 1919, said "Finance should not exist in a socialist community and I therefore apologize for speaking on the subject". Even the Programme of the Bolshevik Party, adopted in 1919, described the abolition of money as a desirable aim:

> ...relying on the nationalization of banks, the Russian Communist Party strives to introduce crucial measures to expand the scope of cashless clearing and to prepare for the abolition of money.

For reasons given above expressions of faith in the abolition of money were not a basic cause of the policy of unlimited inflation, but mainly an ex-post justification of an inevitable process. Still, a general belief in the convenience of abolishing money immediately had some effect in accelerating inflation and replacing the money economy by a moneyless one.

The lack of importance attached to monetary policy (together with the impossibility of defining one) meant that in May 1919 all formal restrictions with respect to money issue were removed. This probably contributed - if marginally - to the ever increasing use of the printing-press.

The role of the People's Bank changed radically from a credit institution into a kind of national Clearing Office, until it was abolished in 1920. The Commissariat of Finance was defined as a book-keeping department, trying to establish moneyless settlements with a view to the total abolition of the monetary system.

As money's role declined, efforts were made to construct a budget in kind. Some Bolshevik economists even thought that no unit of account was necessary to replace money. The majority believed in the need to replace money by a labour unit of account, but the search for such a unit was unsuccessful and no concrete proposal for the establishment of a budget in kind was made.

Theoretical discussions about the moneyless economy were much more an effect than a cause of economic conditions. It seems, however, amazing that so much effort and talent was devoted to work such as the definition of a labour unit of account, when the economy's problems were so critical that they endangered the very survival of the government.

V   Summary and conclusions

The existing literature on War Communism has yielded conflicting interpretations about the influence which ideology had on the development of hyperinflation and the moneyless economy. The Soviet literature on the subject[36] adopts the view that it was the rigorous conditions and military requirements of the period which led the Soviet State into pursuing policies which led in turn to War Communism. Some Western authors[37] share the view that the Bolsheviks had little or no choice, and that War Communism was a product of necessity and not of ideology.

Recent East European literature challenges the Soviet interpretation. It puts forward the view that War Communism was not merely a socialist pattern of war economy imposed by necessity, but was to a great extent a specific economic model, aimed at laying the foundations of socialist economy and having its own established ideological and theoretical background. The most comprehensive work in this area is that of L. Szamuely[38]. Some conservative Western writers[39] carry this view to extremes. They maintain that hyper-inflation and the moneyless economy were exclusively a product of ideology and were deliberately pursued by the Bolshevik leadership, which could have followed alternative policies.

On the basis of the empirical evidence compiled and analyzed in this study, I would support the first interpretation and would argue that there was extremely little room for manouvre for the Bolsheviks during the period 1917-21. The main elements determining the financial disequilibrium in this period have their origin in the very fact that the Bolshevik Revolution - with its specific political aims - had taken place in the Soviet Union, at that specific historical moment[40]. The Bolsheviks themselves had very little power to modify these elements.

Four exogenous elements[41] limited the flexibility of financial and monetary policy at this period (and particularly till the end of the Civil War):

1)   Disruption in production, destruction of assets, and a fall in foreign trade, begun during the War, worsened due to the Civil War and foreign aggression. This drastically limited the base for taxation, as well as increasing the financial needs of the nationalized enterprises.

2)   Expropriation of the means of production and repudiation of debt – measures based on the Bolshevik political aims – greatly limited the base for direct taxation, as well as for loans.

3)   The critical military situation obliged the Bolsheviks to give first priority to maintaining the Red Army. This made reductions in defence expenditure impossible.

4)   The limitations of the fiscal apparatus and the Bolsheviks' lack of experience limited their ability to raise revenues or curtail expenditure.

These factors restricted the Bolsheviks' power to pursue a traditionally 'successful' financial policy[42]. The only feasible improvement was in the field of taxation policy. Mainly during the first year, indirect taxation could have raised higher revenues, had the traditional ideological opposition to it been overcome. However, its effect would have been marginal.

A further factor limiting the scope of financial policy was the financial disequilibrium and accumulated inflationary pressures inherited from the War. Inflation was running at such high levels in 1917 that accumulated pressures alone practically pre-determined the need for high inflation. Furthermore, when the Bolsheviks took power, prices were already rising quicker than money issue. As shown in Table 2.VIII, in 1918 the real yield of money issue fell to one fifth of the 1917 yield. One year after the Revolution, the practice of extracting resources via 'inflation tax' could no longer be implemented[43].

Thus, as the government could not obtain the resources it so vitally needed (particularly to supply the Army) through economic policy it had to resort to extra-economic mechanisms: these were the methods of War Communism. War Communism policies themselves exacerbated financial disequilibria. The double system of pricing (one for sales and another for wages) increased losses in the state sector. Demonetization of transactions limited the base for indirect taxation[44].

At this stage belief in the moneyless economy – though basically an ex-post justification of the disequilibria – accelerated inflation still further, although the influence of this 'ideological factor' cannot be measured. But however great its significance might appear, it occurred at a stage when the disequilibria were already so great that further pressure could make little difference.

Even though hyper-inflation was to a large extent unavoidable, the damage it did to Soviet economy and society in the initial phase of transition to socialism are of importance for other experiences of transition.

Notes

1   For details see P.I. Lyashchenko, op.cit.

2   'The Tasks of the Proletariat in the Present Revolution' in V.I.
     Lenin, Collected Works, Vol. XXIV, Lawrence, London, 1933.

3   V.I. Lenin, Collected Works, Vol. XXVI.

4   E.A. Preobrazhensky and N.I. Bukharin, The ABC of Communism; a popular
     explanation of the program of the Communist Party of Russia, Michigan.
     Ann Arbor, 1966.

5   A good account can be found in E.H. Carr, The Bolshevik Revolution
     (1917-23), Penguin Books, Vol. 2, 1966.

6   Source: E.H. Carr, The Bolshevik Revolution, Vol. 2, op. cit.

7   Can the Bolsheviks retain State Power? in V.I. Lenin, Collected Works,
     Vol. XXVI, op. cit.

8   'The Immediate Tasks of the Soviet Government' in V.I. Lenin,
     Collected Works, Vol. XXVII, op.cit.

9   We shall discuss this in more detail below.

10   K. Shmelev, 'Public Finances during the Civil War' in G.S. Sokolnikov
     and Associates, Soviet Policy in Public Finance 1917-28, op.cit.

11   E.H. Carr, The Bolshevik Revolution (1917-23), Vol. 2, op.cit.

12   Loc.cit. page 197.

13   Data taken from M. Dobb, Soviet Economic Development since 1917,
     London, Routledge and Kegan Paul, 1966, page 100 and E.H. Carr, The
     Bolshevik Revolution, Vol. 2. op.cit. page 198, both based on early
     Soviet estimates.

14   Simultaneously with requisitioning at low prices, the government tried
     to supply the peasants with manufactured goods, also at low prices.
     However this did not change the compulsory nature of state
     collections. The extent to which the state could supply manufactured
     goods to the villages was negligible. Also, grants of manufactured
     goods did not correspond to the amounts of produce requisitioned from
     each individual. The more well-to-do peasant, who supplied most of
     the grain, received no more manufactured goods, and sometimes less,
     than his poorer neighbour.

15   Article by Golanov, S.A., in Vol. II, Na novykh putiakh, quoted in
     Shmelev's article, op.cit. in Sokolnikov, op.cit.

16   Dyachencko   Sovetskie   finansy   v   pervei   faze   razvitya
     sotcialistickeskogo gosudarstva, quoted in Davies, op.cit.

17   The importance of these taxes was their success. In absolute terms,
     they were probably not significant; there are no reliable estimates of
     their volume.

18   This procedure met with strong opposition from Narkomfin, which
     maintained that this type of taxation caused unnecessary resentment
     due to its arbitrariness, and that it disrupted the collection of
     ordinary taxes.

19   It had been expected to raise ten billion rubles by December 1919.
      Approximately 1.2 billion were in fact raised.

20   As initially the Treasury refused to carry out the Government's
      instructions, it was replaced by a new office, issuing allocations
      according to a rough system of priorities. A Special Committee for
      Reduction of State Expenditure was established in 1918; it did not
      operate very efficiently and the complaint was made that vital
      institutions received less than they had in the previous regime, while
      superfluous institutions obtained excessive grants. Apparently in
      1919, some improvements were achieved. The Commission established for
      this purpose reduced excessive claims. Although the figures of
      reduction are quite spectacular (estimated 33% of original demands for
      1919) the doubt always remains whether the departments – knowing that
      their demands would be cut down – did not put forward excessive
      claims.

21   Towards the end, wages were also paid in kind. However,
      demonetization of transactions was much quicker and wider in sales
      than in payments to labour.

22   The lack of coordination between institutions and general
      disorganisation of the state apparatus is illustrated by the cases
      where owners of property about to be nationalized by Vesenkha
      mortgaged it with a branch of the National Bank just before it was
      nationalized.

23   This can be easily understood. Vesenkha, over-burdened with work,
      acted mostly under pressure. The enterprises who had losses were
      permanently pressing for funds, the enterprises with profits would not
      approach Vesenkha. Vesenkha officials did not have the time, the
      experience, or the resources to control enterprises with profits.

24   According to Davies, op.cit. Sokolnikov spoke optimistically in May
      1918 of foreign loan prospects; the events immediately following
      showed how unfeasible this was.

25   As Arnold points out, different monetary units on any given day during
      this period did not have the same purchasing power (money printed in
      different periods had different values). Another interesting
      phenomenon was the large quantities of money and money substitutes
      placed in circulation by agencies other than the central government
      (the 'White' generals, the foreign invaders, Soviet municipal
      governments and others).

26   It has been estimated – by Shmelev, op.cit. – that in 1919
      approximately 75% of foodstuffs was bought at free market prices.

27   Arnold, op.cit.

28   For example, when in 1920 the Commissariat of Finance sent out special
      investigators with instructions to ascertain on the basis of an
      examination of records whether the amounts asked for were really
      needed, the chaotic conditions of those records eliminated the
      possibility of reaching any conclusion.

29   M. Kalecki, 'A Model of Hyper-inflation', in The Manchester School of
      Economic and Social Studies, Sept. 1962.

30   It reduced the wealth and income of particular groups such as affluent
      landlords, less affected by expropriation measures.

31   The hectic revolutionary period hardly made it possible for precise
        theoretical frameworks to be elaborated. Much of the literature
        consisted of newspaper articles, speeches on their brochures.
        Bukharin's book - quoted below - was one of the few exceptions.

32   Quote from Arnold, op.cit.

33   Published in Moscow, 1920. The English version is published by
        Bergman Publishers, Pluto Press, 1971, New York. See the discussion
        of this work in Chapter 1 of this study.

34   This was implied in the much quoted passage of Preobazhensky, where he
        described the printing press as 'that machine-gun of the Commissariat
        of Finance which poured fire into the rear of the bourgeois system and
        used the currency laws of that regime in order to destroy it.'

35   Quote from Arnold, op.cit.

36   See for example, Soviet Financial Systems, Progress Publishers,
        Moscow, 1966; Political Economy, Sikra, Moscow, 1955.

37   Dobb, op.cit. and Carr, op.cit.

38   First Models of the Socialist Economic System, Akademiae Kiado,
        Budapest, 1974. This book quotes extensively from Soviet thinking and
        debates during the period of War Communism and NEP, and devotes a
        large section to the evolution of Lenin's thought.

39   For example, Peter Wiles in his article 'The Political and Social
        Pre-Requisites for a Soviet-Type Economy', Ost-europa, 10(2-3).

40   Many of these elements would be common to any seizure of power by a
        Socialist Revolution, carried out - or defended - by the use of
        extended violence, in an under-developed country. However, the
        circumstances in the USSR were particularly adverse: a very difficult
        economic situation inherited from World War I, strong internal and
        external armed Opposition, no external allies.

41   Exogenous in the sense of external to the policy maker.

42   A successful financial policy is defined here as one through which the
        government is able to obtain the resources it needs without creating
        excessive monetary disequilibria.

43   The relation between the phenomenon of inherited inflation and the
        need to apply War Communist methods is not clearly brought out in any
        of the literature on this period (either Marxist or non-Marxist).

44   The effect on taxation of different factors can be very roughly
        measured. The more substantial fall of taxation - in 1918 the level
        of taxation was equivalent to 5.8% of 1913 level, in real terms -
        occurred as effects of the War, Civil War and foreign intervention.
        The implementation of War Communist policies reduced taxation still
        further. By 1920, the level of taxation reached 0.6% of the 1913
        level; this reduction was smaller - to one fifth of the 1918 level.
        War Communism only accentuated an already disastrous taxation problem.

3

FINANCIAL POLICIES UNDER NEP, 1921-25

I   Introduction

For analytical purposes, the nature of the objectives and policies applied during NEP will be described as if they had been defined in a clear-cut way. It is necessary to point out that a great part of the government policy applied during this period veered in different directions and that there were strong disagreements among the Bolsheviks. Bettleheim[1] maintains that NEP is not - as many Soviet historians claim - merely a new economic policy but a new political strategy which corresponds to a re-structuring of the relation between workers and peasants. NEP was not introduced at a stroke, but constituted a series of measures which grew gradually out of each other; many of its implications were not even visualized when the first measures were introduced.

The first stage of NEP, which covers the period between March 1921 and December 1925, will be analyzed here. This period can be distinguished from the second stage economically, politically and financially. In fact, Soviet historians group together War Communism and the first years of NEP in a stage which extends from October 1917 to 1925, and which they define as a period of social revolution as distinct from the next stage of socialist industrialization[2].

In December 1925, the 14th Party Congress approved the policy of socialist industrialization. This gave priority to industrial development with particular stress on heavy industry. 1925 was also a turning point for agriculture. During this year the greatest appeasement of the peasant was reached - expressed in the 'Face to the Countryside' policy. The peasantry responded negatively, by hoarding grain. The needs of rapid industrialization, coupled with disappointment at the peasantry's reaction to the concessions granted to it provoked, after 1926, a tendency to side with the poor peasants, and a renewed search for direct ways of inducing the richer peasants to part with their surplus.

In 1926, there was a corresponding shift of emphasis in finance and banking, away from stabilization and financing economic recovery towards planned distribution of credit and a reorganization of the banking system. The predominant role played by financial policy was taken over by industrial development policy, and monetary policy became much more passive again, accounting partly for higher inflation and greater shortages after 1925.

II   Political and Economic Framework

1   Political and economic objectives of this stage

Again, the determinant objective was the political one of maintaining power, under prevailing circumstances. The end of civil war revealed the extent of the destruction which it had caused (as well as the additional economic problems provoked by War Communism) and removed the restraints of loyalty which civil war had implied. The peasants' support of the Bolshevik regime and their reluctant submission to requisition had been largely determined by fear of a White comeback and subsequent loss of land. After the civil war ended, mass peasant resistance to requisitioning began, involving uprisings and looting. Lack of food spread political unrest to the factory workers; it also induced part of the population to leave the cities.

The problem was clearly pointed out by Lenin[3] when he began his defence of a tax in kind:

> Comrades, the question of substituting a tax for
> surplus-grain appropriation is primarily and mainly a

political question, for it is essentially a question
of the attitude of the working class to the peasantry.

The essential importance of maintaining the alliance with the peasantry so
that the proletariat might keep state power is stressed in Lenin's writings
and speeches. He emphasized that in Russia the overwhelming majority of the
population were small agricultural producers.   Therefore, Lenin[4]
concluded: 'so long as there is no revolution in other countries, only
agreement with the peasantry can save the socialist revolution in Russia.'

The challenge which the peasantry posed to Soviet power was economic rather
than directly political.   It was insufficient food supplies which most
menaced the survival of the Soviet regime. Lenin pointed out[5]:

> ... What we must fear is protracted starvation, want
> and food shortage, which create the danger that the
> proletariat will be utterly exhausted and will give
> way to petty-bourgeois vacillation and despair.

If the peasantry was not satisfied,

> it will be impossible – economically impossible – in
> view of the delay in the world revolution to preserve
> the rule of the proletariat in Russia...[6] ... it
> will take essentially two things to satisfy the
> farmer. The first is a certain freedom of exchange,
> freedom for the small private proprietor, and the
> second is the need to obtain commodities and
> products[7].

The effects of the measures taken to satisfy the needs of the peasantry were
far reaching; most of the policies adopted during NEP responded – directly
or indirectly – to this purpose.

2   General economic conditions and policies

(a)   NEP policies and their positive effects

Economic conditions and policies during the early stages of NEP were far
more complex than those existing during War Communism. Although general
trends can be distinguished, several important economic variables and
policies fluctuated violently, including terms of trade between agriculture
and industry.

First the general policies of NEP will be described, as well as their
positive effects on the economy's recovery, which coincide with the years
1921–23.   After 1923 – although production continued to recover – the
contradictions inherent in the policies became increasingly explicit, and
began to challenge NEP's success. An exception was in the financial sphere,
where the years 1924–25 marked a period of stabilization. As shall be seen,
there is more than a casual link between the increasing contradictions of
NEP and the success of financial policy.   These financial aspects will be
analysed separately.

One of the NEP's basic aims was to stimulate agriculture. For this, it was
necessary to guarantee the peasants freedom to dispose of their surplus;
with this aim requisitioning was substituted by the tax in kind, which
differed from requisitioning in that the volume levied on the peasantry was
previously fixed, and not arbitrary. The peasant had the security that
beyond the limit of the tax, his produce would not be expropriated; he had
an incentive to increase production so as to maximize his surplus.
Furthermore, tax rebates were offered to peasants who increased the area of

land sown or its productivity. The total tax burden was much lower than the value obtained through requisitioning. The volume effectively collected in 1921 was half the level obtained through requisitioning in 1920[8].

The substitution of requisitioning by taxation in kind had as logical corollary a return to private trade. Initially, the authorities tried to limit trade to local markets, but their efforts were unsuccessful and free trade spread throughout the country.

The right of the peasantry to trade their surplus produce meant that agriculture and industry were linked by market relations. The government's monopoly of purchase and allocation of all agricultural supplies ended. This operation was now carried out by financially autonomous cooperatives and by private traders.   Centralized supply of goods to industrial enterprises was discontinued; state enterprises were allowed to buy and sell on the market. Gradually money-transactions among state industries, as well as between industry and agriculture, were restored.   This process also determined the gradual change from wages in kind to money wages, and the system of rationed supplies declined.   Nationalized enterprises became financially autonomous and were removed from the state budget. The aim of these independent economic units was to make a profit and the state was not obliged to cover any losses incurred.   The Soviet government satisfied another important aspect of the peasants' demands in legally allowing them freedom to choose the form in which the land should be cultivated (communal, individual, cooperative or mixed).

Small industry - especially in rural areas - was given security and opportunities to trade. Some industries which had been nationalized were leased to private persons, cooperatives, or groups of workers. Most of the enterprises leased were very small, with large-scale industry remaining in the state sector.   According to Rozenfeld[9], in 1923, although 88.5 per cent of the industrial enterprises were privately owned or leased to private persons, state enterprises represented 92.4 per cent of industrial production.

The policies of NEP, the favourable terms of trade and the good weather contributed to an excellent harvest in 1922; during this year, total agricultural output reached approximately 75 per cent of the pre-war level[10].

TABLE 3.I

EVOLUTION OF AGRICULTURE AND INDUSTRY

	1913	1921	1922	1923	1924	1925	1926
Grain gross production (mill, quintals)	801.0	n.a	503.1	565.9	514.0	724.6	768.3
Industrial output[a] (mill.roubles, 1926 prices)	10,251	1,925	2,512	3,829	4,469	7,346	10,277

Source: A. Baykov, Development of the Soviet Economic System, Cambridge University Press, 1946.

(a)   Refers to output in large scale industry

As shown in Table 3.I, after 1922 agricultural output continued to make a rapid recovery. By 1925, the grain harvest reached 90 per cent of the pre-war level[11]; other crops surpassed pre-war production by 1925.

The initial recovery of industry was much slower than that of agriculture. As shown in Table 3.I, in 1922 total industrial output (in large-scale industry) was 25 per cent of the pre-war level. (Other sources give slightly higher figures.) The growth of industrial output was seriously restricted at first by lack of fuel, food and raw materials. Gradually these bottlenecks to industrial recovery disappeared and the growth of agricultural output provided a market for industry. The expansion of industrial output was of an easy nature, requiring little fresh investment ᵢ fixed capital. It was mainly achieved by bringing into use labour power, buildings and machinery made idle when production had fallen.

(b)   Contradictions and problems inherent in NEP policies

In its effort to satisfy the peasantry, NEP restored the market economy and also granted other concessions to the peasantry; both these policies caused increasing contradictions.

By restoring a market economy, NEP restored the interdependence of the economic units according to capitalist rules. The economy was capitalist or pre-capitalist except for nationalized industries; but even these were obliged to operate on commercial principles. This provoked short-term, negative effects more characteristic of a capitalist than of a socialist economy. Income distribution became more unequal, as differences in earnings increased within both the countryside and the cities; higher unemployment worsened inequality.

As L. Kritsman said[12]: "The process of differentiation of the peasantry and the process of development of capitalism are one and the same thing ...". The process of differentiation in the countryside was facilitated by leasing of land, hiring of labour and loaning of draught animals and agricultural machines.

Wages were fixed by voluntary contract between worker or trade union and employer. This implied increasing differentials in the level of wages between different industries (high wages in industries with higher profits or in private enterprises). To encourage production, wages were linked to productivity, which increased the scope for inequality. The wage scale itself was broadened considerably, with particularly high wages paid to specialists and managers[13].

As can be seen in Table 3.II, there was a dramatic increase in unemployment during this period. This was caused initially by massive dismissals of workers from nationalized enterprises acting according to commercial rules and by the central government, due to expenditure cuts. After 1923, the increase in unemployment was accompanied by an increase in industrial employment; population growth, accompanied by increasing differentiation in the countryside, forced peasants to seek urban employment. Little was done to alleviate unemployment. Some public works were initiated with the purpose of absorbing it, but for fiscal reasons these programmes were extremely limited.

TABLE 3.II

UNEMPLOYMENT

October 1921	150,000
January 1922	175,000
January 1923	625,000
January 1924	1,240,000

Source: E.H. Carr, The Bolshevik Revolution, Vol. 2, op.cit.

The other negative effect of restoring a market economy was the loss of the
government's centralized control over the economy.   Not only could the
government not allocate resources between sectors, but it was also unable to
orient the economy through indirect mechanisms, such as terms of trade
between agriculture and industry.   It was paradoxical that in an economy in
transition to socialism, fluctuations in relative prices - produced largely
by market phenomena - were more violent than in capitalist countries.

The essential aim pursued by NEP was a recovery of agricultural output, so
as to increase marketable surplus.   The first aim was achieved: by 1925-6,
grain production was about nine tenths of the pre-war level.   However, the
change in the marketable surplus was much less satisfactory: the volume of
marketed surplus of grain was estimated by some sources to be less than half
the pre-war amount.

TABLE 3.III

Evolution of grain output and of its marketed surplus

	Total grain prod. (m. poods)	Grain marketed outside village (m. poods)	% of total harvest which is marketed
Before the war	5,000	1,300	26.0%
1926/7	4,749	630	13.3%

Source: M. Dobb, op.cit. p.217.   Based on figures quoted by Stalin, and
compiled by the Soviet Central Statistical Department.   Some
authors have queried these figures, pointing out that Stalin
understated the level marketed in 1926/27.   For a brief
discussion of recent literature, see A. Nove, An Economic History
of the USSR, Penguin Books, 1980, p.111.

By 1925, it became clear that under NEP the problem would not be
agricultural output but the willingness of the peasant to market it.   The
1925-26 harvest was extremely good (see Table 3.III).   However, that year
the government had greater difficulties than before in purchasing at
official prices from the peasants.

One of the main reasons for the increasing difficulties which the state
faced in buying grain was the growing independence and bargaining power of
the well-to-do peasant, thanks to the economic concessions he obtained under
NEP.   Administrative pressure on the wealthy peasant had been abandoned;
greater economic power gave the wealthy peasant the power to hoard grain,
choosing the time and terms at which he wished to sell it.   Furthermore, the
peasant's higher income enabled him to increase his food consumption.

However, the fall - far below pre-war level - of the proportion of output
marketed was not caused mainly by NEP policies, but by the character of the
1917 agrarian revolution.   Because land was much more equally distributed,
the village was eating more and selling less of its produce; the proportion
of home consumption was larger in the smaller units, and their importance
had increased substantially.

This fall in the marketable surplus is explained far more by the fact that
the big units - which market a much higher proportion of their output -
represented a smaller proportion of the output, than by the fact that the
wealthier peasants were marketing a smaller share of their output than
before the war[14].

As it could not go very far in stimulating capitalist development of
agriculture, NEP was unable to solve the essential problem which the
agrarian revolution had posed. By increasing the bargaining power of the
wealthy peasant, it only made the problem more acute. At the time,
Bolshevik policy towards the peasantry faced further serious dilemmas. The
Soviet Government wished the peasantry to increase production and marketed
surplus; however the more successful 'middle peasants', (that is, those who
in fact increased their output and marketed surplus more) became 'wealthy
peasants', and were then viewed with suspicion as potential class enemies to
the revolution.

Even the definitions and statistics on 'peasant stratification' were
contradictory at the time, being often adapted to suit particular political
circumstances or positions. This was especially true for the definition of
'wealthy peasant', more often known as 'Kulak'. Nove (in An Economic
History of the USSR, op.cit. pp.107-113) points out the difficulty of
distinguishing between the middle peasant and the Kulaks. In fact, the
so-called Kulaks were commonly considered to be the richest five to seven
per cent of the peasantry. As Nove points out, many of the Kulaks were
quite poor, by Western standards. It was only some of the richer Kulaks who
were able to act as usurers, hire labour, or hold on to a large proportion
of their production, thus benefiting from the higher prices occurring long
after the harvest. The total value of grain surpluses that was withheld by
Kulaks seems to have been over-estimated by many Bolsheviks; as a result,
when at a later date measures were taken to requisition grain surpluses from
the Kulaks, the middle peasantry was necessarily also affected.

III   Need for a Stable Currency

With NEP, products again assumed the character of commodities.   Market
relations - as they expanded - could only be conducted in monetary terms.
Money became crucial both as medium of exchange and unit of account.

As Sokolnikov correctly pointed out, a stable unit of account was a
pre-requisite for planning, particularly for planning of a financial nature.
However, with NEP, a stable monetary unit was necessary to the efficient
operation of an economy, under market conditions.   In particular the
effective restoration of the market link with the countryside was difficult
while the peasantry was being paid in rapidly depreciating currency.

The most elementary principles of cost accounting - basic for enterprises
operating on a profit basis - could not be applied without a stable unit of
account.   Furthermore, during hyper-inflation, the devising of ways of
getting out of currency became more profitable than increases in efficiency.

The need for a stable monetary unit was soon officially recognized by the
Party leadership.   In December 1921, the Ninth Congress of Soviets[15]
decided that:

> ... the realization of the new economic policy
> necessitates the adoption of a financial policy that
> is in full accord with it. There arises, therefore,
> the problem of effecting a gradual transition to a
> stable monetary unit.

Narkomfin was charged with 'the task of carrying into effect with the utmost
energy and speed the curtailment and eventually the complete cessation of
note issue'.

However, during the first three years of NEP, monetary stability could not
be achieved.   In this transitional phase, alternative mechanisms were
applied which partially replaced some of the functions of a stable monetary

unit. Initially many were made in terms of 'pre-war rubles'. The value of many transactions was calculated by multiplying the sum expressed in pre-war units by a price index determined by Narkomfin. Later this index was replaced by the rate at which the State Bank was buying gold. Long theoretical discussions were carried out between Soviet economists on the greater convenience of 'gold ruble' vs. 'commodity ruble' (see Yurovsky and Katzenellenbaum op.cit. in Chapter 2). Like the discussions on the labour unit of value during War Communism, this issue was trivial in relation to the essential problems facing the Soviet economy at that moment.

However, the indexes affecting wages did have a controversial practical effect. Local authorities were themselves calculating price indexes mainly adjusted to the limitations of funds available for wage payment. The 'juggling of the price-index' was denounced as causing a decrease in real wages[16]. In that sense, inflation - accompanied by under-estimated price indexes - was indirectly a policy instrument to pull down real wages.

These price-index numbers did serve as measure of value and deferred payments - if very inefficiently. However, they were useless as a medium of exchange, since trade could not be based on an abstract arithmetical standard. By 1922, the need for a stable medium of exchange began to be satisfied with the spontaneous use of gold coins and foreign currency (even state enterprises used them); this showed how essential a stable currency was under NEP.

IV   Political and Economic Forces which Affect Financial Equilibrium

1   Forces which prevent financial equilibrium

Even though the need to establish a stable currency had been politically recognized since 1921, monetary reform and relative monetary stability were not achieved until 1924.

The currency could not be stabilized during 1922 and 1923 because a high proportion of the budget deficit was financed with note issue. The basic reasons were the economy's slow recovery and slow 'monetization'. There was also a time lag between the decision to apply certain policies (i.e. increase taxation), their implementation and the achievement of their full effects. The time lag was particularly long because the economy and the state apparatus were disrupted, and because policy changes were so great.

A pre-condition for stabilization was a reduction in the Budget deficit, requiring a curtailment of state expenditure. Initially, state enterprises were a heavy burden on budget expenditure: the 1922 'sales crisis', which lowered industrial prices, worsened state enterprises' financial results and the budget also had to supply these enterprises with the initial working capital which they lacked. Great efforts were made to create and reconstruct state and local taxation, but significant results were not achieved immediately. The limited extension of private property further reduced the base for direct taxation.

Additionally, there were a number of institutional and organizational obstacles to increasing taxation. The loss of taxation experts, which had occurred during War Communism, could be only slowly made up. The weakness of the tax apparatus was aggravated by lack of 'tax-discipline', both in the socialized and private sectors. The autonomous power of managers in state industry, due to the introduction of commercial principles, made it difficult to enforce tax payments at first; furthermore, these managers had lost the habit of paying taxes, and claimed that they were unable to pay them due to the financially unsound position of most state industry. Some economists and managers even argued that it was absurd for state industries to pay taxes as this 'merely shifted state money from one pocket to another'

- exactly the same phrase was used by many managers of nationalized industry and by some economists in Chile during the Allende period!

Public borrowing was limited due to the economic circumstances. Most of the 'bonds' placed had a compulsory or semi-compulsory nature, other 'bonds' merely anticipated revenue collection, instead of increasing it.   Private saving deposits were revived in 1923, but their significance was very limited.

2   Forces which allow financial equilibrium

The reduction in the budget deficit was achieved both by a substantial increase in state revenue and by curtailing public expenditure.

(a)   State revenue

We shall distinguish tax revenue, non-tax revenue and net revenues from state loans.

Priority was given to the reconstruction of the tax apparatus. Towards the end of 1922, the new tax scheme developed for NEP was practically completed. Simultaneously, special attention was paid to personnel problems, and efforts were made to shift former tax experts back into their work and to train new ones[17].

The evolution of taxation for the period 1922/3-1925/6 is given in Table 3.IV.

TABLE 3.IV

EVOLUTION OF TAX REVENUE 1922/3 - 1925/6 (MILLION ROUBLES)

Type of tax	1922/3 (a)	%	1923/4	%	1924/5	%	1925/6	%
Agricultural tax	176.5	37.2	231.0	29.4	326.2	24.7	251.7	14.1
Promtax on social economy	59.2	12.4	113.1	14.4	92.8	7.0	134.9	7.5
Promtax on private sector					64.5	4.8	94.3	5.2
Income tax on social economy	12.7	2.7	7.9	1.0	33.0	2.5	65.3	3.7
Income tax on population			56.8	7.2	61.3	4.6	86.1	4.8
I. Total direct taxes	248.4	52.3	408.8	52.0	577.8	43.6	632.3	35.3
Excises	103.5	21.8	240.7	30.6	507.8	38.3	841.6	47.0
Customs	66.7	14.1	67.4	8.6	101.9	7.6	150.5	8.4
II. Total indirect taxes	170.2	35.9	308.1	39.2	609.7	45.9	992.1	55.4
Dues and levies	23.1	4.9	67.3	8.6	122.6	9.2	157.9	8.8
Other taxes	32.9	6.9	1.3	0.2	17.6	1.3	8.9	0.5
III. Other taxes	66.0	13.8	68.6	8.8	140.2	10.5	166.8	9.3
IV. Total taxation	474.6	100.0	785.5	100.0	1,327.7	100.0	1,791.2	100.0

Source: Based on data in R. Davies, op.cit. page 82.

(a)   There are no detailed statistics for the first nine months of 1922.

A serious problem in analyzing the evolution of tax revenue is data comparability. Important shifts in the classification of revenues occurred. In 1922/23 and part of 1923/24, the budget was executed in a rapidly falling currency; it was calculated firstly in price-indexes and then in gold roubles. Although this allows comparison in more stable units, the quality and variability of the price indexes used limit comparability. A further complication arises because payments in kind were not abandoned until 1924/25, with these constituting 55 per cent of budgetary receipts in 1922, 10 per cent in 1922/23 and 3 per cent in 1923/24[18].

As can be seen in Table 3.V, during the period 1922-26, there was a substantial increase in tax in real terms. By 1924/25, money taxation reached nearly 50 per cent of Budget revenue.

TABLE 3.V

RATIO OF MONETARY TAXATION
TO 1913 LEVEL (IN REAL TERMS)

Year	Ratio
1913	100.0
1919 (a)	1.8
1920 (b)	0.6
1921 (b)	1.6
1922 (b)	3.0
1924/5 (c)	43.0
1925/6 (c)	54.0

(a)   Table 2.VI in Chapter 2.
(b)   Yurovsky, op.cit.
(c)   Davies, op.cit.

Note: Data for 1922/23 and 1923/24 are excluded because of
           comparability problems discussed above.

The taxation increase achieved was due mainly to a substantial growth in
excises; their participation in total tax revenue increased systematically,
from 21.8 per cent in 1922/23 to 47.0 per cent in 1925/26 (see Table 3.IV).
This increase in indirect taxation was partly explained by the introduction
of excises on a varied number of goods, and the increase in some of their
rates. However, output growth and rapid 'monetization' of the economy were
key factors.

Direct taxation played a greater role than before the war in financing the
budget[19].   However direct taxation grew more slowly than indirect
taxation, its participation in total revenue falling systematically (see
table 3.IV), due to the drastic decrease in the proportion of revenue
collected from agriculture. In 1925/26 the volume of the tax was lower even
in current terms.

Although agricultural production had grown substantially, as we saw, the
level of the agricultural tax was far lower than the value of the compulsory
collections in kind during War Communism.   Furthermore, the level of
taxation as a percentage of the peasantry's income was also far lower than
in the pre-war periods.   According to one Soviet source[20], taxation of
peasants accounted for only 8.1 per cent of their income in 1925-26, as
against 13.7 per cent in 1913.

The decision to maintain such a low level of agricultural taxation was
obviously a political one. The tax raised was lower than that suggested by
'technical' and financial institutions.   Both TSSU (Central Statistical
Administration) and Narkomfin estimated that in 1923/24 600 million gold
rubles could be raised in taxation from the peasants, but a target of only
400 million rubles was in fact set. A proposal from Narkomfin in 1924 to
make the agricultural tax more progressive was resisted, because of
opposition from the richer peasants.   It is interesting that the
'conservative' body, NKF, was advocating higher and more progressive direct
taxation.   In fact, perhaps more than conservative, NKF was less sensitive
to political constraints and objectives than the politicians.

The political leadership believed that too high a tax (particularly on the
richer peasants) would restrict agricultural growth, harming economic
recovery. The XIVth Party Conference in 1925 stated that the progression of
the tax must be such as to 'enable the further development of the economy.'
This was clearly correct in 1921 when the replacement of excessive and

arbitrary requisitions by lower and previously determined taxes helped
economic recovery.   In later years, there was less economic justification
for the agricultural tax to grow less than output (and even less
justification for the absolute level to be lowered in 1925/26).   In fact,
growing inequality in the countryside - together with a general improvement
in economic conditions - provided a base for higher and more progressive
direct taxation.   On the contrary, this lenient tax policy, together with
other concessions, contributed to increases in the peasantry's purchasing
power far greater than the supply of consumer goods available to them.
After 1924 the main owners of grain surpluses, the richer peasants, had
neither the financial need nor an immediate interest in selling grain. Due
to the increase in their cash holdings, they could afford to withhold their
surplus from the market.   Not only was an excessively lenient tax policy
unnecessary but it was probably disfunctional to the economic goal of
achieving an increase in marketable surplus.   It is interesting that during
War Communism, too high a level of taxation was provoking a decrease in
marketable surplus, while five years later, too low a level was giving rise
to the same effect.

Excessive concessions also had an adverse political effect.   By increasing
the richer peasants' prosperity, they augmented their power and influence.
As Olga Narkiewicz[21] points out, during NEP two types of rural
administration co-existed: an ineffectual network of rural soviets and a
strong communal administration (the latter controlled by well-to-do
peasants).   One of the main reasons for the rural soviets' weakness was
sparse financial support from the Budget.   The communes had considerable
financial resources which allowed them to take effective action; they even
financed part of the soviets' expenses, which gave them great control in
their management and increased the richer peasants' influence.   An increase
in agricultural tax, together with higher budget allocations to the soviets,
would have probably increased the rural soviets' political power and
autonomy (decreasing the influence of the richer peasants).

Thus,   the   exaggerated   appeasement   of   the   well-to-do   peasant   was
disfunctional also to the political objectives of the Bolsheviks.   It had
the undesired effect of increasing the   richer peasants' power and
influence, as well as their control of local governments.   Stricter taxation
policy on the well-to-do peasantry - and fewer economic concessions - may
well have obliged them to market a greater part of their grain production
and curtailed their power and influence.   This might have prevented, or at
least diminished, the later use of administrative and violent political
measures to assure the grain supply and limit the power of the more
prosperous peasants.   (For an interesting discussion of this topic, see R.
Medvedev, Let History Judge, Macmillan, 1971.)

The politicians' attitude towards low direct taxation on the peasantry could
have several explanations[22].   One is the inevitable time lag between a
change in economic and political conditions, their perception by policy
makers and the necessary change in policy.   Furthermore, politicians -
particularly in a situation where the struggle to maintain power is so
intense - tend to overestimate the importance of the short-term effects of
their policies, neglecting their long-term effects.

Another level of explanation concerns the underlying political and social
forces.   The analysis that Engels[23] made (in a different historical
context) applies quite well; he pointed to the restrictions facing the
leader of a revolutionary party who takes over power, when the movement is
not yet ripe for the rule of the class which he represents.   The political
leader is

> confronted by an insoluble dilemma: what he can do
> contradicts his whole former behaviour, his principles
> and the immediate interests of his party; what he

ought to do is impracticable. In a word he is
compelled to defend not his own party, not his own
class, but that class for whose rule the movement is
already ripe at the time in question. He must in the
interests of the movement itself defend the interests
of an alien class and put off his own class with
phrases and promises, assuring it that the interests
of this alien class are identical with its
interests...

This analysis seems to fit the Soviet situation, where the political
leadership's range of manoeuvre was restricted by pressures from the richer
peasants.

Direct taxation on the urban population was not an important source of
Budget revenue (see Table 3.IV). One of the reasons for this was more rapid
expropriation of private capital in the cities than in the countryside; in
the former, most property passed to the state. With NEP, a new bourgeoisie
developed; however, their income was difficult to detect and tax, being
based mostly on quick speculative profits. Thus, Promtax was collected
every six months. Although this implied a higher collection cost, it was
necessary as at the time many enterprises did not survive much longer than
six months. Lack of experience with direct taxation was an additional
problem.

However, a higher level of revenue could probably have been extracted from
the urban private sector - mainly from trade, where profit margins were very
high. The initial rates of income and property tax were very low and their
progressiveness limited. (The maximum rate for the income tax introduced in
1922 was 15 per cent. At the end of 1923, this was increased to 25 per
cent.) When, after 1925, their rate and progressiveness were increased, the
private sector was shrinking rapidly. Cooperatives, whose development was
being successfully stimulated, were granted exemptions from direct taxes.
This policy was determined by the belief that favourable tax treatment was
necessary first to stimulate economic recovery and later to promote the
development of certain sectors, i.e. cooperatives. As in the former case,
lenience in taxation policy seems to have been carried too far. It is again
difficult to assess whether this was due to the leadership's errors or lack
of interest, or was determined by the influence of Nepmen and cooperative
members on the political and financial leadership.

Soviet economists[24] put forward the argument that the base for direct
taxation was limited, because of former expropriations. This argument is
important - but much less so than during War Communism. In particular, it
had less validity in the countryside where private ownership predominated;
production growth and increasing inequality caused by the action of market
forces, offered a significant base for direct taxation.

Holzman believes that the taxation pattern which emerged during NEP can be
largely explained by the difficulties encountered in reconstructing the tax
apparatus, which had virtually disappeared. This explanation is too
'technocratic'. It may have some validity in explaining difficulties in
taxing 'the new urban bourgeoisie' and initial problems in taxing the
peasantry. However, it cannot explain the slow growth of agricultural tax
and, even less, its decline during 1925/26; these were obviously political
decisions.

Finally, it should be pointed out that the decision not to tax the more
prosperous peasants more, implied as a counterpart an increasing reliance on
indirect taxation to finance the budget. This laid the burden basically on

the poorer peasantry and the industrial proletariat.

Non-tax revenue played a relatively minor role in financing the budget, representing in 1922/23 oly 4.9 per cent of total state revenue; this level more than doubled during the next three years (see Table 3.VI).

TABLE 3.VI

PERCENTAGE OF TOTAL STATE REVENUE FINANCED BY NON-TAX REVENUE

	1922/23	1923/24	1924/25	1925/26
Deductions from profits	0.8	2.1	4.1	4.2
State property (timber, ores, etc.)	2.1	2.8	4.2	6.3
Other non-tax revenue (a)	1.9	7.7	5.1	2.5
Total non-tax revenue	4.9	12.6	13.4	13.1

Note: Some of these data differ from other sources, due to differences in classification and definition.

Source: R. Davies, op.cit. page 82.

(a)   Includes net revenue (gross revenue minus gross expenditure) from transport and ports in 1924/25. In all other years, this item received a net allocation from the budget.

Growth in non-tax revenue was partly due to an increase in 'deduction from profits' mainly originating in state industry. Until 1922, state industry had a global loss; it made a small profit in 1922/23, which increased substantially the next year. Furthermore, the share of profits paid into the Treasury increased steadily from 15.8 per cent in 1923/24 to 21.0 per cent in 1925/26[25].

Other branches of the socialized economy yielded relatively little revenue. Net profit from state domestic trade was extremely small, due mainly to the small profit margin earned by wholesale state trade institutions. The government's success in controlling wholesale prices was accompanied by failure to control prices in the retail trade, which was mainly privately owned. The margin between retail and wholesale prices grew rapidly; by November 1924, it reached 45 per cent, which was two and a half times as great as in 1913[26]. The sacrifice - in terms of lower surplus retained in the state sector - demanded from nationalized industry and state wholesale distributors was not being mainly transferred to peasants and workers (which was the policy objective) but to the private retail trader.

During this period, net revenue from state loans represented a decreasing proportion of total budgetary revenue. According to Davies (op.cit.), net revenue from state loans represented 5.3 per cent of total state revenue in 1922/23, falling gradually to 0.7 per cent in 1925/26.

Because of prevailing political conditions and inflation, it was difficult to place bonds voluntarily on a large scale. Up till 1925, most of the bonds placed amongst the population were compulsory, and collected in the same way as direct taxation[27]. Voluntary loans were very short-term and had a high cost for the state; this was reflected in future lower net revenue, already apparent by 1925[28]. From 1925, voluntary bonds were issued at interest rates comparable to the market rate.

In a different category were bonds purchased by state enterprises.

Socialized undertakings were obliged to invest part of their revenue in
state loans, allowing the government to accumulate temporarily free
resources.

As a result of the savings banks' reorganization, deposits rose. However,
savings were much smaller than before the war.

(b)   State expenditure

Another essential element for balancing the budget was the curtailment of
government expenditure. In what follows, we shall describe the measures
taken by the government, their impact on the budget, as well as their
economic and political implicatiions.

A first group of measures was aimed at restricting the number of
institutions supported by the State Budget. In 1921 and 1922; most state
enterprises were gradually removed from the State Budget and placed on a
commercial basis[29]. The financial powers of local soviets were restored.
The right to collect local revenues for local use was extended. Local
budgets were separated from the state budget, which could - but was not
obliged to - make loans to cover their deficit. The local budgets became
responsible for an increasing number of local expenditures, such as
administration, education and health. Social security functions were also
taken from the budget, and financed by contributions from enterprises.

Great efforts were made to reduce expenditure of institutions financed by
the budget. The political situation allowed a reduction in defence
expenditure. The government also introduced measures to limit
administrative personnel. In 1921, institutions on the budget were ordered
to reduce their staffs by 50 per cent; in 1922, further cuts were ordered,
and 'norms' of administrative personnel were made binding to all state
institutions.

A technique was gradually developed and imposed for compiling and approving
budget expenditure, determined by revenue. During the civil war, the
expenditure budget was based on what the different commissariats thought
they needed; the budgets of NEP were determined by the amount of expected
revenue. This was partly due to improvements in budgetary techniques. It
was feasible mainly due to the increasing power of financial institutions
within the government, and to the political support they received.

During budget discussions, there were conflicts between Narkomfin and other
government bodies. In 1922/23, after several months of controversy, NKF
persuaded the other institutions to accept its figure for budget
expenditure; this implied a substantial cut on expenditure demands. (The
expenditure proposed by the different institutions added 2,200 million
pre-war roubles, the figure proposed by NKF was 1,334 million pre-war
roubles, and the actual figure was 1,460 million pre-war roubles.) In later
years, Narkomfin proposals were more readily accepted, implying substantial
reductions in the deficit[30].

Bitter institutional discussions were carried out mainly between NKF and
Gosplan. After 1923, Gosplan defended the development of heavy industry,
recommending important investments. NKF was determined to restrict this
item. Gosplan also defended the industrial proletariat, demanding higher
wages. NKF relied on its own calculations for price indexes and often did
not release sufficient funds to industries still dependent on state finances
to honour wages fixed in collective agreements; both mechanisms allowed the
Ministry of Finance to lower effective real wages.

During these years, the budget was the only plan. It greatly influenced the
real variables in the economy, and this was reflected in the predominance of

financial institutions over others.

First, we shall examine the levels of government expenditure, comparing them
with those of former periods. For reasons already analysed, monetary budget
expenditure was very low under War Communism. With NEP, there was a
substantial increase in expenditure, remaining, however, far below the
pre-war level. It is interesting that budgetary expenditure in real terms
during 1924/25 was slightly lower than that of the first nine months of
1922, in spite of economic recovery. This reflects the effort made - and
the success achieved - in curtailing budget expenditure.

TABLE 3.VII

BUDGET EXPENDITURE

Years	Budget expenditure (millions of pre-war roubles)	Yearly budget expenditure as % of 1913 level
1913	3,400 (a)	100.0
1920	148 (a)	4.4
1921	350 (a)	10.3
Jan. - Sept. 1922	1,707 (a)	49.9
1924/25	1,407 (b)	41.1
1925/26	1,930 (b)	57.0

(a)   K. Shmelev, op.cit. in Sokolnikov et al., op.cit. Values expressed in
      million pre-war gold roubles.

(b)   Based on Davies, and reduced to millions of pre-war gold roubles with
      the Retail Prices Index of the Institute for the Study of Market
      Conditions, quoted in Yurovsky, op.cit.

There are several limitations to the sectoral analysis of state expenditure.
One is the already mentioned problem of data comparability. Also, the state
budget did not cover completely the financing of state undertakings and
local budgets.

60

TABLE 3.VIII

STATE BUDGET EXPENDITURE 1922/23 - 1925/26 (MILLION ROUBLES) (a)

	1922/23		1923/24		1924/25		1925/26	
	Amount	%	Amount	%	Amount	%	Amount	%
Industry	121.0	11.4	143.2	9.6	150.9	8.3	219.5	9.4
Electricity	23.3	2.2	50.8	3.3	51.7	2.8	68.3	2.9
Agriculture	50.6	4.8	58.3	3.9	171.4	9.4	209.8	8.9
Net expenditure on transport & ports	142.9	13.4	68.5	4.6	0	-	3.3	0.1
Other expenditure on net economy. (b)	53.0	5.0	84.7	5.6	181.6	9.9	175.2	7.4
Total national economy	390.8	36.8	405.5	27.0	555.6	30.4	681.1	28.7
Transfer to local budget	78.0	7.3	133.0	8.9	265.3	14.5	437.0	17.5
Social and Cultural	83.0	7.8	133.1	8.9	198.7	10.8	275.9	11.7
Defence	230.9	21.7	402.3	26.8	443.8	24.3	638.0	26.9
Administration (c)	230.3	21.7	245.2	16.4	242.7	13.3	261.6	11.0
Other expenditure (d)	50.2	4.7	180.3	8.9	123.3	6.7	99.5	4.2
TOTAL EXPENDITURE	1,063.2	100.0	1,499.4	100.0	1,829.4	100.0	2,369.8	100.0

(a) Based on data in Davies, op.cit. page 83. Self-balancing expenditure on transport and ports, and on loans have been eliminated; the data include only net expenditure (and therefore are lower than those in Davies).

(b) Includes trade, municipal economy and housing.

(c) Includes institutions administering the national economy, and social and cultural activities.

(d) Includes grants to social insurance.

Administration Expenditure. It is remarkable that the share of administration expenditure fell from 21.7 per cent in 1922/23 to 11.0 per cent in 1925/26, that is, by 50 per cent. There are changes in the expenditure classification which limit data comparability. Throughout this period local budgets increased their volume and responsibilities. Thus, part of that expenditure formerly classified as administration was registered in local budgets. However, this does not alter the basic conclusions.

The main explanation lies in the power and ability of the government and financial authorities to control (and even sometimes reduce) government employment and wages. Curtailment of administration expenditure was made easier by the decline of the central government's functions of regulating the economy, due to the nature of NEP itself.

TABLE 3.IX

HEALTH AND EDUCATION EXPENDITURE

	1923/24	1925/26
State and local health and education expenditure (million roubles) (a) (b)	363	756
% of total State expenditure (c)	24%	32%

(a)   Sources: A.M. Gordin's article 'Development of Local Budgets in the U.S.S.R.', in Sokolnikov, et al., op.cit. and Table 3.VIII.

(b)   Does not include expenditure through social insurance organizations.

(c)   Total expenditure is defined as in Table 3.VIII.

Defence. Defence expenditure was much lower than during War Communism. Furthermore, the share of defence in budget expenditure and per-capita defence expenditure in real terms was substantially lower than before the war[31]. This was a political decision, stemming from the peaceful national and international situation.

Health and education. State expenditure on health and education was financed to a great extent by local budgets. As can be seen in Table 3.IX, an increasing proportion of resources was allocated to these items between 1923/24 and 1925/26. In spite of general austerity, priority was given to these sectors.

Transfers to local budgets. This is the item with the quickest growth rate. In spite of a rapid growth in local revenues, local budgets required increased grants to finance rapidly growing expenditure, a large proportion of which went on administration, public education and health.

Transfers to the national economy. The State Budget played a large but quickly decreasing role in financing the national economy. Initially substantial expenditures were made on grants to transport and communication which before the war had yielded considerable net revenue. The need for high subsidies at the beginning of NEP was caused by the low prices charged for these services, reduced levels of activity and inefficient management. The need to subsidize transport and communications decreased rapidly, mainly because the operating ratio improved[32].

Another important item was the financing of industry. The Budget allocated industry a larger proportion of its funds at the beginning of this period, when it endowed it with initial working capital and financed losses. As industry began making profits, using finance from other sources, budget grants lost importance. 1925/26 marked a break through: grants to industry began to grow quicker than budget expenditure, now financing fixed capital.

After 1923/24, state enterprises were financed mainly by bank credit, the great majority of which was never repaid. Although formally different, the economic implications of budget grants and increases in non-returnable credits are the same. The latter are financed either by increases in the banks' capital (through a budget grant) or by an increase in money issue. Budgetary grants increases are also financed - if there is a budget deficit - with money issue. Unfortunately, data available for credits to state undertakings are scarce, and limit the following analysis.

TABLE 3.X

FINANCING OF STATE UNDERTAKINGS

	1922/24 (a) %	1924/25 %	1925/26 %
Budget grants (b)	55	31	43
Increase in level of credits to state undertakings (c)	45	69	57
TOTAL	100	100	100

(a)   The two years are taken together due to data availability.

(b)   Source: Based on data in Davies, op.cit. p.82.

(c)   Source: Gordin, op.cit. in Sokolnikov, op.cit.

Table 3.X shows that bank credit, already important in 1922/24, had a predominant role in both 1924/25 and in 1925/26. Total financing of state undertakings (including both budget grants and increases in bank credit) grew from 1922/24 to 1924/26 at approximately the same rate as total budgetary expenditure (see Tables 3.VIII and 3.XI). The increase in bank credits compensated for the relative fall in budget grants.

Payments from state undertakings to the budget grew more rapidly than the resources transferred to them. Therefore, the net flow of resources from the budgetary and banking system to state undertakings grew less between 1922/24 and 1924/26 than did total government expenditure.

TABLE 3.XI

RESOURCES FLOWING TO AND FROM STATE UNDERTAKINGS

(million roubles)	1922/24	1924/26
Budget grants plus increase in credits (a)	1,264.8	2,002.3
Payments to State Budget (b)	137.5	620.0
Net flow to state undertakings	1,127.3	1,382.3

(a)   Source: As for Table 3.X.

(b)   Includes Promtax, income tax on socialized economy and deductions from profits. Data differ according to source, but quoted ones are based mainly on former tables, and assumptions taken from Davies, op.cit.

Between 1923 and 1926, several factors made the financial results of state undertakings particularly favourable; however, many of these had only a 'once-for-all-effect'.

During these years, the level of activity in state undertakings increased rapidly. This expansion required little fixed capital investment, as it was achieved by using idle labour power, and capital. The budget did not have to finance losses and provide working capital, as during War Communism and 1921/22; neither did it finance significant capital investment - as occurred increasingly after 1926.

Complete data for all state undertakings are not available to show these tendencies. We shall illustrate them with the railway sector, because of data availability and of its large impact on the budget. According to Reingold (op.cit. in Sokolnikov, op.cit.), net profits in the railroads grew from 37 million roubles in 1923/24 to 185 million roubles in 1925/26[33]. This was partly due to an increase of 72 per cent in freight shipments, which did not require significant investment until 1926/27.

Forced to follow commercial principles and often under pressure from reduced financial resources, the state enterprises had to take measures which improved their results. One of these was the widespread dismissal of workers; later, as production increased, employment grew - but much slower than production[34]. The magnitude of workers' dismissal can again be well illustrated by the railroads: railway workers were reduced from 1,240,000 in 1921 to 720,000 in 1922[35].

Wage control was another measure taken to ensure better financial results. It is very difficult to analyze real wages' evolution. In addition to problems of comparability, there are problems such as the discrepancy between official wage rates and effective ones - limited by the funds actually available for payments and the non-inclusion of 'socialized wages' (social expenditure) which increased during this period.

However, it is clear that the wage level was far below the workers' expectations. The wage policy imposed provoked widespread opposition among industrial workers, reflected in waves of strikes and unrest; these were particularly serious when the authorities tried to lower real wages.

In 1922 and 1923, industrial wages were paid according to arbitrarily manipulated local price-indexes. Often, funds were not available to meet wage payments even at these manipulated rates, and the enterprise would fall into arrears; due to rapid inflation, this decreased real wages further. More than half the strikes during 1922 and 1923 were officially attributed to delays in wage payment. At the end of 1925, a wage freeze was applied, which implied a decrease in real wages. Again, this provoked a massive wave of workers' unrest.

For the railways, current results were further improved by a substantial increase in tariffs (in real terms). In nationalized industry, the situation was more complex. The terms of trade were unfavourable to industry during the first nine months of 1922. Afterwards, violent fluctuations occurred, but practically during the whole period 1923/26, the level of industrial wholesale prices was higher (in terms of 1913 prices) than the overall wholesale price index.

Curtailment of public expenditure implied certain decisions which though economic in nature had an inevitable political content (although they were implemented mainly through the action of 'spontaneous' market forces).

The level of unemployment tolerated and the amount of aid given to the unemployed was a crucial decision. The need to diminish expenditure in public services and state undertakings, following commercial principles, led to workers' dismissals; this had a direct effect on the level of unemployment[36], which rose from 150,000 in October 1921 to 1,240,000 in January 1924 (see Table 3.II). There is a significant correspondence between the peak of unemployment reached during the period and the success of the stabilization policy.

Little was done to better the unemployed's plight. Some public works were initiated to relieve this problem, but due to the wish to curtail expenditure, these programmes were extremely limited. In May 1923, less than one per cent of the unemployed in Moscow and Petrograd were employed. Only a small proportion of unemployed were covered by insurance benefits: in January 1923, 26 per cent of the total registered unemployed in Moscow, 14 per cent in Petrograd and 11 per cent in the twelve other major cities received this payment, which fluctuated on average between 13 per cent and 45 per cent of the minimum standard wage.

Unemployment benefits were granted discriminately, responding not so much to principles of social justice as to political needs and pressures. Subsidies were paid in a higher proportion to skilled workers, whose dispersal was undesirable for future industrialization. Subsidies were also given in higher proportion to organized workers, mainly those who had belonged to large enterprises, where industrial discontent would have been politically more dangerous[37].

There are two aspects worth noting about the level of unemployment tolerated, and the lack of aid given to the unemployed. First, it implied a decision contradictory to Marxist principles. Marxist analysis denounced unemployment as one of the worst characteristics of capitalism, which, by denying the worker the possibility of selling his labour power, denied him the chance of earning his living. However, unemployment was accepted in a country beginning its transition to socialism. It is difficult to evaluate whether the decision to 'postpone' consumption by the unemployed was necessary or inevitable. Technically, it would have been possible to reduce dismissals and/or increase subsidies to the unemployed, without affecting the stabilization programme (by increasing taxation, for example, on the peasantry). Whether this was politically feasible is another matter. Second, the imposition of this policy implied that the interests of the unemployed were not effectively represented within the party or the Government. This issue was not even discussed much at Party Congresses or Conferences.

The weak position of the unemployed in the Soviet power structure is linked to the nature of the trade unions. During NEP trade union organizations did not uphold the interests of the unemployed very strongly[38]. This was partly because their members were in a better position than most workers[39]; also, they realized that increases in subsidy payments might imply lower real wages for the employed (the trade unions tended to defend the interests of employed workers more than those of the working class as a whole).

To a great extent, the trade unions' position towards unemployment was explained by their lack of strength and autonomy. The independence between trade unions and the state apparatus introduced with NEP[40], was a source of weakness rather than of strength for them, as it limited their chances of influencing government decisions 'from inside'. Their ability to challenge government decisions 'from outside' was restricted by party control over their actions[41]. Thus, not only was the level of unemployment tolerated as a controversial political decision, but its acceptance required special political conditions.

Another political decision implicit in the curtailment of government expenditure was wage control. On the two occasions when the workers resisted wage policy, the trade union leaders - following the party line - opposed both the workers' demands and their strikes, and the workers' movements were repressed. The government, however, did increase real wages after the strikes.

In a planned socialist economy[42], once the plan for production of consumer goods has been decided, total real wages are not influenced by subsequent modifications of money wages. The situation was very different during NEP.

The economy was not wholly socialized; workers in the state sector were a minority of the active population; levels of output were not planned, but determined by market forces. All this allowed scope for an autonomous trade union wage policy, as the short-term interests of the workers in state enterprises contradicted the NEP line of concessions to the peasantry. The political control exerted by the party over the workers via the trade unions helped impose a line which, although contrary to their short-term interests, had been defined as necessary for keeping the proletariat in power[43].

From the view-point of social justice, wage control in state undertakings was more justifiable than high levels of unemployment. On average, industrial workers had a higher level of income than the peasantry.

Another crucial decision concerned the volume of resources allocated to capital investment. Due to idle capacity, it was possible during these years to increase output without significant investment. After 1922, sectors within the Government and the Party advocated a greater allocation of resources to capital investment — particularly in heavy industry. The view triumphed that this investment effort should be postponed.

Once this development strategy was adopted by the political leadership, there was no point in increasing grants to heavy industry during these years. An increase in industrial investment could have been financed from lower consumption growth — mainly in the countryside. As discussed, the decision was taken by the political leadership at the time not to follow this strategy. Alternatively, increased investment could have been financed with note issue, removing the possibility of financial stability. However, had the levels of inflation existing at the beginning of NEP been maintained, not only the essential relations between town and country, but also all exchange within the economy based on market relations would have been endangered.

Thus, Narkomfin policy of controlling grants to heavy industry was not only consistent with the strategy chosen (recovery based on alliance with the peasantry), it also contributed to making viable the economic mechanism chosen (use of market forces). Had NKF increased grants to heavy industry (without other changes), this would have implied a different development strategy (more industralization) and a different economic mechanism (less reliance on the market, and more physical planning and allocation of resources), inconsistent with the political leadership's decisions.

The ability to reduce administration expenditure substantially was not only due to the government's capacity to control employment and wages. It was made easier because government's intervention in regulating economic activities declined, due to the nature of NEP. The centralized allocation of food, raw materials and industrial products introduced during War Communism was replaced by allocation through the market, thus sharply reducing the need for state bureaucracy. Finally, the level of defence expenditure was essentially a political decision, conditioned by the favourable internal and international situation.

V   Monetary Evolution and the Monetary Reform

The monetary situation during the early years of NEP will be described first. The process ending with the monetary reform of 1924 will then be described and assessed.

1   Disequilibria during 1921-22

During NEP's first year, the economic situation continued to be unfavourable for monetary stability, and the budget deficit was similar to that under War Communism[44]. This level of budget deficit implied growth rates in currency circulation even higher than under War Communism (see Table 3.XII). During 1922, currency in circulation increased nearly a 100 fold.

Prices also rose at a spectacular rate, although less than money. From July 1921 to the end of 1922, the volume of currency increased by approximately 850 times, whilst prices increased by 263. This was partly due to production growth. An additional — transitory — factor was that state enterprises and cooperatives were liquidating their stocks, allowing industrial sales to grow faster than output. Perhaps the most important element was the rapid monetization of exchange.

Consequently real government revenue from issue increased; from 33.7 million roubles in the first half of 1921, it grew to 115.4 million roubles during the second half of 1921, and to 123.5 and 171.0 million roubles during the first and second halves of 1922[45]. The real value of total money in circulation increased from 29.1 million roubles in July 1921, to 89.9 million roubles in December 1922.

TABLE 3.XII

CURRENCY CIRCULATION AND PRICES (1920–1922)

Year and Quarter		Quarterly issue as % of currency circulation on first day of quarter (a)	Price index, 1913=100 on first day of quarter (b)
1920	1st	51.4	2,420
	2nd	50.2	4,770
	3rd	45.6	8,140
	4th	56.8	9,620
1921	1st	44.3	16,800
	2nd	39.1	35,700
	3rd	93.2	80,700
	4th	287.2	81,900
1922	1st	362.9	288,000
	2nd	294.1	2,524,000
	3rd	166.1	5,795,000
	4th	134.3	7,342,000

(a)   Davies, op.cit. pages 31 and 53.

(b)   Arnold, op.cit. Refers to Labour Statistical Index.

2   Initial steps towards monetary reform

Monetary reform was carried out in two stages[46], the first of which (from October 1922 to February 1924) was characterized by the co-existence of two currencies. It was thought that each currency had an indispensable role. The economy urgently needed a stable currency, and this was satisfied by the gradual introduction of the Tchervonetz. The budget deficit had been substantially reduced, but not eliminated; the issue of the old money was believed to be essential to cover this deficit, as the use of the new money for this purpose would have undermined its stability from the beginning.

The Tchervonetz was to be issued only to cover commercial operations of the State Bank and advances to Narkomfin (with 25 per cent ratios of cover of precious metals and foreign currency). Great importance was attached by the financial authorities to this cover in gold and foreign currency and to the limitation it imposed on State Bank credits to the Treasury.

At first, the Tchervonetz was used mainly as a unit of account and store of value, and was used as a medium of payment only to a limited extent. When the State Bank granted loans in Tchervonetz, the enterprises exchanged them with the Bank for roubles, which they used for making payments. One of the reasons was scarcity of Tchervonetz of low denomination; the other, initially important, was unfamiliarity with the Tchervonetz.

The system of two currencies circulating simultaneously had certain beneficial results. It gave the economy a comparatively stable currency and avoided the imminent danger of penetration of foreign currency and pre-war gold coinage into circulation. However, the longer the two-currency system lasted, the more its disadvantages became evident. The increasing issue of roubles (in 1923, their volume grew 11.3 times[47]) used in a decreasing sphere of circulation led to an explosive growth of the 1923 price index[48]. Although they represented a rapidly falling proportion of total money in circulation (at the beginning of 1924, 23 per cent of total money[49]), their presence was sufficient to disorganize monetary circulation and have disruptive effects on the whole economy.

One of the main objectives of introducing the Tchervonetz had been to provide a basis for economic calculation. However, often it was much more profitable to buy Tchervonetz one hour earlier, than to dedicate time and effort to calculating costs. Endeavours to conduct business on profitable lines were mainly reduced to attempts at successful currency transactions.

The rouble even had an adverse effect on the Tchervonetz's stability. Because of the prevailing mode of payments and settlements (traders had to accept roubles which they exchanged for Tchervonetz the next day) and the difference between official and market rates of exchange, traders protected themselves from losses of exchange by increasing prices also in terms of Tchervonetz.

The peasantry had particular difficulty in exchanging the rapidly falling rouble for the more stable Tchervonetz. They reacted by marketing only that part of their produce which was strictly necessary to pay for the commodities which they wished to purchase on that day. This reduced the supplies of agricultural produce on the market. Thus an inadequate monetary system was curtailing the fulfilment of crucial economic goals. Finally, the usefulness of the rouble to cover the budget deficit diminished, as its value fell so drastically - much faster than the note issue.

It is noteworthy that, in 1923, even though general economic conditions improved rapidly, there were increasing problems in the financial sphere. The year 1923 differs markedly from the preceding period (1917-1922) when disruption in the production sphere explains to a great extent disruption in the sphere of circulation. It also differs from the following period (1924-25) where the improvement in the production sphere is reflected in a relatively stable financial equilibrium.

3   The Monetary Reform of 1924 and its effects

At the beginning of 1924, the financial authorities thought that the basic premises for successful currency reform had been achieved. The budget deficit had fallen steadily; it was hoped that no issues would be needed to balance the budget in the next financial year (1924-25)[50]. Great importance was also attached to the increase in reserves of gold and foreign currency during the last year[51], due to improvement in the balance of payments[52]. The decision to carry out the Monetary Reform at the beginning of 1924, without waiting for further improvements in economic conditions, was based on the urgent need to end disruption in the financial sphere[53].

The Monetary Reform was introduced through a series of decrees enacted in the months of February and March 1924. The first step taken was to issue new paper currency - the Treasury notes - which was accorded the right of legal tender. There was no formal link between the new treasury gold rouble and the Tchervonetz rouble. The relationship was established by the readiness of the State Bank to accept the new Treasury notes at a fixed rate, without limitation as to their sum. A limit was placed on the aggregate issue of Treasury notes, which was not to exceed one half of the amount of the Tchervontzi in circulation. The printing of Soviet roubles was stopped, and a fortnight later, the rate of redemption for the Soviet roubles (or money tokens) was fixed. The mintage and issuing of silver copper coins was re-established. Some importance was placed on the fact that they corresponded exactly to the coins existing before the Revolution, which, it was believed, would enhance the trust which the population would have in the new money.

Before appraising the general economic effects of the Monetary Reform, the principles and concepts on which it was based will be evaluated. Two aspects will be stressed: the orthodoxy of the Monetary Reform and the erroneous concepts which were applied in its implementation.

The shift in attitude towards financial policy had been complete. The Bolsheviks passed from distrust in the role of money during the transition to socialism to a belief in its predominant importance. Thus, it is interesting to compare the declaration of the Commissar of Finance in 1918: 'Finance should not exist in a socialist community and I must therefore apologize for speaking on the subject', and in 1925: 'The financial strengthening of the Soviet state is, naturally, a necessary condition to a firm rule, to an ability to ensure the defence of the country, keep up an administrative machine, provide for the cultural needs ..... the strengthening of currency at a given moment becomes a necessary condition to the strengthening of power'. The principles on which financial policy was carried out followed canons of extreme orthodoxy. Several traits of the financial policy closely followed Western principles existing at the time or even the tradition applied in Russia during the 19th Century. In part this was caused by a wish to win the confidence of the capitalist world, so as to facilitate foreign trade and perhaps even foreign loans. This acceptance of orthodox measures was further explained by the presence of experts at Narkomfin, bred in the conservative tradition of the previous century; also, nobody had ever defined before how stabilization should be carried out in a socialist country, which made the return to the traditional, well-known patterns easier. Thus, Yurovsky wrote: 'One can break with one tradition, but one must adhere to some other'.

The most orthodox principle applied was the gold-cover support built up for the Tchervonetz. Whatever the usefulness of the gold standard in the capitalist world, it had little sense for a socialist country. The regulating role of the flows of gold on foreign trade (via price level) was impossible in the Soviet Union; the monopoly of foreign trade by the state achieved this objective through a more direct mechanism. The impact which gold cover could have on the internal confidence of the Tchervonetz was limited by the predominance of nationalized enterprises; it is doubtful that the peasantry - unacquainted with the more sophisticated details of the monetary system – would be favourably influenced by a higher level of gold-cover. As regards foreign acceptance, the Tchervonetz played a minor role in foreign trade, which was carried out mainly in foreign currency.

The need to build up gold and foreign currency reserves provoked a restriction in imports and increasing exports. The building up of reserves may have been justified at the time as it gave a greater margin of manoeuvre for emergency situations. But to reduce the level of imports with the sole objective of providing gold reserves to give cover for the currency seems both too costly and senseless in a socialist, underdeveloped country, with an urgent need to recover and grow. Another negative aspect of the Monetary Reform was the slow pace at which it was introduced. If the Bolshevik government had acted with greater flexibility, it could have entered the second stage of the Monetary Reform earlier.

The interpretation of the Monetary Reform and its success by financial experts (such as Katzenellenbaum and Yurousky) was too 'technocratic'. It over-emphasized the significance of the different limits and ratios imposed by the financial authorities[54]. Too little importance was placed on the circumstances which allowed these limits to be imposed. The ability to establish these limits – and to have them respected – was an expression of the power of the financial authorities and the predominance of financial policy.

As soon as the influence of financial authorities and policy decreased, these limits lost their validity. This occurred when investment for industrialization began on a large scale. A good example was the limit in the ratio between Treasury issue and Tchervontzi, to which the financial experts attached great importance at the time[55].

Finally, the evolution of the monetary situation after the Reform will be briefly outlined. As can be seen in Table 3.XIII, between the beginning of 1924 and the end of 1925, the total means of payment had increased by more than three and a half times. The increase in prices was much smaller. Particularly slow was the growth in the level of wholesale prices (the level even fell for a time); retail prices grew by 26 per cent between January 1924 and January 1925.

TABLE 3.XIII

MONEY AND PRICES (1924–25) (a)

Date	Total Means of payment (b)	General Wholesale Index of Prices (c)	General Retail Index of Prices (d)
Jan. 1924	658.7	169.0	180.0
Mar. 1924	832.0	193.0	203.0
Jan. 1925	1,384.7	172.0	205.0
Oct. 1925	2,316.4	174.2	215.0
Jan. 1926	2,382.0	183.3	226.0

(a)   Source: Davies, op.cit.

(b)   Includes total currency in circulation plus bank deposits (in millions of roubles on the first of the month).

(c)   Wholesale price index of Gosplan.

(d)   Retail price index of the Institute of Study of Economic Conditions.

This divergence between growth of means of payment and level of prices can be explained at two levels. First, the financial authorities' hopes of an increase in monetary demand due to higher trade turnover and confidence in the new monetary unit were fulfilled. Second, prices remained relatively stable due to the price control policy. Control was more effective on wholesale prices, as the majority of wholesale trade belonged either to the state or to cooperatives. Increasing demand pressures and the predominance of the private sector in retail trade made the control of retail prices somewhat more difficult; however, till the end of 1925, retail prices did not grow too much. Therefore, the two main measures taken by the government to achieve price stability differed markedly. On one hand, it carried out an orthodox financial policy, based on principles such as the gold standard. On the other it increasingly applied direct price controls.

VI   Summary and Conclusions

NEP pursued the political objective of maintaining power. The Soviet State was unable to extract through administrative measures the level of agricultural surplus crucial for its survival. This obliged the Bolsheviks to establish a political alliance between peasants and workers. To obtain the peasantry's support (which would allow the Soviet State to extract the required surplus), two conditions had to be met: a) restoration of the market, so that the peasant could sell his produce, and b) economic concessions to the peasantry.

The economic mechanism chosen (the market) and the economic strategy adopted (recovery based on consumer goods) were therefore essential to the achievement of the basic political aim, and consistent with the existing class alliance.   The financial policies followed during NEP will be evaluated in the light of their usefulness in ensuring the operation of the economic mechanism and the economic strategy adopted.

These criteria of evaluation will first enable us to dispute the widely expressed view in the Soviet Union at the time that financial institutions and financial policy in general, were bulwarks of conservatism and pre-revolutionary influence.   In assessing this view, it is necessary to distinguish between the financial institutions and their policies.   It is true that both NKF and Gosbank were predominantly conservative institutions; many of their personnel were officials from Tzarist times.   In mid-1922, only 18 out of 15,000 tax-workers were Communist Party members[56].   In Gosbank, the presence of a former Kadet minister and other experts trained in the tradition of nineteenth century finance was significant.   This problem, common also in other institutions, was more serious in financial institutions as few Bolsheviks had knowledge or experience of financial matters.

The State bureaucracy opposed socialist aims. Its ideology was reflected in the fact that only nine per cent of the employees coming from the Tsarist Regime and 13 per cent of the newly hired declared that they favoured the Soviet Regime – in a poll carried out during 1922 among State employees[57]. However, while the state bureaucracy had some influence on policy-decisions, these were basically made within the Party[58].   It therefore cannot be said that financial policies were conservative due to the ideology predominant in financial institutions.

The main criticism of financial policy and its alleged conservatism was based on its restrictive nature.   This criticism was incorrect.   In an economy in transition to socialism, even when the 'commanding heights' of the economy are state-owned, the role of financial policy remains essential while there is no physical planning and allocation of resources. In such a context, the only way to detect real resource constraints and possible incompatibilities between different goals is by detecting financial disequilibria. It is the role of the financial authorities to make explicit to the political authorities the existing constraints and the need to choose an economic strategy consistent with existing resources. These decisions should be taken by the political leadership; the role of the financial authorities is mainly to make clear the need and urgency of making such a choice. Furthermore, if certain restrictive decisions had not been taken during NEP, hyper-inflation would have continued, endangering the very viability of the economy under market relations. The use of the market made the existence of a relatively stable monetary unit essential, to serve as measure of value, medium of exchange and temporary store of value. Some restraint in financial policy was therefore not 'conservative', but helped to make viable the economic mechanism chosen by the political leadership at this stage.

The contrast with War Communism, where the role of finance was more passive, is interesting. At that stage, a more autonomous financial policy would have been disfunctional to the basic economic and political aims, whereas during NEP, the more autonomous role of finance was functional to the main goals of this stage. The restoration of monetary stability was feasible both because conditions were favourable and deliberate decisions were taken.

In this period, the Bolsheviks were in a relatively favourable political position. Their power position had been consolidated both externally and internally, and three 'exogenous'[59] elements increased their area of manoeuvre in financial policy:

1)   The end of civil war and imperialist aggression allowed a gradual economic recovery, providing a wider base for taxation and diminishing the financial needs of the nationalized enterprises.

2)   The end of the war allowed a higher proportion of this augmented output to be used for non-defence purposes.

3)   Bolshevik experience allowed for greater control over the fiscal apparatus.

NEP policies themselves increased the flexibility of the role played by financial policy. Terminating the double system of pricing reduced losses on the part of the nationalized enterprises. The increasing monetization of transactions provided a growing base for monetary taxation. One of the negative effects of NEP - the growth of inequality - provided a broader base for direct taxation.

Other elements contributing to monetary stability were determined by certain government decisions. An example was the decision to use the market mechanism and accept its effects so as to achieve financial equilibrium. The economic effects (on employment, wages, level and distribution of investment, several of which reproduced the characteristics of capitalism) appeared as consequences of 'spontaneous' market forces. The effects of the decision were less strongly felt - both by those who took them and those affected - because they were not explicitly taken by the central government, but made in many decentralized units as a result of central government policies. Furthermore, the ability to impose these effects (i.e. level of unemployment and wages) depended on the government's political control and on the relative weakness of different social groups or sub-groups. These decisions were easier to impose because a monolithic political organization (the Communist Party), whose power was consolidated, faced different social groups at a very atomized level[60].

The other element on which the new class alliance was based, was the
strategy of making economic concessions to the peasantry. As was discussed,
the exaggeration of these concessions - particularly during the end of the
period studied - was disfunctional to the Bolsheviks' economic and political
aims.   A stricter taxation policy on the wealthier peasants and less
concessions in general might have obliged them to market a higher proportion
of their production, and then power and influence would have diminished.
This may have prevented - or diminished - the need later to use
administrative and violent measures to assure the grain supply and curtail
the power of the wealthier peasants. Too lenient an economic policy in
this period restricted future prospects, making excessive concessions
disfunctional not only in the short-term, but even more so in the long term.

In relation to more specific policy instruments, two errors will be pointed
out (of policies disfunctional to political and economic aims).

Since 1924, the government had successfully controlled wholesale industrial
prices.   However, due to excessive demand and the predominance of private
capital in the retail sector, control over retail prices was less effective.
By the end of 1924, the margin between retail and wholesale prices had more
than doubled in relation to 1913.

This erroneous policy was described as 'a scissor which cut in pieces both
industry and the good relations with the peasantry'.   The sacrifice - in
terms of lower surplus retained in state industry and wholesale trade - was
not transferred to the peasant (the policy objective) but remained in the
hands of the private retail trader - whom the Soviet government wished to
discourage.   It was precisely in this period that a policy of replacing
private retail trade for cooperatives was begun.

Controlling wholesale industrial prices when control of retail prices was
not feasible, therefore went against both political and economic goals.
This error seems to have been based on a misunderstanding of the limitations
of effective state control over economic variables at this stage.   This
mistake was not unique to the Soviet experience. It is, for example, very
common among populist governments in Latin America, and will be analysed in
some detail for the Chilean case.

Another erroneous economic policy also favoured the private sector,
discriminating against nationalized industry.   The licensing fee
corresponding to the trade and craft tax rose progressively with the size of
the firm, thus discriminating against state enterprises, which were usually
larger.   The conservative nature of this more 'technical' measure may have
been due to the ideology of the financial institutions; the political
leadership would have lacked both expertise and interest to tackle this
issue.

An interesting point emerging from an analysis of NEP, is that the
correctness of a policy during transition to socialism lies not only in its
formulation, but largely in the timing and extent to which it is applied.
The problem of lags in policy making and implementation in response to
changes in economic and political conditions is common to all economies, but
is sharply accentuated in an under-developed economy in transition to
socialism.   In such a situation, a particularly high degree of flexibility
is necessary in policy making.   The violently changing political and
economic framework - both externally and internally - demands particularly
rapid and drastic changes in economic policy.   Unfavourable conditions
impose restrictions which magnify the negative effects of excessive lags.

Furthermore, excessive analysis of policy decisions in terms of 'ideology'
may hinder the policy-maker from taking rapid and flexible action. (This
criticism is not levelled at the use of ideology or political criteria in

establishing political aims. It refers to the choice of concrete economic
policies according to ideological criteria, and not according to their
contribution to the achievement of political and economic aims.)

'Ideology' is wrongly used at two levels:

1) A certain policy - resulting from specific circumstances - is justified
ideologically as correct per se and accepted as desirable independently of
circumstances.   This delays the introduction of new policies, more
appropriate to new circumstances. An example is the belated and reluctant
abandonment of War Communism, although this analysis has the benefit of
hindsight.

2) As the struggle for power is so crucial, exaggerated importance is given
to making concessions to social groups in order to obtain their short-term
support. Though some concessions may be necessary, their level and extent
are often exaggerated. It is mechanistically believed that the greater the
economic concessions, the larger will be the support obtained.   The
'boomerang effect' of excessive and prolonged concessions to the peasantry
was discussed above.

This problem can be generalized to other underdeveloped countries in
transition to socialism. On the one hand, there is a vital need for very
flexible policies; at the same time, so called 'ideological elemements' and
inexperience tend to limit the ability to generate flexible policy-makers.
In this sense, the study of former experiences, of their errors and
achievements, acquires particular importance. Though historical experiences
cannot be applied mechanically, much can be learned and much precious time
can be saved by studying them.

Notes

1   In Les luttes de classes en URSS, Maspero, Paris, 1974.

2   Source: D. Lane, The end of inequality? Stratification under state
     socialism, Penguin Books, London, 1971.

3   'Report on the substitution of a tax in kind for the surplus-grain
     appropriation system', V.I. Lenin, Collected Works, Vol. XXXII.
     (op.cit. in Chapter 2).

4   Op.cit. in (3).

5   'Summing up Speech on the Tax in Kind', V.I. Lenin, Collected Works,
     Vol. XXXII, op.cit.

6   Op.cit. in (3).

7   Op.cit. in (3).

8   Estimate from different Soviet sources, quoted in E.H. Carr, The
     Bolshevik Revolution, Vol. 2, op.cit.

9   Source: Y.S. Rozenfeld, Promyshlennaya Politika S.S.S.R., (1926)
     quoted in E.H. Carr, The Bolshevik Revolution, Vol. 2, op.cit.

10   Id. as (9).

11   There are certain discrepancies between different sources, but the
     general tendencies are quite clear.

12   L. Kritsman in Vestnik Komministicheshoi Akademii, quoted in E.H.
     Carr, Socialism in One Country, Vol. I, Pelican Books, London, 1970.

13   According to A. Bergson, (in his work, The Structure of Soviet Wages,
     Harvard University Press, 1944) wage inequality in 1926, though far
     greater than during War Communism, was still lower than during the
     pre-war period. Other economists (i.e. the Soviet economist Kostin,
     quoted in D. Lane, The End of Inequality op.cit.) state that wage
     differentials in the Soviet Union during 1925-26 were similar to those
     of pre-revolutionary Russia.   Unfortunately, there is little
     conclusive evidence.

14   This can be seen clearly from the Stalin-Nemchimov data on grain
     output and marketing, by type of holding, quoted in M. Dobb, op.cit.
     p.217.

15   Collected Decrees 1922, quoted in Arnold, op.cit.

16   Strumilin Na Khozyaistvennon Fronte (1925), quoted in E.H. Carr, The
     Interregum 1923-24, p.22, Pelican Books, Baltimore, USA, 1969.

17   In spite of these efforts, the tax apparatus remained weak during NEP.
     According to Holzman in Soviet Taxation, Harvard University Press,
     Cambridge, Mass., 1962, and Soviet sources (i.e. articles in
     Sokolnikov et al., op.cit.) this was an important reason for the
     introduction of simple and easily enforceable taxes.

18   Data taken from 'Budget Expenditures during the years 1922-3 to
     1927-8', article by A.M. Gordin in Sokolnikov et al., op.cit.

19   According to data from Davies, op.cit. in 1922/23, direct taxation

represented 52.3% of total tax revenue and only 11% of total tax revenue in 1913. According to another source (O. Solovei, 'Pre-War and Present Financial System', in Sokolnikov et al., op.cit.) the proportion of direct taxation reached c. 25% in 1913.

20   Solovei, op.cit., in Sokolnikov, op.cit.

21   The Making of the Soviet State Apparatus, Manchester University Press, 1970.

22   What is analyzed here is the exaggeration of tax concessions which was disfunctional to Bolshevik aims.

23   F. Engels, 'The Peasant War in Germany', in Classic European Historians, edited by L. Krieger, University of Chicago Press, 1967.

24   For example, Reingold, op.cit.

25   Source: Reingold, op.cit. in Sokolnikov et al., op.cit.

26   Source: Y. Rozenfeld, Promyshlennaya Politika S.S.S.R., quoted in E.H. Carr, Socialism in One Country, Vol. 1, op.cit.

27   The difference was that they entailed an obligation to pay back the loan, plus interest.

28   The sharp fall in net revenue during 1925/26 is explained mainly by large increases in interest and repayment. See R. Davies, op.cit. page 126.

29   The only exceptions were railways, posts and telegraphs.

30   Based on Soviet sources, quoted in Davies op.cit. pp.62 and 63.

31   Data can be found in articles by Solovei and Gordin, op.cit. in Sokolnikov et al., op.cit. and in Davies, op.cit.

32   The operating ratio total operating expenses to gross receipts of railroads dropped from 100.3% in 1922-23 to 85.6% in 1925/26. They were still far above pre-war levels. (Information based on quoted article by Reingold, in Sokolnikov, op.cit.)

33   State industry profits also grew rapidly. According to Reingold, they increased from 200 million roubles in 1923-24 to 610 million roubles in 1925-26.

34   Between 1922 and 1926, industrial output grew by 309%, industrial employment increased by 185%. (Source: A. Baykov, op.cit.)

35   E.H. Carr, The Bolshevik Revolution, Vol. 2, op. cit. According to data in Baykov, op.cit. in this period employment in census industry fell from 1,185,000 to 1,096,000, while gross output increased by approximately 30%.

36   An estimate made in January 1924, calculated that dismissal through redundancy explained 47% of all cases of unemployment.

37   A similar criterion was applied for dismissing workers. At the beginning of 1923, the decision was taken — in the interest of rationalization — to close down the Putilov engineering works in Petrograd. But this factory had been one of the great Bolshevik strongholds in 1917. The political authorities postponed its closing,

in spite of the heavy losses which it caused. Rykov confirmed that it had been kept open for 'political reasons'. Source: L. Trotsky, The History of the Russian Revolution, Vol. 3, London, Gallancz, 1933.

38   On several occasions, trade union leaders expressed the view that an increase in unemployment subsidy was not feasible under the circumstances.

39   At a time when only one-seventh of all unemployed received unemployment subsidy, one-half of unemployed trade unionists obtained it.

40   During War Communism, trade unions participated in the State apparatus. For a good description, see E.H. Carr, The Bolshevik Revolution, Vols. 1 and 2, op.cit.

41   In March 1922, it was approved that only party members of long standing could be elected to leading posts in the trade union organization.

42   With no private property of means of production.

43   The above-mentioned quote of Engels, from The Peasant War in Germany, is again particularly relevant.

44   During 1921, and the first quarter of 1922, the proportion derived from money issue was still around 85% of total government revenue (very similar to the 1920 level). Sources: Katzenellenbaum and Yurovsky, op.cit.

45   Source: Yurovsky, op.cit.

46   For detailed descriptions of the Monetary Reform, see Yurovsky, op.cit., and Katzenellenbaum, op.cit. Their description is particularly interesting because they were largely responsible for these reforms.

47   Source: Davies, op.cit. p.53.

48   In terms of roubles.

49   This figure refers only to the distribution of the stock of money. As roubles circulated faster than Tchervonetz (their velocity of circulation was higher), their significance in the total flow of money supply was somewhat higher.

50   It was believed that the favourable effects of the Monetary Reform itself would accelerate growth of output - and therefore improve the budgetary situation.

51   The holdings of gold and foreign currency rose from 15 million gold roubles on January 1923 to about 150 million gold roubles on January 1924 (Source: Carr, The Bolshevik Revolution, Vol. 2, op.cit. from Soviet sources).

52   The real importance of gold backing for the stability of the currency will be discussed below.

53   In December 1923, the Commissar of Finance, Sokolnikov warned, '...the chief danger is not that we shall remain without the Soviet roubles, but that we shall not find within ourselves sufficient strength and

understanding to give it up in due time. Should we not do so, our circulation of money will become so chaotic that it will be far more difficult to clear up...'

54   As representatives of financial institutions, obviously their role was to defend the stability of these limits. However, in their theoretical analysis, they could have shown a broader understanding.

55   When the pressure for larger government expenditure and deficit became stronger, means were found to satisfy them, despite the legal restrictions. First, an increasing proportion of resources was granted through the banking system. Then, the legal restrictions were changed: the ratio between Treasury Issue and note credit was raised by later decrees from 50% to 75% and later to 100%.

56   In 1922-25 great efforts were made to ensure that Communists predominated among the new personnel employed by NKF.

57   Source: Marcel Lubman, Le Leninisme sous Lenine, quoted in C. Bettleheim, Les luttes de classes en URSS, op.cit.

58   For descriptions of policy decisions which illustrate this, see for example, works of E.H. Carr, op.cit. and Bettleheim, op.cit.

59   Exogenous to the policy maker.

60   One could contrast this with the Chilean experience (see Chapter 5), where there was no monolithic political organization (there were many parties in Popular Unity), its power was not consolidated, there were alternative polditical parties, and the different interest groups were organized and bargained at a much more aggregate level.

THE ROLE OF SHORT-TERM AND FINANCIAL POLICIES
IN CZECHOSLOVAKIA, 1945-48

In this chapter, the economic and political set up will be examined in which
Czechoslovakia's National Front Government, established after Liberation,
operated.   It begins with a very brief description of the Czechoslovak
economy during the German occupation.   After outlining the main political
features of this period, the political and economic targets of the
Czechoslovak Communist Party will be described.   The evolution of the
economy and the planning apparatus during 1945-48 will be briefly outlined.

Then, the initial solution of financial disequilibria via the 1945 Monetary
Reform will be examined.   The causes for further disequilibria will be
studied, as well as the economic and political forces behind them.   The
evolution of money and Balance of Payments will be described.   Finally, the
appropriateness of the financial policies pursued to the goals of the
Communist Party will be evaluated.

The emphasis here is on the role played by financial policy in achieving the
targets of the Czechoslovak Communist Party during this period.   It could be
thought that economic and financial policy played a highly determining role
in the Czechoslovak transition to socialism, given that it was non-violent
and that it was the sole example of transition in an advanced capitalist
country with a traditional bourgeois democratic political system.   However,
the importance of financial policy was limited by the almost overwhelming
importance of political elements.   The main determining political factors
were Czechoslovakia's position within the Soviet sphere - resulting from the
Yalta and Potsdam conferences - and the Czech Communist leadership's belief
that the interests of the working class were best served by a policy in
harmony with the Soviet Union's strategic requirements.   Thus, financial
policy - while recognised as important - seems to have played a role even
more determined by political considerations in Czechoslovakia than in the
Chilean case, which we analyse in the next chapter.

I   Economic and Political Framework

1   The Czechoslovak economy during the German Occupation

The Czechoslovak economy during World War II will be examined briefly,
stressing the financial aspects.   Although great damage was caused to the
Czechoslovak economy by the German occupation its scale did not reach that
suffered by the Soviet Union, Poland or Yugoslavia.   The different treatment
accorded to the Czech provinces and to Slovakia was related to the
difference in the status accorded them by the Germans; while the Czech
provinces were a 'Protectorate', Slovakia was 'autonomous', with an
established quisling government.

The harnessing of the Czech economy to the needs of the German war effort
caused important changes in the ownership, organization and structure of
industry.   Germany established control over Czech industry by amalgamating
its leading industries with large German concerns, confiscating some
industrial establishments, and placing all industries and financial
institutions udner the supervision of German officials.

Total industrial production in Czech lands fell initially, but increased
again after 1941.

TABLE 4.I

INDEX OF GROSS INDUSTRIAL OUTPUT IN CZECH LANDS (1939=100)

1941	1942	1943	1944
92	101	113	118

Source: Stručný hospodářský vývoj Ceskoslovenska do roku 1955 ('Brief
          Survey of Czechoslovak Economic Development till 1955'),Kolektiv
          Pracovníku Vysoké Školy Ekonomické Nakladatelství Svoboda,
          Prague, 1969.

Industrial recovery implied a radical change in structure, gearing it
towards the German war economy. A massive shift towards heavy industry,
particularly armaments, occurred. Light industry suffered loss of labour
force, suspension of production programmes and non-renewal of equipment.

Agricultural production fell in the Czech lands quite substantially. For
example, between 1939 and 1944, cereal production fell by 28 per cent.
Animal stock fell also. Industrial evolution in Slovakia was rather
different. Initially, industrial production grew very sharply; in 1943, it
was 62 per cent above the 1937 level, according to Přehled Hospodářskéko
vývoje Československa v letech 1918-1945, ('Survey of Czechoslovak Economic
Development, 1918-45'), Kolektiv Vysoká Škola Ekonomická, Prague, 1961).
Industrial output fell well below the pre-war level after 1943, partly
because of direct military operations.

By the end of the war, transport had deteriorated substantially in the whole
of Czechoslovakia. Over half of locomotives, 68 per cent of passenger
carriages and 75 per cent of freight trucks had been lost, destroyed or
severely damaged. The exploitation of the Czech economy by the German Reich
to finance its war effort was mirrored in the monetary and financial sphere,
by a rapid increase in the quantity of money and a fall in foreign exchange
reserves.

The Czech economy was exploited through both the clearing system and the
payment of cheques and issuing of credit. The rate between the crown (Czech
currency) and the mark was established at a level undervaluing the crown.
Germans (both civilians and military) increased their purchase of Czech
goods with marks; the Czech National Bank could not use these marks, but had
to deposit them in Berlin in a frozen account. Similar measures were
applied to foreign trade. The trade surplus for the Czech lands was
extremely high during 1939-45, representing 27 per cent of total exports.
This surplus was frozen in accounts at Berlin and used by Germany to finance
its imports[1].

The Czech National Bank was obliged to honour cheques issued by German
authorities to finance their current expenditure and purchase of property in
the Czech lands, and for financing German industry outside Czechoslovakia.
The total exploitation was reflected in the evolution of frozen claims of
the Czech National Bank at the Reichsbank. The total sum at the end of the
war surpassed the total taxation revenue collected in the Czech lands
between 1939 and 1949.

TABLE 4.II

TOTAL FROZEN CLAIMS OF THE CZECH NATIONAL BANK IN GERMANY

(milliard crowns) (a)

End of 1940	6.9
" " 1941	12.8
" " 1942	17.3
" " 1943	34.2
" " 1944	59.7
Liberation	105.0

Source: Přehled hospodářského vývoje Československa v letech 1918–1945, op.cit.

(a)   Milliard refers to thousand millions.   Outstanding claims of Czech commercial banks against Germany amounted to a further 45 milliard Kčs in 1944[2].

The Slovak economy was exploited through both the clearing system and fiscal policy.   The rate fixed between the Slovak crown and the German mark was even more unfavourable than in the Czech case.   However, the exploitation of Slovakia occurred only through foreign trade, as the mark did not ciruclate internally.   Total Slovak funds frozen in Germany were much lower than in the Czech case.

Slovakia's total government expenditure grew more rapidly than in the Czech lands.   This was mainly due to militarization of the economy, war collaboration with Germany and maintenance of a Police State apparatus.   The increase in state expenditure was not completely financed by taxation growth.   The deficit was mainly financed by money issue.

The growth of frozen claims in the Reichsbank and the high level of war expenditure in Slovakia explains the rapid growth of money in the hands of the private sector, this increased in Czechoslovakia from 14.2 milliard Kčs at the end of 1938 to 107.6 milliard Kčs at the end of the war[3].   The rapid growth of money, accompanied by a fall in the supply of goods for the internal market (due to a reorientation of production towards the war effort and limited imports) created strong inflationary pressures.

To stop these pressures leading to large price increases, the German authorities imposed price controls.   The official retail price index rose by 72 per cent during the same period[4].   Inflation manifested itself in a decrease in the quality of goods and in widespread scarcities and black markets.   During the Occupation it was impossible to calculate an index for black market prices.   After Liberation, it was estimated that by the end of the War, on average black market prices were 40 or 50 times the official ones.

2   The political context: political and economic
     targets of the Czechoslovak Communist Party

We shall here outline the main political elements, stressing those related to the use of financial policies for the power struggle[5].

During and after World War II, there was a fundamental 'shift to the left'

in the Czechoslovak political scene. The surrender of Czechoslovak
territory at Munich caused distrust of the Western powers. Conservative
parties were discredited by the collaboration of some of their followers
with the Nazis; the left played a key role in domestic resistance. A
fundamental shift in Czech foreign policy occurred in December, 1943, with
the signing of the 20-year Soviet-Czechoslovak Treaty[6].

The Communists were becoming the most decisive force in Czechoslovak
politics; this was recognized by Beneš (President of the Republic, 1935-48)
when he told them in 1943, 'You will be the strongest element of the new
regime'[7].

After 1929, the Czechoslovak Communist Party leadership followed the shifts
in Comintern and Soviet policy. As Klement Gottwald, then General-Secretary
of the Czechoslovak Communist Party, admitted[8], 'Our highest revolutionary
staff is really Moscow'.

Since the Seventh Congress of the Comintern in 1935, the key task for
Communist Parties was to unite all sections of the working class,
irrespective of what organization they belonged to, and to forge links
between workers, peasants, petty bourgeois and middle strata. Communist
parties were encouraged to develop this popular front strategy in accordance
with their specific, national conditions.

After the war, the Soviet Union was immensely weakened by the losses and
damage it had suffered. The strategy its leadership adopted until the
Spring of 1947 was a continuation of the anti-fascist coalition, based on
the premise of the possibility of inter-allied co-operation. The Soviet
Union encouraged foreign communist parties to pursue a similar policy of
national fronts uniting all anti-fascist forces. The policies of the
Czechoslovak Communist leadership clearly followed this pattern.

In March, 1945, several major aspects of the Czechoslovak post-war
government and programme were accepted by all the anti-fascist parties. The
government would be composed of a single, National Front of all the
anti-fascist parties (Communists, Social Democrats, National Socialists,
Czech People's Party and Slovak Democratic Party). Parties that had
collaborated with the Nazis were to be banned; this again shifted
Czechoslovak politics to the left. It was agreed that Germans and
Hungarians who had not been active anti-fascists were to be transferred out
of Czechoslovakia. After strong opposition from other parties, Communist
proposals were accepted advocating radical revisions in the Army structure,
purging it of pro-fascist elements and linking it very closely to the Soviet
Red Army. It was on this programme that Czechoslovakia began to function
after Liberation.

During 1945, the Communist Party laid greater emphasis on the direct
mechanisms of powers, linked to controlling political and state
institutions. Economic transformations, such as nationalization, were
considered secondary; furthermore, on nationalization, the Communists
emphasized their desire to be 'at the head' of the nation, rather than too
far to the left[9].

The initial programme supported by all political parties proposed taking
over the property of Germans, Hungarians and collaborators, and placing them
under national administration. Pressures for nationalization seem to have
started at trade union level. Only later did the Communists support
immediate nationalization. In October, 1945, a nationalization decree was
approved by the government; 16.4 per cent of industrial enterprises
employing 61.2 per cent of persons engaged in industry were
nationalized[10]. Simultaneously, all joint stock banks and private
insurance companies were nationalized. Enterprises remaining in the private

sector would not be liable to nationalization.

Immediately after Liberation, a decree was passed without opposition to
confiscate all land belonging to Germans, Hungarians and traitors.   Under
this decree, nearly a quarter of the country's territory was confiscated.

Communist and Western historians of the period agree that the Czechoslovak
Communist Party leadership was pleased at the end of 1945 that the national
and democratic revolution had followed their strategy in all fundamental
aspects. From late 1945 until mid-1947, the relative international calm led
the Communists to base their strategy on continued support for the National
Front Government.   Gottwald, then the Communist Deputy Prime Minister,
expressed this at the Party Congress held in March, 1946[11]: 'The new,
democratic, popular republic and its political and economic structure
correspond to the interests of all the working strata of our nation.'

In the economic sphere, the Communists emphasized economic reconstruction as
the main task. Thus, Gottwald, in September, 1945, stressed: 'as the first
task of the national and democratic revolution, the recovery of the economy
from war damage'[12].

In March, 1946, the Communists ratified their full support for the remaining
private sector.   Their attitude was reflected in the resolution passed by
the government in July, 1946, declaring 'the action of nationalization
finished and granting constitutional protection to small and medium
enterprises'.

The Communist Party programme for the May 1946 National Assembly elections
adopted the policy and tone of its congress. As a result of the elections,
the Communists obtained 38 per cent of the popular vote, surpassing other
parties by far.

During 1947, the Cold War began.   In March, the Truman Doctrine was
announced heralding an ideological crusade against communism.   In June, the
Marshall Plan was announced, offering massive American aid to help European
reconstruction; it also aimed to weaken communist influence in Europe.   The
Soviet Union reacted very strongly; it was agreed at a conference in Poland
of ten European Communist parties in the late summer, that those parties in
Eastern Europe were to take power; this would quickly seal the whole Soviet
sphere of influence from Western penetration.   In this operation,
Czechoslovakia was very important both economically and militarily.

The Czechoslovak Communist Party veered sharply to the Left. On his return
from Poland, Slansky, general secretary of the Czechoslovak Communist Party,
declared that the most important task was 'to bolster the National Front,
from which of course, exponents of domestic and foreign reaction must be
expelled'[13].   This theme was to become one of the main Communist tactics
in their attempt to dominate the government.

From then on almost every sphere of state life became an arena for sharp
political struggle.   We shall not examine here important institutional
aspects, as they do not fall within the scope of this study.   In the
economic sphere, the change in Communist strategy coincided with economic
difficulties.   As we shall detail below, problems in agriculture and
financial disequilibria led to increasing black markets and speculation.

The Communists, following their overall strategy, blamed the capitalist
sector for the economic problems.   Frejka, Chairman of the Communist
National Economic Comittee and one of their main economic spokesmen,
said[14]:

                the harmful activity which, in this year of bad

harvest, was practised by the capitalist sector mainly
in the field of supply convinced us that it is a
foreign element in our popular democratic economy.
This forces the people's democracy to conduct a daily
struggle   against   the   private   capitalist
representatives of the reaction... The capitalists
know well that in our country a new path leading from
the people's democracy to socialism has been taken.
They know well that each step in consolidating our
economy and increasing the living standard of the
masses is a deadly blow to their existence, because
such an evolution broadens the trust in the new regime
and mainly in the Communists, strengthens the workers'
confidence and induces them to continue the path
towards   socialism.   Therefore,   the   nests   of
capitalism, which   provide   the   base   for   the
reactionaries, want the disruption of the people's
democratic economy because of their class interests.

Based on this diagnosis of the economic problems, the Communists proposed to
severely restrict the capitalist sector in agriculture, industry and trade.
These proposals found strong support in the Communist controlled trade union
movement.

As we shall detail below, in this period the Communists - as well as the
other parties - made important use of financial issues as part of the
increased political struggle.

3   Economic evolution, 1945-48

First, the successful reconstruction of the Czechoslovak economy up till
1947 will be described.   This coincided with a period of collaboration
amongst political parties in the National Front.   The economic difficulties
and contradictions which arose mainly after mid-1947 will then be examined.
They coincided with - and were partly related to - increasing political
tension internationally and nationally.

(a)   Post-war reconstruction

A severe limitation to post-war economic reconstruction was the labour
problem.   Employment had fallen during the war; in October, 1945, industrial
employment was 80 per cent of the 1937 level.   In 1945-46, the labour market
was affected by the transfer of three million Germans from Czechoslovakia.
Particularly in industry, these problems were overcome quite rapidly.   The
fall in the number of German workers in industry was compensated for by an
increase in Czech and Slovak workers[15].   The situation was more serious in
agriculture, which lost a large number of German workers.

Immediately after Liberation, the government successfully focused its
efforts on sectors crucial to economic recovery - coal mining and transport.
An important role in satisfying Czechoslovakia's urgent needs and helping
reconstruction was played by economic aid provided by the United Nations
Relief and Rehabilitation Administration (UNRRA).   Approximately 70 per cent
of its cost was financed by the United States.   Total UNRRA aid to
Czechoslovakia during 1946 and 1947 reached US$ 260 million[16].   It
provided basic foodstuffs, medicines, transport, material, livestock and
other items.

As can be seen from Table 4.III, economic recovery was extremely rapid[17].
By 1948, total national income surpassed the 1937 level and per capita
income surpassed it by 18 per cent (due to the drastic population decline).
Disposable national income was higher, due mainly to the inflow of economic

aid provided by UNRRA.   Industrial growth was particularly rapid.

(b)   Economic difficulties

Difficulties arose during 1947, both internally and externally.   Internally,
agriculture posed the most serious problems.   Total agricultural production
fell in 1947, due to a very large decline in crop production (see Table
4.III), which in 1947 reached only 62 per cent of the pre-war level.

Shortage of fodder crops reduced livestock yields and livestock decreased in
1948.   The bad harvest affected internal supplies of foodstuffs as well as
exports.   Food rations were cut substantially, in some cases to below 1945
levels[18].

At the beginning of 1948 the fall in agricultural output was attributed by
politicians and planning institutions mainly to the drought.

Throughout 1948, the emphasis changed; in October, the new Administration
blamed sabotage of production by capitalist elements as the main cause[19].
Later evaluations of the agricultural problems of the period introduce
additional factors[20].   One of the most serious problems faced by
agriculture was the sharp fall in employment.   A further limit to output
growth was the maintenance of the procurement system, prevalent during the
war so as to obtain cheap food supplies for the towns.

TABLE 4.III

INDICATORS OF CZECHOSLOVAKIA'S ECONOMIC EVOLUTION

Indicator	1937	1945	1946	1947	1948
Index of National Income (at 1937) prices	100	n.a.	83	95	101
Index of Disposable National Income (at 1937 prices) (a)	100	n.a.	87.1	99.8	102.5
Index of per capita National Income (at 1937 prices) (a)	100	n.a.	93	111.3	118
Index of per capita Disposable National Income (at 1937 prices) (a)	100	n.a.	97	118	120
Index of Industrial Production	100	50	70.8	87.0	103.3
Index of Agric. Production (a)	100	n.a.	76.0	74.5	74.4
Index of Crop Production (a)	100	n.a.	86.3	61.6	87.8
Index of Livestock (a)	100	n.a.	69.4	82.7	65.8

(a)   Source: Průběh Plnění Dvouletého Hospodářského Plánu (Appraisal of the
      Two Year Plan's Fulfilment).   Státní Úřad Planovací.   Prague, 1948.
      In future, referred to as PPDHP.

Another element influencing the level of agricultural output was land reform. Production was affected, due largely to the new owners' lack of experience. The living standards of new small-holders - mostly coming from the poorest sections of the rural population - improved; investment and supplies to the cities from the reformed estates fell.

Externally, difficulties arose as an effect of the restriction of Western foreign aid. At first, the outlook seemed promising. Besides UNRRA aid, Czechoslovakia received loans from Western countries such as Canada, the United Kingdom and the United States, as well as from the American Export-Import Bank. Additionally, a large credit from the International Bank (for US$ 50 million) was being negotiated in 1946. In June 1946, the US Government extended a US$ 50 million credit to Czechoslovakia for the purchase of surplus US army stocks. However, economic contacts with Western powers were disturbed by the deteriorating international situation. In mid-September 1946, the US stopped deliveries to Czechoslovakia from the previously agreed military credit (only $10 million had been drawn) and in the same month negotiations about the International Bank loan were interrupted[21].

As a result largely of Soviet pressure, Czechoslovakia refused to participate in the Marshall Plan. It justified this refusal by referring to the Plan's ideological nature (oriented against the Soviet Union and supporting right-wing, anti-socialist forces). The discussion about the Marshall Plan was one of the events of 1947 which typified the connection between the increasing tension at an international level and in Czechoslovakia itself[22].

Following its rejection of the Marshall Plan and the problems faced in agriculture, Czechoslovakia needed external credit badly. This was provided by the Soviet credit approved in December 1947 (see below).

4   The Planning Apparatus and Economic Management

Between April 1945 and July 1946, the Economic Council was formed as an auxiliary organ of the government; its main tasks included the elaboration of an economic plan and the assignment of concrete tasks to the ministries. In fact, it held very few meetings and never started to prepare a plan.

Although the Economic Council was virtually inactive, its two auxiliary organs soon began to function. The General Secretariat, was mainly concerned with short-term co-ordination, while the State Planning Office was geared mainly towards preparatory work for formulating the Two Year Plan. Its work tended to be somewhat limited to description, with little attention paid to analyzing the discussion of different alternatives.

The draft of the first Czechoslovak plan was not only born, but also elaborated, within the National Economic Commission of the Communist Party. Though Communist Party specialists did not work out all the plan's details, they defined its political and economic directives. In fact, the Communist Party National Economic Commission fulfilled the function of a top planning organ. The Two Year Plan was used by the Communist Party as propaganda for its 1946 electoral campaign; after the elections the Communists had it accepted as part of the Government Programme.

For the implementation of the Two Year Plan, the planning organs were reorganised. The newly established Central Planning Commission became the supreme planning organ. It was formed by the Prime Minister, the chairmen of the State Planning Office, and economic experts representing political parties. This allowed various interests to be harmonized[23]. Due to the lack of concreteness, the Plan had in many cases little real influence on enterprises. As Goldman pointed out: 'in many factories the Plan was left in the leading planning organs, and life in the factories remained just as it was before the Plan'.

The nationalization decrees accorded nationalized enterprises independent
legal status; they were managed on commercial lines. After equipping these
enterprises with basic capital and reserve funds, the state did not take
responsibility for their obligations. The enterprises were not directly
linked to the state budget, but had balance accounts at the Finance Ministry
where part of the profits (after deductions) should flow. These funds were
to balance losses of other nationalized industries, finance programmed
investments, and pay for compensation of nationalized property. The
surplus, it was intended, should flow into the State Treasury. In practice,
the nationalized sector incurred losses.

General directorates were set up to oversee the direction of the different
national enterprises. These centralized financial resources, marketing,
foreign trade, technical development and investment. Their directorates
became the managing and planning centres of their industrial branches.

Increasing centralization obeyed the needs of rapid post-war economic
reconstruction. According to some Czech authors[24], the high degree of
centralization was influenced by the type of economic management in the
Soviet Union and the wish to obtain quicker and more spectacular results
than was thought could result from the use of more indirect mechanisms (such
as financial and price mechanisms). Even though the State intervened
strongly during this period in the administration of enterprises, this did
not correspond to the precise fulfilment of a detailed and coordinated plan.

Not only did centralized physical planning have very limited effectiveness,
but financial planning (on a macro-economic level) was not integrated in the
planning process. The Plan was based only on physical production targets,
and the role of finance was regarded as completely passive. It was said at
the time[25] that:

> Financing the Two Year Plan is a similar problem to
> financing a war. The final aims are completely
> contrary, but the basic problem is similar. It is
> basically a problem of mobilizing labour and means of
> production (inputs, energy and productive capacity)
> for the production of war goods or investment goods.
> To ensure that this production level is achieved, does
> not depend on whether the necessary financial
> resources are available. To assure such production,
> it is first of all necessary that the physical
> preconditions be fulfilled. If these are given then
> the investment is feasible. The Two Year Plan itself
> had already stated[26]: ..In connection with the
> question of what total value of investment is possible
> and advisable, we frequently hear an erroneous view
> put forward based on the assumption that the volume of
> investment is determined by the financial means
> available. This is not the case however.
>
> If all the physical instruments of investment are
> available, investment can be carried out and it is the
> proper and only task of financial policy to mobilize
> the financial means required to realize the investment
> policy for which the physical resources are available.
> This planned investment should not be held up by
> insufficiency of financial means.

Several other opinions were expressed during the period on the subject. The
most naive one was that of the State Planning Office's representative[27],

who said: 'in the People's Democracy, because it is a planned economy, there can be no inflation unless the authorities wish it'. Left-wing politicians repeated the same argument. In the same book, Dr. V. Erban (Communist deputy of the National Assembly) said that 'inflation was a ghost raised by the reaction'. He added: 'In a planned and directed economy, inflation is not possible - unless the government has agreed on it. We know that the People's Democracy will not take such a decision'.

Even more serious, the General Director of the National Bank (Dr. L. Chmela) also misunderstood these problems. He said[28] that 'the problem of financing was only a technical problem'. Printing of money he called 'anticipation of future savings or pre-investment'. According to Dr. Chmela, the most important element was not the size of credit expansion, but the instruments through which it was carried out.

In all these opinions, there is a serious confusion between a planned economy with effective centralized control[29] and that existing in Czechoslovakia during the period. As we saw, at the time, physical planning was not operating adequately so as to assure equilibrium at the level of physical resources. There was no financial plan to assure equilibrium between production and consumption; lack of coordination between financial policies as well as pressures from different groups and sectors within society expressed themselves in disequilibria. Furthermore, there was a struggle for power which was reflected in excessive demands and pressures from different social groups.

The insufficient attention devoted to financial policy during this period was perceived and correctly criticized by some economists within the planning apparatus. For example, Jaroslav Krejčí[30], explaining the factors behind the 1947 inflationary pressures, said:

> A further cause is the insufficient extent of our planning. The main limitation is that till now a whole set of aspects were excluded from planning. This refers mainly to the financial aspects, ranging from price policy to credit and taxation policy.

II   Initial solution of financial disequilibria and causes of further imbalances

1   The 1945 Monetary Reform

The Czechoslovak monetary reform was one of many carried out in Europe after Liberation, mainly to dispose of excessive liquidity which had arisen as an effect of the war.

Czechoslovak monetary reform had three phases. At first, a major portion of banknotes and bank deposits were blocked; certain basic allocations were made to individuals and business firms so that normal economic activity could continue; funds, or part of them, were gradually released either through individual requests, through blanket releases, or other means[31].

In November, 1945, a new currency was introduced, its rate to the old crown being 1:1. The old currency was placed on blocked accounts. Deposits, life insurance policies and state bonds were also frozen. From the funds placed on blocked accounts, 500 Kčs per person were freed. Enterprises received new currency equivalent to the amount of their monthly wages and payments. After initial exchange of money, 24,000 million Kčs were left in circulation. Funds on blocked accounts not converted in December, 1945, amounted to 258,000 million Kčs[32]. Public institutions, state enterprises, political parties and other legal institutions were allowed to draw freely from their accounts. Special withdrawals for social reasons to benefit particularly the old and the sick, were allowed if approved by a special commission. According to some authors[33], there was fraudulent and illegal de-blocking of funds, particularly to groups linked with the Democratic Party in Slovakia.

The freezing of deposits was not only an anti-inflationary measure, to neutralize pent-up demand, but also a means of redistribution of private property. A general levy on property and a higher and progressive levy on increase of property during the war was introduced.

2   Sources of financial disequilibria

Following the 1945 monetary reform, there were two main sources of money supply expansion: de-blocking of funds and credit expansion.

(a)   De-blocking of funds

Excluding the amount freed during the monetary reform, total released deposits reached 33,500 million crowns towards the end of July 1947, composed as follows:

TABLE 4.IV

COMPOSITION OF RELEASED DEPOSITS

(million Kcs).

Social reasons	14,026
Public institutions	17,750
Special government decrees	480
Charge for Allied Army	1,250
	33,506

Source: Dolanský, J. Výklad Min. Financí k státnímu rozpočtu na rok 1948. ('Exposition of the Finance Minister on the 1948 Budget'). Ministerstvo Financí, Prague, 1947.

Several measures were introduced to control the excessive release of de-blocked funds. At the end of August 1947, a Liquidation Monetary Fund was created, taking over all blocked deposits. Stricter controls were imposed on fund releases. Small sums were even re-frozen, as examination showed that their release had not been in accordance with legal prescriptions. After August, 1947, the amount of de-blocked funds decreased substantially.

(b)   Budget deficit

The level of the budget deficit, as well as State revenues and expenditures will be discussed next. A more detailed analysis - especially of taxation policy and its class implications - will follow.

For 1945-48, the State Budget results were as follows:

TABLE 4.V

PLANNED AND EFFECTIVE STATE BUDGET DEFICIT

(in million Kcs of every year) (a)

	(1) Planned deficit or surplus	(2) Effective deficit or surplus	(3) (2) as % of National Income
1945	(b)	- 11,928	n.a.
1946	- 26,208	- 15,287	9
1947	27,905	- 9,320	5
1948	- 13,827	- 7,202	4

(a) M. Tuček, Vývoj československých financí v letech 1945-52 op.cit. Czechoslovak National Bank monthly Bulletins.

(b) There was no budget.

It can be seen that after the war the budget deficit was a relatively high proportion of National Income. However, the effective budget deficit was smaller than the programmed one. This was mainly due to higher receipts of taxes than expected[34].

The structure of the tax system will be analyzed and compared with the pre-War one.

TABLE 4.VI

COMPOSITION OF TAXATION (1937 and 1945-48)

	1937	1945	1946	1947	1948
Direct taxes (of which wage tax)	20.4	64.1	45.1 (19.4)	39.9 (14.6)	40.5 (12.7)
Turnover taxes	28.6	11.8	19.4	23.9	26.2
Dues	21.5	8.1	11.1	10.4	11.2
Other indirect taxes	20.8)		14.7	12.4	10.8
Customs duties	8.0)	16.0	0.5	1.4	1.5
Monopolies	0.7)		9.2	12.0	9.8
Total:	100.0	100.0	100.0	100.0	100.0

Source: Bulletins of Czechoslovak National Bank and Dolanský, op.cit.

In analyzing the distribution between direct and indirect taxes, there is a problem in the classification of dues. It will be assumed here that the proportion of dues which are direct taxes for the years 1937 and 1945 (where no detail is available) is the same as the 1946-48 average proportion.

TABLE 4.VII

STRUCTURE AND LEVEL OF DIRECT AND INDIRECT TAXES

(a)   Percentage composition of taxation

	1937	1945	1946	1947	1948
Structure of taxation					
Direct taxes	26.0	66.3	47.5	43.3	43.8
Indirect taxes	74.0	33.7	52.5	56.7	56.2
Total	100.0	100.0	100.0	100.0	100.0

(b)   Evolution of taxation in real terms

Direct taxation	100	269[c]	215	260	265
Indirect taxes	100	49	86	173	174
Total taxes:	100	107	118	198	200

Source: (a)   Table 4.VI.

(b)   Dolansky, op.cit. in (34).

(c)   Deflated by wholesale price index, published in Statisticky
Zpravodaj, op.cit. are based on the period May-December, but
extrapolated so as to be comparable with the other years.
Source: Bulletins of Czechoslovak National Bank.

The proportion of direct taxation in the total during the National Front was
much higher than before the War. As will be seen, this was mainly due to an
increase in direct tax rates, particularly of income and profit tax.   It
would seem that this increase in direct taxation during the People's
Democracy in relation to the pre-war situation reflected the 'shift to the
left' in Czechoslovak society.   During 1945-48 the share of direct taxes
fell. The reason was a very rapid growth in indirect taxation mainly caused
by quick economic recovery.

Comparing individual taxes (see Table 4.VI) with the pre-war period two
changes stand out: there is a fall in the proportion of customs duties, due
partly to the decline in foreign trade, but mainly because of a fall in
tariffs, as many popular consumer goods were exempt from duties; and the
income from monopolies grew substantially. This reveals a tendency to shift
the taxation burden from essential goods (ie. food) to non-essential goods
(ie. liquor).

The main changes in the tax system during the 1945-48 period were:

Reform of income and profit tax: In December 1945, a similar taxing system
to the pre-war one was introduced, but with much higher progressiveness.

Reform of indirect taxation: Some modifications were introduced in February
1946 to simplify the structure and increase rates on some non-essential
goods.

Property tax on blocked funds: As we saw, a property tax to exhaust blocked
funds was passed, establishing strongly progressive taxation on property
increase and taxation of property, beyond a certain limit. The incomes from

this tax had the role of an accounting operation, to liquidate blocked funds, and were not a source of State revenue.

Reform of wages, agriculture and artisan tax: The Communists assumed the initiative of further tax reforms before the 1946 elections. The general objectives were to simplify the tax structure (each income should be affected by one tax) and to re-distribute the 'tax burden' (earned and unearned incomes should be treated differently).

Of the Communist proposals only the reform of the wages tax was approved before February 1948 (other reforms being opposed by the other parties in the government).

Till 1947, taxes on wages were treated in the same way as on profits. The wages tax approved in June 1947, led to a lowering of the workers' tax burden. The rates were, however, very progressive. The wages tax excluded incomes obtained for overtime and for good achievement; thus the progressiveness of the tax did not affect productivity incentives.

The introduction of a lower tax for workers implied a substantial fall in the cost of living index for working class families (see Table 4.XVIII). As the middle strata began opposing the government - and particularly the Communists - this Party designed, as part of its March 1946 electoral platform a series of measures designed to favour them. One was the modification of the tax on artisans, small traders and peasants. It proposed to tax these groups like workers. The other parties did not support these proposals, a fact that was used against them by the Communists, particularly in January and February, 1948.

It seems to have been an incorrect political tactic of the right-wing not to have tried to maintain middle class support through this tax.

Discussions on a millionaire's tax: The discussions on millionaire's tax and tax on conspicuous consumption occupy an important place in the economic and political evolution of the period. For example, Opat, op.cit. in (22), calls the struggle for the millionaire's tax 'the best catalyst in the evolution to socialism.'

To compensate for the effect of the 1947 drought on peasants' incomes, the Communists and Social Democrats proposed subsidies on purchase prices and compensation to poor peasants. This was accepted unanimously by all the National Front parties. The total subsidy was estimated at 6,500 million Kcs. The Communists proposed financing the expenditure by a tax to be paid by the millionaires (people whose property assets surpassed 1 million Kcs); they also proposed a tax on conspicuous consumption. The slogan used by the Communists was 'let the wealthy pay'. The government accepted the tax on conspicuous consumption; it simultaneously rejected the millionaire tax[35,36]. The National Socialists and the People's Party strongly opposed it, initially offering no alternative form of finance. They proposed that the additional expenditure should result in a bigger deficit.

Initial opposition to the millionaire's tax was extremely strong. The National Socialists gave several reasons for their opposition. They expressed doubts as to whether it would achieve the desired yield; they claimed that the tax would not only affect millionaires, but also small and medium entrepreneurs; that it would affect 'honest savers' more than speculators (whose capital increase could not be detected) and that it would break the basic trust and saving morale of private entrepreneurs. The Communists reacted strongly to the rejection of the millionaire's tax. Their first action was to publish in Rude Pravo (their newspaper) the list of Ministers who voted against the tax. For the first time since 1945 a government crisis threatened.

An important role was played by the united trade unions (Revolucni Odborove Hnuti-ROH). Mass meetings were organised in factories, which passed resolutions to support the Communist position. In the presidium of ROH the Social Democrats presented a motion - approved unanimously by representatives of all political parties - to support a millionaire's tax. The declaration had a clear class content: '...The Presidium of ROH demands that the weight of the necessary measures be laid on the exploiters and the recently enriched strata...' A new wave of meetings at the factory level followed.

As a result of public opinion pressure, the National Socialists and Social Democrats began modifying their position. The Communists drafted another proposal, which included taxing high incomes, wealth and excessive profits. Taxpayers whose 1947 income or wage surpassed 240,000 Kčs had their tax increased by 20 per cent; taxpayers whose income surpassed 240,000 Kčs and who owned property worth over 1 million Kčs would pay the 20 per cent surcharge, plus an additional property tax. The tax on extraordinary profits was to affect all those whose property grew between November 1945 and December 1947, by more than 300,000 Kčs. All growth exceeding that limit would be taxed away. These proposals were approved by the Government. As Dolansky op.cit. pointed out, the final version implied certain minor concessions.

The effective yield of the tax was lower than expected - only 4 milliard Kčs in 1948. This was mainly because of the large unplanned expropriations carried out after February, 1948. It is difficult to estimate the potential yield, had these unforeseen property changes not occurred. There were, however, also technical difficulties in the application of the tax.

The final yield of the tax does not justify the political struggle it caused. It seems that the importance of the 'millionaire's tax' was more political than financial, and the struggle over it coincided with increasing national and international tension and a sharp veer to the left in the Communist Party strategy.

The technical objections put forward by the right-wing about the tax's yield had some validity, but their main reason for opposing the tax was political. They were unwilling to tax the wealthy more, and they may also have been pursuing (as the Communists claimed) a medium-term political objective by allowing a larger budget deficit to cause further disequilibria in the economy[37].

The Communists gained most politically, as they used the discussion about the tax (which they broadcast through the mass media and workers' organizations) to discredit other political parties. This followed an explicit political decision taken by the Communist leadership in mid-September 1947, which defined, as the main task to:

> use the discussions on the millionaire tax to gain Social Democratic and National Socialist workers for joint actions, mainly through trade union organizations, to increase aid to the left-wing Social Democrats and support the formation of a left-wing oriented group in the National Socialist party, which would oppose the existing reactionary leadership[38].

Their political gains stemmed not so much from the approval of the tax itself but from the effect of the discussion, particularlý within the trade unions. The Communist message was simple:

> The struggle was not about 5 milliard, but about the question whether the regime would continue to govern

in favour of the working class or in the selfish
interest of a small minority of millionaires - which
would imply a return to the past.

Workers of all parties supported the Communists in this, non-Communists
following its line because they felt it served their short-term interests
better.   More important for the Communists was the fact that the struggle
over the millionaire's tax increased sympathy for their position amongst the
working class, by revealing the inherent contradiction between workers' and
capitalists' interests.   This implied that their long term interests
(suporting revolutionary change which would solve these inherent
contradictions) were also best represented by the Communists[39].   Also, of
great importance for the forthcoming power confrontation, it showed that in
a political conflict, particularly on issues of interest to the majority of
the people, the Communists had the workers' suport and could mobilise this
support on their behalf; such pressure would shift the Social Democrats'
position, ensuring the Communists a majority in Government.

The basic reason for the large state deficit in 1945-48 was the increase in
the level of State expenditure.   Average budgetary State expenditure in
1946-48 was nearly three times the 1937 level.

TABLE 4.VIII

LEVEL OF BUDGETARY STATE EXPENDITURE

(1937 million Kčs) (a)

1937	8,453
1945	n.a.
1946	20,280
1947	24,930
1948	22,710

(a) Source: Tuček, op.cit.   The deflator used is the wholesale price
                index.

The item which grew most was administration of the national economy and of
the State.   The Finance Minister, Dolánsky[40], pointed out that the main
reason for this growth was an increase in state functions (i.e. management
of and planning of nationalized enterprises and removal of the German
population).   The number of state employees increased substantially, from
425,000 in 1937 to 642,000 in 1948.

The financial evolution of State enterprises (i.e. those already belonging
to the State in 1945) was as follows:

TABLE 4.IX

BUDGETED FINANCIAL RESULTS OF STATE ENTERPRISES

(million Kčs of each year)

	Current incomes	Current expenditures	Current surplus	Invest-ment	Net flow to State enterprises
1946	23,574	21,213	+ 2,361	9,513	− 7,152
1947	41,630	33,665	+ 7,965	9,606	− 1,641
1948	41,868	33,129	+ 8,639	12,183	− 3,544

Source: Dolánsky.   Výklad na státni rozpočet 1949, 1948 and 1946, op.cit.

Between 1946 and 1947 the current surplus increased rapidly as current incomes increased quicker than expenditures. This was due both to price increases and to a rapid recovery in production. While total current expenditure grew by 60 per cent between 1946 and 1947, wage expenditure increased by 74 per cent over the same period. In no year did the current surplus generated cover investment.

Initially, it was hoped that nationalized enterprises would have a net profit, which would be transferred to the State Budget. However, in 1946 and 1947 nationalized enterprises suffered net losses, reaching 1,335 milion Kčs in 1946 and 208 million Kčs in 1947. As the right wing parties refused to agree that these losses as well as investment should be financed from the Budget[41], they were mostly financed with credit via the banking system (see below). Losses of nationalized enterprises by sectors in 1946, (the only year for which data are available) can be seen in Table 4.X.,

TABLE 4.X

PROFITS AND LOSSES OF NATIONALIZED INDUSTRY (MILLION KČS) IN 1946)

Industrial Sector	Net Result
Mining	− 1,284
Metallurgy	− 619
Engineering	− 601
Chemical	+ 414
Paper	+ 71
Textile	+ 297
Leather and Rubber	+ 229
Sugar	− 219
Other Sectors	+ 377
Total	− 1,335

Source: Mrázek, op.cit.
           Minus (−) means net losses.

The greatest losses were in mining, metallurgy, engineering and the sugar industry.

Several explanations were given for the nationalized enterprises losses[42]. Initially, an important element was that national enterprises began to operate without their own appropriate financial means. A great part of

their assets had been depreciated or were uncollectable (war damages, claims
for military deliveries). Another important element was price policy. A
policy of low prices was followed for basic raw materials, mainly produced
by nationalized enterprises (i.e. coal, iron and steel); prices for the
products of light industry - largely in the private sector - were increased
more (see below).

The reasons for this price policy are not very clear. According to most
Communist historians, it was caused by the control by bourgeois interests of
the Central Pricing Commission. However, it is not clear why the Communist
Party did not press more strongly for price increases for the nationalized
sector (for detailed discussion see below).

Furthermore, nationalized industry faced particularly difficult problems.
Given the nature of the branches where nationalized industry predominated
(i.e. engineering), greater efforts were necessary for reconversion to peace
time production. Production levels in nationalized enterprises seem to have
recovered as quickly as in private enterprises. In 1946, of the five
sectors where nationalized industry was most important, four surpassed the
average recovery of industrial production (in comparison with 1937). By
1948, recovery of levels of output in all the main branches of the
nationalized sector was higher than the average for industry.

TABLE 4.XI

EVOLUTION OF INDUSTRIAL OUTPUT AND PRODUCTIVITY PER WORKER (a)

Industrial Sectors	Particiption of the sector's employment in nationalized industry	1946 output base 1937=100	1948 output base 1937=100	1946 pdt base 1937=100 (b)	1948 pdt base 1937=100 (b)
Mining	100.0	91.2	113.3	68.8	80.7
Energy	99.1	140.0	183.9	114.3	136.0
Metallurgy	99.4	68.7	109.0	74.0	100.6
Chemicals	76.4	77.7	124.0	76.5	105.9
Engineering	72.6	73.3	120.5	n.a.	n.a.
All Industry	61.2	70.8	103.3	79.6	99.7

Sources: (a) Mrázek, op.cit. PPDHP, op.cit.

           (b) pdt = productivity per worker. This figure is obtained by
                dividing the output index by the corresponding employment
                index, both with base 1937=100.

The evolution of productivity was, however, less satisfactory in
nationalized industry, especially in 1946. In that year productivity
declined more (in comparison with 1937) in three of the four sectors
analyzed than the average for industry. The situation had improved
substantially by 1948.

There are several explanations for the initially somewhat slower recovery of
labour productivity in the nationalized than in the non-nationalized
sectors. As pointed out by Kalinová and Brabec[43], there was a tendency in
nationalized enterprises to 'hold' labour reserves for eventual future need
and so as not to be anti-social. Protective measures, such as the social

policy of the workers' committees, trade unions and party organizations impeded dismissals or even transfers of workers within the enterprise. This led to a high level of 'social over-employment' (as the Czechoslovak economists called it). It was considered legitimate that nationalized industry should carry out the social function of paying unnecessary workers for un-worked hours.

An additional problem which also explains the low rate of productivity was the high proportion of the increase in workers in nationalized enterprises going to unproductive work. There was a significant transfer of workers – mainly skilled – to administrative work, partly related to the wish of certain workers to increase their social status and living standards. This can be attributed largely to the administrative system used to manage the economy, and to the desire of the different political parties to be represented in certain jobs.

After the 1945 wage reform wages were centrally controlled by government directives. The official wage policy – supported by the trade union movement – supported wage stability, and linked wages to productivity through a system of norms. This system became a mechanism for wage increases in nationalized industry. As wage rates were fixed, workers concentrated on fixing norms which made earnings increases easier. In nationalized enterprises, conflicts arose between the 'fixer of norms' (representing the state's interest) and the representatives of nationalized industry. Excessive wages were obtained by the fixing of low or 'easy' norms, causing so-called 'black wages', achieved both by pressure from below (by workers) or from managers of enterprises wishing to win the worker's support. Through these mechanisms the original wage policy was destroyed.

An undoubtedly important factor in determining the unsatisfactory financial results of the nationalized enterprises was the insufficient attention given to value relations by the enterprises' management. For the fulfilment of planned targets specified in physical units, these managers often considered credit financing to be the duty of the banks. The management of nationalized enterprises often regarded it unnecessary to justify their credit needs on financial grounds. Furthermore, there was competition between banks. If one bank demanded detailed economic information, the enterprise could turn to another bank which proceeded less strictly. Sometimes, credits were almost forced upon enterprises. Banks 'lured' enterprises by offering them various advantages. The situation in the money market aided this; after the 1945 monetary reform, deposits grew quicker than credit demand, and the banks had excessive liquidity.

Apparently, the National Bank did not – or could not – control the total levels of credits given by the banking system. No mention is made in the literature about the possibility of strengthening the National Bank's control over the nationalized banks to regulate the volume of credit. As a solution to the problem, the Communist Party advocated reorganization of the nationalized banks, and a detailed proposal was set out in their 1946 Action Programme. It included proposals for individual nationalized and state enterprises to obtain credit for operational purposes at only one bank, concentrate their financial affairs at that bank, and not grant credits to each other.

As a first step, the Communist Party proposed the establishment of special bodies for the state supervision of banking. In 1946, the Central Administration of Banks, an institution controlled by the Finance Minister, was established. The other Communist proposals were rejected by the Government. Communist historians explain this as an effort by the right wing parties to hold existing positions within the credit system as well as to discredit nationalized enterprises. The emphasis laid by the Communists on the role of bank reorganization seems somewhat exaggerated. These structural changes would not necessarily have assured a solution to the problems. Furthermore, nowhere do Communist economists mention the possibility of macroeconomic or global controls of credits to nationalized enterprises, which could have been exercised via the National Bank without recourse to reorganizing the banking system.

On this point, the Polish experience is interesting[44]. Following the 1947 drought, the Polish banking system introduced very strict restrictions on credit to state and industrialized enterprises, forcing them to obtain cash by 'throwing merchandise on the market'. As one banker put it, there was 'almost a direct flow from machine to the market'; stocks were minimized. Direct price control was also attempted in Poland during the 1947 difficulties. But, as Douglas, op.cit., points out, (based on interview material) the fighting of speculators directly in the market proved far less effective than the 'stock-pile' operation caused by tight credit. The policy followed in Poland shows the effectiveness of credit controls in such situations, and that the possibility of credit control does not depend exclusively on the approval of a law on bank re-organization.

The level of credit received by nationalized enterprises between 1946 and 1948 was very high.

TABLE 4.XII

CREDIT GRANTED BY BANKING SYSTEM IN BOHEMIA AND MORAVIA

(million Kčs)

	End of 1946	March 31 1948
Nationalized enterprises	20,800	33,300
Cooperatives	4,600	8,700

Source: PPDHP, op.cit.

Credit finances working capital or investment; it also subsidizes losses. As relatively little investment was carried out in the nationalized sector, (particularly during 1946) a great part of the credit went either to provide working capital or to subsidize losses.

It seems probable that, especially during the 1945-46 period, the flow of financial resources devoted to subsidizing losses was higher than that reflected in the official results of nationalized enterprises (see above). The real extent of losses may have been disguised by the enterprises by accounting devices. Unfortunately, there is insufficient information available to determine the real level of losses.

III   Monetary policy and balance of payments

1   Evolution of money after the Reform

The evolution of money after the 1945 Reform reveals a large increase in the money supply.

TABLE 4.XIII

MONEY SUPPLY

(million Kčs)

Money Supply	End of 1945	End of 1946	End of 1947	% increase 1947/1945
Notes and coins	28,197	46,577	61,699	118
Current Account	11,501	42,471	54,327	372
Total	39,698	89,048	116,026	192

Source: V. Bušek and N. Spulber (eds), Czechoslovakia, Praeger, USA, 1957, article 'Domestic Trade, Banking and Finance' by E. Ames (based on data from Czechoslovak National Bank, Monthly Bulletin).

The factors affecting the change in the money supply are as follows:

TABLE 4.XIV

EXPLANATION OF CHANGES OF MONEY SUPPLY BETWEEN END OF 1945
AND END OF 1947 (a)

Variations of:	million Kčs
Total money supply	76,328
Credits granted by National Bank and other Banks	+ 58,954
Increase in savings deposits	− 26,670
Blocked deposits(b)	+ 34,018
Variation in foreign assets	+ 2,148
Other	+ 7,878

Source: (a) Same as Table 4.XIII.

           (b) Slight discrepancies with data above are due to different sources in Ames, op.cit.

The main source of increase in the money supply was credit expansion. Of this, a large proportion went to finance the Budget deficit (see above). Much of the additional credit expansion can be attributed to increases in credit to nationalised industry (see Table 4.XII). The financing of the state sector (fiscal sector, state and nationalized enterprises) covers a predominant part of the expansion of credit. The other important source was de-blocking of funds. Slightly more than half of this de-blocking went to finance public institutions (see Table 4.IV). Thus, the increase in the money supply in 1945–47 mainly financed the state deficit and the nationalized enterprises.

2   Evolution of Balance of Payments

The evolution of foreign trade will be analyzed first.

TABLE 4.XV

VALUE OF FOREIGN TRADE

(million Kčs, current prices)

Year, quarter of Year		Import	Export	Balance
1937	Total	10,980	11,972	+ 992
1946	Total	10,308[a]	14,283[a]	+ 3,975
1947	1	5,006	5,461	+ 455
	2	7,808	7,511	− 297
	3	7,570	6,592	− 978
	4	8,536	8,986	+ 450
1947	Total	28,920[a]	28,550[a]	− 370[a]
1948	1	11,218	7,605	− 3,613
January		4,168	2,364	− 1,804
February		3,604	2,382	− 1,222
March		3,446	2,859	− 587
	2	10,389	9,625	− 764
	3	7,851	8,799	+ 939
	4	8,411	11,632	+ 3,221
1948	Total	37,869	37,652	− 217

Source: PPDHP

(a) Does not include imports financed through UNRRA and reparation deliveries.

These data are not exactly compatible with the IMF Balance of Payments Yearbook due to variations in coverage, valuation and timing. The IMF data are not used here because they provided no information for 1946, nor do they give any quarterly breakdown.

Only during 1946 was the trade balance positive. However, if the UNRRA donations are included as imports, the 1946 trade balance would become significantly negative[45]. There was a small deficit during 1947, which would be significantly larger if the UNRRA donations were included.

TABLE 4.XVI

VALUE OF TRADE

(million Kčs - 1937 prices)

Year, quarter of year		Total Imports	Foodstuffs and Beverages Imports
1937	Total	10,980	1,206
1946	Total	3,883	955
1947	1	1,509	166
	2	2,255	248
	3	2,254	435
	4	2,415	623
1947	Total	8,434	1,473
1948	1	3,037	968
	2	2,810	642
	3	2,464	453

Source: Statistical   Bulletin,   Statní   Úřad   Statistický.   Prague,
Czechoslovakia, 1949.

As can be seen in Table 4.XV, during the first quarter of 1948 the trade
account had a large deficit; this was generated mainly in January and
February, 1948, that is, in the crucial period when the power question was
being defined.   The total level of imports was so high during the first
quarter of 1948 that it almost equalled (at constant prices) the whole of
1946 imports (see Table 4.XVI).   As regards the composition of foreign
trade, the most spectacular change in comparison with the pre-war situation
is the increase in imports of foodstuffs and beverages, which rose from 11
per cent of total imports in 1937 to 21.3 per cent in 1946 and to 26 per
cent during the first quarter of 1948.   Total foodstuffs imports during the
first quarter of 1948 were higher (at constant prices) than for the whole of
1946.

It was these massive imports of foodstuffs which allowed an adequate supply
to the population, in spite of problems in agriculture.   As we saw, part of
the difficulties existing in agriculture were caused by a more rapid growth
in consumption as compared with production during 1947.   Thus, as regards
agriculture, Czechoslovakia 'lived above its means' in the crucial period
1947-48, when the power struggle was most intense.   It did so initially, at
the cost of damaging internal agricultural production; it continued doing so
mainly by running a large trade deficit.   This policy has obvious limits.
However, as the power struggle was relatively short (and there was
sufficient external financial support available), it was feasible[46].

Increased imports of foodstuffs coincided with normal levels of imports of
raw materials, allowing industrial activity and employment to be maintained.

Although not mentioned at all in the literature on the period, the fact that
the population could be properly supplied with food, in spite of
difficulties in agriculture, was of tremendous political importance.

Disruption in the supply of foodstuffs would have undoubtedly challenged the effectiveness of the National Front government and weakened the Left's position. The political importance of the credit granted at that time by the Soviet Union must be stressed. This credit, which reached a maximum of 2,971 million Kčs during the second quarter of 1948 and 1,654 million Kčs by the end of 1948, was approximately equivalent to the trade deficit of the first quarter of 1948. It was very short-term, and a large part was paid by the end of the year after the power question was decided, yet it provided sufficient economic relief at the moment of maximum political tension. The import policy pursued could not have been maintained for long unless credit support were supplied by the Soviet Union. The import policy followed was politically correct in that it was functional to the political objective of adequately supplying the population at time of maximum political tension. It was feasible because the Soviet Union supplied the credit, and the fact that credit was supplied by the Soviet Union and not by the Western powers was of particular political strategic importance to the Czechoslovak Communist Party.

The Communist press was filled with news about the delivery of wheat, the Soviet credit which financed it, and the role of the Czechoslovak Communist Party in obtaining these credits.   Moreover, the subject was repeatedly raised at mass meetings.

Yet according to the United Nations Economic Survey of Europe after the War (Geneva, 1950) between May 1945 and December 1946, Czechoslovakia used up US$ 49 million (2,500 million Kčs), all from Western sources; the total credit granted during the period was much larger: US$ 162 million.

As can be seen in Table 4.XVII, the 1947 net deficit was equivalent to 7,245 million Kčs. It was financed again exclusively from Western sources. These included receipts from UNRRA, long-term loans from Canada, UK, US, Brazil, Egypt and Australia and bilateral short-term payments agreements.

TABLE 4.XVII

FINANCING OF INTERNATIONAL TRANSACTIONS (1947)
(million Kčs)

Net deficit	7,245
Receipts from UNRRA	4,000
Drawing on long-term loans	1,953
Payments agreements	1,292

Source: Balance of Payments Yearbook, IMF, Washington, 1949.

During 1948, the external financing was provided mainly by the Soviet Union. The credit granted during 1948 was much smaller than those granted in 1947 or 1946 (see IMF Balance of Payments Yearbook, 1949 and 1950).

The total contribution of Soviet aid and credit during the period 1945-48 was small in comparison with credits and aid granted to Czechoslovakia by Western countries.   Due to the change in the international political situation and to a deliberate Soviet policy, it was that country which gave all the support in the critical moment of struggle for power.   Therefore, Soviet credit policy was effective politically not because of its volume, but because of the moment at which it was given and the way in which the news of the credit was used politically by the Communist Party.

IV   Evaluation of financial policies

We shall evaluate here financial policies pursued, not only from the point of view of their economic effects, but in relation to their contribution to

the main political and economic objectives pursued at the time by the
Communist Party.

1   The 1945 Monetary Reform

The 1945 monetary reform achieved its aims. The ratio of black-market to
official prices fell substantially from 15:1 before the Monetary Reform to
around 3:1 after it; it increased the incentive to work and the peasants'
willingness to market their produce. It thus helped economic recovery.

Some Communist economic historians emphasize that the monetary reform was a
compromise which favoured the bourgeoisie in many respects; they claim that
it did not lead to more permanent monetary stability. According to Blažej
and Tuček[47], this happened mainly because, for the Communists, monetary
reform was not a key problem in the struggle for power, like the
nationalization programme. This explanation can be questioned on two
levels: historical correctness and theoretical validity. As we saw in
Section 4.I.2. it is not correct that in 1945 the Communists gave such high
priority to nationalization; their main economic target clearly was rapid
economic reconstruction. If recovery was the main aim, then the monetary
reform was an important and effective instrument in achieving it.

Analytically there is no necessary dichotomy between structural changes and
a minimum of financial equilibrium. Furthermore, the belief that financial
disequilibria are not relevant to the question of power is basically
incorrect; its validity depends on the concrete historical circumstances and
on the role which economic policy is obliged to play in the power struggle.
In Czechoslovakia, in 1945, it was particularly important that the economy
should recover at sufficient speed to satisfy the different classes which
supported the National Front Government. Some degree of financial stability
was a pre-requisite for this.

The real reason why the monetary reform, which was necessarily directed at
monetary stocks and not at flows[48], did not stop inflation was the
monetary evolution after the reform. These new financial developments
caused inflationary pressures originating only partly in the Monetary Reform
itself - insofar as de-blocking of funds contributed to the increase in the
money supply[49].   The greatest proportion of de-blocked funds were for
public institutions and social reasons. De-blocking for the first purpose
can hardly be blamed on pressures from the bourgeoisie; as regards the
second, there is little information about effective criteria applied in
granting them.   Although socially just, they seemed slightly vague with
perhaps too much discretionary power given to the National Bank[50].   An
example of corrupt de-blocking was the agreement between the Democratic
Party and some capitalists to de-block funds for the latter if part of them
were given to that Party. (Although this point is stressed in the Communist
literature it had relatively little impact - the amount claimed to have been
de-blocked was 100 million crowns.)

It can be concluded that the Monetary Reform achieved in the short-term its
purpose of diminishing pent-up demand inherited from the War, thus
contributing to the Communist Party's aim of economic recovery.   During
1946-48, as a result of the expansion of the money supply, inflationary
pressures reappeared.   These cannot be attributed - as the Czechoslovak
Communist historians do - mainly to the fact that the monetary reform was a
compromise with the bourgeoisie (although this argument has some validity).
The main element which explains the expansion of the money supply after the
Monetary Reform (see Table 4XIV) is not de-blocking of funds (of which an
important part goes to public institutions) but credit expansion - geared
mainly to the state sector and nationalized industry.

Czechoslovakia   103

2   Price Policy

Policies followed for wholesale and retail prices will be described and
evaluated.

The 1945 prices and incomes reform, carried out simultaneously with the
monetary reform, attempted to achieve equilibrium between supply and demand
and eliminate losses in some sectors. A general but strongly differentiated
increase was applied to prices and incomes, reaching about three times the
pre-war level on average. The reconstruction of prices favoured livestock
production: incomes from property were frozen, especially rents; war
rationing of goods and price control were maintained.

The 1945 price and monetary reform achieved the objective of reducing the
demand gap, reflected in the sharp fall in the ratio between black market
and official prices (see Table 4.XVIII). Persistent excessive buying power
is shown by the continued existence of the black market.

TABLE 4.XVIII

COST OF LIVING INDEX OF CZECHOSLOVAK WORKERS (1939 = 100)

Month	Year	Total	Food	Black market prices (a) Official prices
V	1945	187.7	n.a.	
IX	1945	n.a.	n.a.	
I	1946	323.8	352.8	(c) 1,500
III	1946	328.4	353.9	333
VI	1946	326.7	348.7	289
IX	1946	321.4	336.2	231
XII	1946	324.0	336.0	206
I	1947	324.8	337.1	
II	1947	326.3	339.0	
III	1947	325.9	338.2	186
IV	1947	308.1	306.3	
V	1947	307.1	306.4	
VI	1947	307.9	308.7	214
VII	1947	296.1	315.0	
VIII	1947	292.2	305.3	
IX	1947	293.1	305.7	271
X	1947	293.9	305.9	
XI	1947	297.9	311.5	
XII	1947	299.0	316.0	318
I	1948	304.0	325.3	354
II	1948	305.3	327.8	415

Source: **Statistical Bulletin**, Státní Úřad Statistický and Kožušník,
op.cit.

(a) Data for Bohemia and Moravia. Official prices = 100.

The second objective (eliminating losses in certain sectors) was not achieved. In branches where the private sector's participation was largest, prices rose most. Relatively low prices in state and nationalized industry were one of the main causes of their losses. This erroneous price policy was not completely corrected until 1948. Unfortunately, there are scarce data to prove this trend, which is however, widely described and discussed in the economic literature of the period. An indicator of differential price policy is the much less favourable price policy for minerals — where nationalized industry predominated — than for textiles where private enterprize was predominant (see Table 4.XIX); this was particularly marked during 1946, even though it characterized the whole period[51].

TABLE 4.XIX

INDEX OF WHOLESALE PRICES (GEOMETRICAL AVERAGE) MARCH 1939 = 100

Year and Month		Raw materials and finished products			
		Minerals	Textiles	Average	Average General Index
1945	V	n.a.	n.a.	n.a.	154.2
1946	I	213.8	417.4	266.6	266.9
1946	XII	265.3	475.0	307.5	300.7
1947	XII	295.2	453.7	321.7	306.2
1948	XII	357.7	485.0	349.0	325.2
1946 Average		241.2	495.2	290.7	287.7
1947 Average		274.6	469.8	313.2	302.5
1948 Average		314.7	470.4	333.5	316.7

Source: Kožušník, op.cit.

The price policy followed (favouring the private sector) can be partly attributed to technical problems; the Central Pricing Office could not carry out all necessary calculations. The main reason seems to have been that there was no correct understanding of the issue and its importance. Communist economic historians stress[52] the influence of capitalists on the Central Pricing Office as the main explanation. Were this the main cause it is unclear why the Communists did not press for changes in the pricing policy as they had enough power within the economic apparatus[53]. The Communists did not make an important issue of this at the time. The importance of pricing policy for nationalized enterprizes and its effect on their financial results (and on the money supply) was probably not fully perceived by the Communist economic experts. It is possible that its importance was realized more fully ex-post; for an inadequate price policy the blame was laid on the influence of bourgeois elements.

Better prices for the nationalized sector could have yielded higher revenues than the widely discussed millionaire tax. As the total value of sales of nationalized enterprises for 1947 was approximately 120 million Kčs[54] an additional price increase of three per cent would have yielded approximately the same revenue as the millionaire tax. The effect on income distribution would probably have been similar to increases in direct taxes. Price increases in nationalized industry — mostly producing inputs — would have reduced the profit margin in private consumer goods and wholesale trade, whose prices were growing anyway due mainly to excesive demand[55].

The trade union movement pressed the government to lower retail prices[56], and strikes occurred in different enterprises to support this demand. It is interesting that strikes were used mainly to demand lower prices and not higher wages. This reveals a considerable degree of working class solidarity, rather than a narrow defence of local factory interests. In fact, lower prices were practically the only economic issue on which workers went on strike during this period; strikes over wages were very rare. The aims of the trade union leadership were being accomplished. In 1945, E. Erban, General Secretary of ROH[57] stated:

> We are building the trade unions as a united movement
> including all wage-earning people; what they have in
> common is primary and fundamental whereas the special
> interests of indidivual categories of working people
> are derivative and secondary.

The trade unions' attitudes can be attributed to unity and centralization in their organization. As Zinner[58], Bloomfield and others show, this was facilitated by the mood for unification of the trade union movement after the War. Pre-war fragmentation had had disastrous consequences for the labour movement; trade union unity during the resistance showed its effectiveness. After the war, the trade union movement was organized on the principle of one union representing all members in any one enterprise. The union structure was pyramidal; it was highly centralized, permitting great concentration of power in the central organ, URO (Central Trade Unions Council). Centralization had its theoretical roots in the Stalinist conception of mass organizations as 'transmission belts' for Party directives; it required united, centralized mass organizations which were easily controlled[59].

The Communist Party began proposing retail price reductions in March, 1946, and this became a Communist slogan in the election campaign. Communist proposals on price cuts were implemented by the new government, after some opposition. During 1946 the government lowered prices of some foodstuffs, and as a result, the foodstuffs price index fell substantially. But the general cost of living index remained stable (see Table 4.XVIII) and in February 1947, Communist Party proposals for further cuts in the price of food and other consumer goods were approved. These measures were reflected in a reduction of the general cost of living index between March and June, 1947 (see Table 4.XVIII).

When prices did not cover costs plus an accepted profit margin, the difference was compensated for by the Ministry of Finance. These subsidies were from a fund financed by a special tax on gross sales. Differential treatment was given to different categories of enterprise, and the sectors where nationalized industry predominated were exempt. Private small producers paid lower rates than larger firms. During 1947, the total revenue of the 'Price Intervention Fund' reached 2,734 million Kčs (source: J. Dolánsky, Výklad státnimu rozpočtu na rok 1949, op.cit.).

The Price Intervention Fund was really a discriminatory turnover tax; it seems to have been one of the most imaginative financial policies designed during the National Front Government to extract surplus from the private sector. Its yield was relatively high and was rapidly obtained. Its approval was made easier by linking it to retail price reduction. A further reduction in the cost of living index for working class families was achieved through lowering the wage tax (see above). From a fiscal point of view this form of lowering retail prices was less desirable than that carried out before; it was financed by Budget deficit growth and not by increased taxation.

We shall now evaluate the policy of price reduction itself.

The pressure on the aggregate demand side is shown by the rapid growth in money supply (see Table 4.XIII). As a result of excessive demand, the fall in the official price index had been accompanied since March 1947 by an increase in the ratio of black market to official prices. Between March and September 1947, the cost of living index fell by ten per cent, but the ratio of black market prices to official ones rose by 45 per cent (based on Table 4.XVIII).

According to existing Czechoslovak analysis on the subject[60] one of the main aims of price reductions was to redistribute income to workers. However, as Kalecki[61] pointed out, subsidizing wage goods financed by taxation of profits will not affect total net profits - unless there is idle capacity and unemployment in the wage goods sector[62]. The argument is similar to the Kaleckian analysis of the effect of an increase in nominal wages discussed in Chapter 5. If there is no excess capacity in the wage goods sector, prices will be demand determined. According to Kalecki, price controls (or subsidies of wage goods financed by direct taxation of profits) can, in such situations, lead only to scarcities of goods, haphazard distribution and black markets.

However, under particular conditions, lowering retail prices can affect income distribution. In Czechoslovakia, at the time, a considerable proportion of consumer goods was physically distributed through rationing. According to L. Kalinová and B. Brabec, (op.cit.) during 1946 many working class families could not use the rations allocated to them fully as their incomes were insufficient, so lowering retail prices allowed them to spend their rations. When a significant proportion of goods is distributed by rationing, at official prices, a reduction in retail prices may imply higher real wages. In Czechoslovakia, it assured effective consumption by the workers of essential goods distributed through rationing.

A policy of price reduction or controls will have clear positive redistributive effects only if accompanied by physical distribution of consumer goods[63]. The negative effects of price controls without effective rationing will be analysed in the Chilean case (see Chapter 5).

Reducing retail prices was clearly a political success for the Communists, as they had proposed this policy. The adverse effects of this price reduction were the increased size of the black market as well as higher prices there (see Table 4.XVIII). This coincided with increasing political tension and changing Communist strategy. The blame for the growth of the black market was laid by the Communists on the capitalist elemnts and responsibility within the National Front was put on the parties defending the private sector (see Frejka's quote in section 4.I.2). No mention was made by the Communists of the effects which monetary and price policy had had. The Communists explained in simple terms to the masses who the 'real culprit' was, proposing to eliminate the black market by eliminating the 'culprit'.

The Communist's proposal to end the black market was based on the nationalization of wholesale and retail trade. Politically, what is relevant is not only whether a certain policy leads to an increase in financial disequilibria, but, probably more important, who can be blamed for these imbalances at the moment of greatest struggle. At the beginning of 1948 in Czechoslovakia, the Communists had sufficient command of the situation and organized working class support to blame the capitalists for the effects of financial disequilibria, and use the situation as a justification for further nationalizations.

3   State employees' wages

Before evaluating the issue of state employees' incomes, we will examine
their evolution in the period 1945–48, compared with that of other groups.
As can be seen from the footnotes to Table 4.XX, there are some problems in
comparing the data, although the general tendency is clear.   Between 1945
and 1946, real earnings of all state employees fell substantially.   In 1947
their real earnings rose, remaining, however, well below pre-war levels.   In
other sectors the evolution was completely different.   Wages of workers in
industry and agriculture increased steadily during the period 1946–48.   By
1947 real weekly earnings for industrial workers amply surpassed the pre-war
level, as did wage rates in agriculture.

TABLE 4.XX

EARNINGS IN REAL TERMS

State employees(a)			1945	1946	1947	1948
I	(b)	(c)	113.3	62.3	69.1	75.6
		(d)	70.4	38.7	42.0	44.3
II	(b)	(c)	126.9	69.7	78.2	87.1
		(d)	80.9	44.5	49.2	52.2
III	(b)	(c)	123.2	67.7	75.6	84.9
		(d)	81.9	45.0	49.5	53.2
IV	(b)	(c)	124.9	68.7	76.5	86.0
		(d)	78.9	43.4	47.5	51.2
Industrial workers						
Weekly earnings (e)			n.a.	122.7	145.0	158.0
Wage rates	(f)		n.a.	n.a.	95.1	102.6
Agricultural workers						
Wage rates	(f)		n.a.	n.a.	177.4	206.5

(a)   Employees' gross earnings. Base 1937=100. Source: PPDHP op.cit.

(b)   State employees ordered from high-ranking to low-ranking, for details
see PPDHP

(c)   Highest wage

(d)   Lowest wage

(e)   March 1939 = 100.   Refers to Czech industry.   Source: article by
Kalinová and Brabec, op.cit.

(f)   March 1939 = 100. Source: PPDHP

The issue of state employees' earnings had been discussed in the Government
and in ROH since May 1947, without concrete proposals being reached.   In
January 1948, a representative of ROH was told by the President and the

Finance Minister that the maximum limit for increase in state employees'
incomes was to be 3 milliard Kčs.   Accepting this limit, ROH proposed a
monthly tax-free rise for all public employees of 300 Kčs.   This proposal
was supported by the Communists.

During the government meeting on this issue, higher wage increases were
proposed.   Two alternative proposals were made: the National Socialists
proposed increasing public employees' salaries by 25 per cent at a cost of
approximately 6 milliard Kčs; the Social Democrats' proposal implied larger
differentials than that of ROH, costing a total of 4 milliard Kčs, and was
approved by the government[64].

The ROH leadership reacted violently, accusing the government of trying to
disrupt the economy and isolate the trade unions, who would jump to the
offensive.   The president of URO Zapotocký, stated[65]:

> When by its position the bougeoisie forces the trade
> union movement to mobilize its forces for struggle,
> then it should also know that if we are freed to
> mobilize the masses of ROH, we will not limit
> ourselves to defence, but will struggle for the
> formation of a completely new solution to all the
> basic questions.

This was followed by demands for further nationalization; a massive
conference of workers' representatives was called.   In this reaction URO was
following the tactical line elaborated by the Communist leadership which
they had presented to URO.

The URO's decision aroused great interest at factory level.   Many suporting
declarations were issued, initially with the emphasis on incomes policy, but
as time passed and the political crisis grew more acute, the emphasis was
increasingly on nationalization.   By the time of the mass meeting of the
Workers' Committees, the issue of state employees' wages was pushed into the
background by more pressing political matters.

As we saw, there was an objective economic base for the issue: deterioration
of real earnings, both in absolute terms and in relation to other types of
worker.   This offered the right-wing parties the opportunity to break
Communist dominance of the working class and of ROH, by fostering factional
divisions and defending the interests of one group of workers.   The Right
therefore acted here correctly according to the political criteria.   It
supported economic improvement for a relatively important sector of workers
which had clearly been neglected by the National Front Government.

The right - especially the National Socialists - drew a large proportion of
their supporters from public employees[66], who had no independent mass
organization.   The right was unsuccessful in its attempt to challenge the
leadership and policies of ROH, which was dominated by the Communists.
Proposals that trade unions should restrict their role to the defence of
sectional interests had only limited support in ROH; they were crushed by
administrative methods given the unions' over-centralized power structure.
Thus, although the Right had a correct issue to fight on, it was unable to
extract political dividends from it because of its limited control over mass
organizations.

For the Communist Party the issue was not a particularly favourable one.   It
was correct to oppose measures which could increase inflationary pressures,
though their impact was relatively limited.   In this case - and unlike that
of the millionaire's tax - the Communists could not attack the right-wing
parties for defending the interests of a small minority; on the contrary,
the Communists risked alienating a relatively important sector of the middle

strata. The Communists therefore took up an economic issue which was less favourable to it, yet used it very efficiently from a political point of view. This was to a great extent because they had organized mass support.

V   Concluding Observations

In evaluating financial and monetary policies from the point of view of the role they played in the power struggle two levels can be distinguished. One analyses the declarations of those responsible for financial and economic policy. As we saw (section 4.I.4), the leading authorities in planning and financial institutions grossly misunderstood some of the key issues of financial policy. The most naive opinion was expressed by the Communist representative at the State Planning Office when he stated that in the People's Democracy there would not be inflation unless the government wished it. This argument fails to appreciate the difference between a planned economy with effective centralised control and that existing in Czechoslovakia during the period, with inadequate physical planning, no financial plan and a struggle for power going on. Furthermore, as we saw, even the General Director of the National Bank expressed the view that the problem of financing was 'only a technical problem'.

It seems apparent that the views of those responsible for financial policy were incorrect, inapplicable to the period through which Czechoslovakia was passing, and theoretically very weak. However, this does not mean that the financial policies themselves were incorrect. Similarly in the case of the Soviet Union during NEP – see Chapter 3 – many of those in charge of financial policy were very conservative, but this did not imply that the financial policy carried out was necessarily conservative. The correctness of the financial policies pursued is evaluated here mainly in relation to their contribution to the principal political and economic objectives pursued at the time by the Communists[67].

As we saw in section 4.IV.1, the initial stabilization of the currency achieved as a result of the 1945 Monetary Reform was functional to the Communists' goals of economic reconstruction and the strengthening of the National Front Government. After the monetary reform, financial disequilibria grew; their effects became more acute during 1947, as the money supply continued to increase and as supply difficulties developed.

Three financial policies had an important impact on the growing financial disequilibria. One was the high level of state expenditure. This arose mainly from the growing requirements of planning and from post-war functions which the state apparatus had to take over. Second, prices for nationalized and state enterprises were too low. As was pointed out, higher prices for these enterprises would have had a considerable impact on improving the financial situation. Third, the retail price policy followed also accentuated the effects of financial disequilibria. In conditions of excessive aggregate demand, the Communists successfully proposed to the government a policy of lowering retail prices. As we saw, in conditions of excessive aggregate demand, a reduction in official retail prices does not diminish total profits, but transfers them to 'black market profits'. However, given that a large proportion of goods was distributed as rations at official prices, the policy had a direct positive impact on real consumption by the working class.

As regards the two issues presented by the Communists as crucial to prevent inflation – the millionaire's tax and state employees' earnings – their effective importance was far more political than economic or financial. It is politically understandable that the Communists should provoke discussions on these issues with such zeal, as they coincided with the period when the struggle for power became most intense.

The relevance of financial disequilibria in the context of the Czechoslovak power struggle will be briefly examined. It seems evident that policies leading to financial disequilibria in an economy with price controls would cause increasing black markets and speculation. If acute, these phenomena could have disrupted the functioning of the economy, damaging the Communists, the largest party in the Government.

In Czechoslovakia, the financial disequilibria generated did not lead to such undesired effects, for several reasons. First, the financial disequilibria were not so large as to threaten to disrupt the economy completely. Second, in the crucial moment of struggle for power the effects of financial disequilibria (black market, speculation, scarcity) were blamed by the Communists on the private sector and on the right-wing parties. The Communists also suggested a solution to the effects of disequilibria: further nationalizations. They proposed to eliminate the 'culprit', thus justifying further nationalizations. By 1948 the Communists had sufficient command of the situation (given not only their own size, but the international context, their influence over the army and police and organized working class support) to be able to blame the capitalists for the effects of financial disequilibria and profit from the situation.

Finally, financial disequilibria are less important when resources are allocated physically (both in production and consumption). In the Czechoslovak experience, the physical planning of production did not seem to operate so efficiently; however, the rationing system had great importance in assuring minimum supplies to the workers.

Czechoslovakia 111

Notes

1   As regards third countries, all foreign currency flows (in payment of
    foreign trade) went through a central clearing in Berlin - which froze
    Czech surpluses.

2   Source: V. Průcha and K. Jech, 'Outline of Economic Development in
    Czechoslovakia, 1945-48', in The Czechoslovak Economy, 1945-48, Acta O
    economica, State Pragensia Pedagogical Publishing House, Prague, 1968.

3   These data refer to notes and coin. Current account deposits
    approximately doubled in this period. Source: article by V. Průcha
    and K. Jech, op.cit.

4   Source: Přehled hospodářského vývoje Československa v letech 1918-45,
    op.cit.

5   For an interesting recent discussion of the political developments,
    see J. Bloomfield, Passive Revolution. Politics and the Czechoslovak
    Working Class, 1945-48, Allison and Busby, London, 1979.

6   See bibliography of Bloomfield, op.cit. for Czechoslovak
    interpretations.

7   Klimeš et al, Cesta Ke Květnu: Vznik lidové demokracie v
    Československu ('On the Way to May : the Origin of People's Democracy
    in Czechoslovakia'), Prague, 1965, p.55.

8   K. Gottwald, Spisy, ('Works'), Vol. 1, Prague, 1953, p.322.

9   See L. Frejka, Náš hospodářský program ('Our economic programme'),
    Brno, 1948.

10 For details on nationalization, which lie outside the scope of this
    study, see Bloomfield, op.cit. Chapter 6. Also see K. Kaplan,
    Znárodnění a socialismus (Nationalization and Socialism), Práce,
    Prague, 1968 and O. Mrázek 'Course and results of the nationalization
    of industry', in The Czechoslovak Economy, 1945-48, op.cit.

11 Sněm budovatelů: Protokol VIII řádného sjezdu KSČ, březen 1946
    ('Assembly of Construction Proceedings of the Eighth Communist
    Congress, March 1946'), Prague, 1946.

12 K. Gottwald, 'O dalsi ceste narodni a demokraticke revoluci' ('The
    further road along our national and democratic revolution') Spisy,
    Vol. XII. The theme was repeated many times, see, for example,
    Gottwald's speeches in March 1946, September 1946, and January 1947,
    in "Spisy", op.cit. Vol. XIII.

13 Rudé Pravo, 7th October, 1947.

14 Frejka L. Československe hospodářstvý : na cestě K Socialismu ('The
    Czechoslovak economy on the road to Socialism'), Prague, 1948.

15 For data, see J. Goldman and others, Planned Economy in
    Czechoslovakia, Orbis, Prague, 1949.

16 For data on UNRRA donations; see UNRRA, The History of the United
    Nations Relief and Rehabilitation Administration, prepared under the
    direction of G. Woolbridge, New York, 1950.

17 There are little data available for 1945. Therefore, it is necessary

to make comparisons with 1937.

18   For details, see PPDHP, op.cit.

19   For example, První československký pětiletý plán, Prague, 1948.

20   For example, 'The Post war problems of Czechoslovak Agricultural
        Production', by A. Vaclav in The Czechoslovak Economy 1945–48, op.cit.

21   This was mainly justified by the US because of Czechoslovak support
        for the USSR at the Paris Peace Conference.

22   For an account of the government discussions and the influence of the
        Soviet Union on this decision, see for example J. Opat O novou
        demokracii (The New Democracy), CAV, Prague, 1966 (for the Communist
        point of view) and H. Ripka, Czechoslovakia Enslaved, London, 1950
        (for the National Socialist point of view). Also see J. Bloomfield
        op.cit. Chapter 11.

23   For details, see Fiser D., Teoretické Otázky Vrcholných Plánovacích
        Orgánů (Theoretical questions about planning institutions), NCAV,
        Prague, 1965.

24   For example, B. Urban, "Dva ekonomické aspekty československé cesty k
        socialismu" in Českolovenska revoluce v letech 1944–48, ("The Economic
        Aspects in the CSSR road to Socialism") CAV, Prague, 1966.

25   Planned economy in Czechoslovakia, Orbis, Prague, 1948.

26   The Explanatory Memorandum on the Bill and the Text of the Two Year
        Economic Plan Act, Orbis, Prague, 1947.

27   Article in Financování dvouletky (The Financing of the Two Year Plan),
        edited by E. Sommer, Olomouc, 1947.

28   Article in op.cit. in (27).

29   Furthermore, even well-established socialist countries have suffered
        some inflationary pressure, but discussion lies outside the scope of
        this study.

30   Jaroslav, Krejčí, 'Investice, zaměstnanost a národní důchod', in
        Plánované Hospodářstvy, Year 1, 2, 3, Prague, March, 1948.

31   The other type of monetary reform – followed by most East European
        countries – reduced assets at the outset without blocking any
        proportion of it.

32   Source: Bulletin of Czechoslovak National Bank, Prague, 1946.

33   For example, M. Tuček, Vývoj československých financí v
        letech 1945–52, (Evolution of Czechoslovak Finance, 1945–52), SPN,
        Prague, 1953.

34   For detailed figures, see J. Dolanský, Výklad Min Financí K státnímu
        rozpočtu na rok 1949 (Exposition of the Finance Minister on the 1949
        Budget), Ministerstvo Financí, Prague, 1948.

35   Sources: for the discussion on the millionaire's tax – Tuček op.cit.
        Opat., op.cit. Ripka, op.cit. and Těsnopiscké Zprávy o Schůzích
        Ustavodárného Národního Shromaždění, Republiky Československé,
        (Speeches at the National Assembly of the Czechoslovak Republic)
        Prague, 1947.

36   National Socialists, People's Party and Democratic Party
      representatives voted against the millionaire tax. The Social
      Democrats abstained.

37   The right-wing parties seemed to adopt a similar tactic to that in
      Allende's Chile (see Chapter 5). They were relatively willing to
      allow laws which implied an increase in state expenditure, or a fall
      in the tax burden either for workers - in Czechoslovakia - or for
      small entrepeneurs - in Chile, but opposed strongly increased taxes on
      the wealthy.

38   Source: Archiv U.V. - K.S.Č., quoted in Růžička Karel, 'ROH v boji o
      rozšíření moci dělnické třídy,' (ROH in the struggle for broadening
      working class power'), Práce, Prague, 1963.

39   Thus the Czechoslovak Communist Party avoided a common contradiction
      in situations of transition to socialism when workers follow their
      short-term interests (ie. demanding higher wages in nationalized
      enterprises), and endanger the achievement of a goal which serves
      their long-term interests (provoke inflation which makes the
      transition to socialism more difficult).

40   J. Dolanský, Výklad k rozpočtu na rok 1949, Prague, 1948, op.cit.

41   Source: J. Dolanský, Výklad k rospočtu na rok, 1948. Min Financi,
      op.cit.

42   There are no complete data or analysis available of nationalized
      industry losses, nor of the variables which determine them for the
      period 1946-48.

43   Lenka Kalinová and Václav Brabec, 'K Některým stránkám vývoje
      struktury a postavení československé třídy v letech 1945-48', (On
      certain aspects of the evolution of the structure and position of the
      Czechoslovak working class in the years 1945-48) in Odbory a naše
      revoluce, Práce, Prague, 1968.

44   See D.W. Douglas, Transitional Economic Systems. The Polish-Czeck
      Example,, Routledge and Kegan Pane, London, 1953, p.150.

45   The total UNRRA donations are estimated here at US $ 260 million, US $
      80 million (that is 4,000 million Kcs) in 1947, and US $ 180 million,
      that is, 9,000 million Kcs) in 1946. (Source: UNRRA, The History of
      the United Nations Relief and Rehabilitation Administration, op.cit.)

46   The feasibility of applying this kind of policy is related not only to
      the magnitude of the gaps (between consumption and production) but
      also to the time during which those gaps have to be maintained, and to
      the foreign finance available.

47   Z. Blažej, "Význam naši peněžni reformy". ("The meaning of our
      monetary reform"). Politicka ekonomie, 1953, c.3. Tucek, M. "K.
      historickym korenum nove menove reformy". (The historical role of our
      new monetary reform"). Politická economie 1953, c.4.

48   According to J.G. Gurley, 'Excess liquidity and European Monetary
      Reforms 1944-52'), American Economic Review, Vol. XLIII, March, 1953,
      it was a common problem that as a result of monetary reforms during
      the period, the authorities focussed their attention on 'stocks' to
      the neglect of flow variables.

49   It had been originally established that the de-blocked funds would be

matched by proceeds from the sale of confiscated property from former Germans; a special Fund for National Reconstruction had been established for this. However, re-settlement of the boundary zone did not proceed in an orderly manner, and the money was not paid by the new settlers. It seems that the quest for popularity by different parties - and in particular the Communists, prevented them from exacting payments from the new settlers. Source: Interview information provided by Professor Jaroslav Krejčí.

50   For detailed outline, see B. Spáčil, Vázané Úklady a jejich uvolňování, (Blocked funds and their freeing), 1947, Orbis, Prague.

51   Another indicator can be found in metallurgy, where nationalized industry predominated, while in June, 1947, import prices had an index of 387 (1939 = 100), final products has a price index of 178 (1939 = 100). Source: Mrázek, op.cit.

52   For example, D. Fišer, op.cit. above, and others.

53   The fact that Communists could for example impose their line on retail prices (see below) shows their influence on the government apparatus.

54   Source: Třetí dvouletní zprávy o průběhu dvouletého plánu, (Third report on the achievements of the Two Year Plan), UPV, December 1947.

55   For a more theoretical discussion of these issues, see Chapter 5, section 5.I.4.

56   During the first analysis of wage policy carried out by ROH (in February 1946), it was concluded that 'it is indispensable to carry out a lowering of retail prices'. Source: URO foil U.K.S. P/716, quoted in article by L. Kalinová and V. Brabec, op.cit.

57   Article published in Práce, 10.6.45.

58   P. Zinner, Communist Strategy and Tactics in Czechoslovakia 1918-48, Pall Mall Press, London, 1963.

59   According to J. Bloomfield, op.cit. p.163, on issues such as wages the trade union structure helped impose discipline from above, yet many sections understood their necessity and were prepared to accept it voluntarily.

60   The main work on this subject is Kožušník, op.cit.

61   'Class Struggle and Distribution of Income', in Selected Essays of the Dynamics of the Capitalist Economy, Cambridge University Press, 1971.

62   In Czechoslovakia in 1947, the main wage good - food - had serious supply problems. Industrial wage goods seem to have had somewhat more supply flexibility in 1947 (see Table 4.III).

63   This point is clearly made for developing countries in K. Griffin and J. James, Supply Management Problems in the Context of a Basic Needs Strategy, A Report prepared for the Word Bank, Queen Elizabeth House, Oxford, 1978.

64   Source: Belda et al, Na rozhran dvou epoch (On the frontier of the two eras), Prague, 1968.

65   Source: Archiv U.R.O., protocol of January, 1948 meeting.

66   For detailed data see K. Kaplan, <u>Znárodněny a socialismus</u>, op.cit.

67   During 1945–48, the Czechoslovak Communist Party successfully led a
      revolution which transformed the country's economic social and
      political system to a socialist one. The extent to which during that
      period and later, the Communists seriously represented and interpreted
      the interests of the Czechoslovak people or even its working class,
      has been genuinely questioned, both from within the party itself and
      from outside. This theme is strictly outside the scope of this study.
      However, it seems necessary to point out that basically I agree with
      those analysts who claim that the Czechoslovak working class was a
      largely willing accomplice to the revolution, but not its driving
      force. The decisive impetus for the revolution came from above and
      abroad, and this had very negative consequences for post–1948
      developments.

CHILE'S POPULAR UNITY SHORT-TERM AND FINANCIAL POLICY

In this chapter, the economic and political framework within which Chile's Popular Unity had to operate will be described first. This will include a description of the economy's main characteristics before 1970, as well as of Popular Unity's diagnosis of the Chilean economy. After describing the political and economic objectives of Popular Unity, the design of the short-term policy will be briefly described and its functionality to the goals of Popular Unity evaluated critically.

Then, the causes of financial disequilibria will be examined, as well as the political and economic forces which conditioned it. The evolution of money and Balance of Payments will be described, as well as their effects. Finally, specific financial policies will be evaluated and possible alternative policies briefly discussed.

This chapter criticizes Popular Unity's short-term and financial policy for not contributing to the achievement of the economic and, more important, the political aims of transition to socialism. However, this does not at all imply an attempt to explain the eventual overthrow of the Allende Government with reference only - or even mainly - to economic strategy. Obviously, political elements not sufficiently analyzed here (as they are studied only in relation to the financial and short-term economic policy) played a crucial role; these political elements include a wide range of actions both by the internal and external opposition[1] (see also chapter 1). The argument presented here claims only that the economic policies pursued weakened Popular Unity in its power confrontation with the opposition, and that alternative policies might have placed Popular Unity in a more favourable position for this confrontation, thus increasing its chances of survival and of achieving its aims.

The analysis carried out here does not enter into the somewhat futile debate favoured by some foreign observers, on whether the Popular Unity exercise was viable or doomed from the start. Rather, it attempts to understand particular important aspects which led to the loss of viability of the Popular Unity project, as well as the search for alternatives which would have reversed its probability of survival and success. Although at times reaching somewhat difficult conclusions, a similar approach has been used by senior participants in the Popular Unity Government (in particular, see P. Vuskovic, Una sola lucha, Editorial Nuestro Tiempo, Méjico, 1978, pp.37 and 103; S. Bitar, Transición, socialismo y democracia, la experiencia chilena, Siglo XXI, Méjico, 1979, p.17, and several articles in S. Sideri (ed.), Chile 1970-73 : Economic Developdment and its International Setting, Institute of Social Studies, Nijhoff, 1979.

I   Economic and political framework

1   The Chilean economy before November, 1970

In the 1960s, Chile's Gross Domestic Product, at market prices, grew at an average annual rate (4.3 per cent), below that for the whole of Latin America (5.5 per cent)[2]. In the second half of the 1960s (1965-70) this trend was even more marked: while Chile's Gross Domestic Product grew at an average annual rate of 3.8 per cent, the total for Latin America grew by 5.7 per cent[3]. In this period, production of services grew at a faster rate (4.0 per cent) than that of goods (3.5 per cent). The highest growth in the goods production sector was in mining (4.9 per cent) and manufacturing (3.6 per cent); the lowest in construction (0.7 per cent) and agriculture (3.0 per cent)[4] (see also Table 5.XIII).

During the 1960s, inflation continued - as in former decades - to be a persistent feature of the Chilean economy. In the period 1965-70, the consumer price index grew at an average rate of 26.0 per cent[5].

Over the period 1967-70, the growth rate of GDP fell to 2.8 per cent annually; this implied a per-capita growth rate of Gross Domestic Product of a mere 0.8 per cent (see Table 5.I).

TABLE 5.I

GROWTH OF TOTAL AND PER-CAPITA GROSS DOMESTIC PRODUCT

Total GDP		Per capita GDP	
1965-70	1967-70	1965-70	1967-70
3.8%	2.8%	2.0%	0.8%

Sources: Same as those quoted in notes 2 and 3.

The depressive tendencies during this period were mainly determined by government action; as inflationary pressures increased in 1967, the Government followed a deflationary policy[6]. In the course of 1970, the depression worsened. As a result, by December 1970, unemployment in Gran Santiago reached 8.3 per cent of the labour force, the highest for ten years (it had averaged 6.6 per cent over the decade[7].)   This deepening of recessive tendencies was caused by demand factors: one was the drastic fall in the price of copper; another was the drop in private investment, provoked by the political circumstances.

The economic situation worsened in the period September-November 1970.   The main reason was the accentuation of 'the campaign of economic terror'[8], which depressed economic activity further. However, the main effect of the 'campaign of economic terror' was to provoke financial panic. As a result, certain sectors of the population withdrew their banking and savings deposits.   The Central Bank strongly increased its money issue to prevent the banks getting into cash difficulties; it also supported non-banking savings institutions, with similar cash problems.   Furthermore, private enterprises restricted their credit to buyers; this put additional pressure on the banks stimulating them to increase their credit to the private sector.   The Central Bank re-financed part of this expansion.   Due to measures taken by the Central Bank[9] and to a decline in political tension, this financial crisis was to a great extent brought under control by December 1970[10].

The impact of the financial crisis is reflected in the monetary indicators. During 1970, money issue grew by 70 per cent; the quantity of money held by the private sector increased by 61 per cent[11]; this can be compared with the tendency observed for the first eight months of 1970, which projected a probable growth for the year of 61 per cent for money issue, and 45 per cent for money held by the private sector. In fact, as a result, in 1970, money held by the private sector grew more than in previous years[12].   It can be concluded that the financial crisis created some additional inflationary pressures. However, the financial disequilibrium created by this crisis was relatively limited; its order of magnitude was incomparably smaller than that inherited in other experiences of transition to socialism[13].

The external sector's evolution for the second half of the 1960s will now be examined; the data in Table 5.II allow comparisons with 1960 levels.

TABLE 5.II

BALANCE OF PAYMENTS, 1960 AND AVERAGE 1966-70

(US $ million)

		1960	Average 1966-70
Current account balance		-164.6	- 96.6
Exports of goods and services		550.5	1,115.4
Imports of goods and services		-663.2	-1,016.2
Net remittances of profits and interests abroad		- 64.6	- 198.8
Net private transfer payments		12.7	3.0
Capital account		164.6	96.6
Net external financing (a+b+c+d+e)			
(a)	Net external non-compensatory capital	82.6	226.6
i)	Direct investment	29.0	33.6
ii)	Long and medium-term loans	50.5	303.4
iii)	Amortization payments	- 41.5	- 139.8
iv)	Short-term liabilities	10.2	25.4
v)	Official transfer payments	34.4	4.0
(b)	Domestic non-compensatory assets	- 8.7	- 12.2
(c)	Errors and omissions	45.6	- 28.4
(d)	Allocation of SDR's	-	4.2
(e)	Net compensatory movements (increase + -)	45.1	- 93.6
i)	Balance of Payment loans, trade arrears, deferred payments, IMF position and other liabilities	59.9	41.4
ii)	Amortization payments	- 31.4	- 82.2
iii)	Movement of foreign offical reserves	16.6	- 52.8

Source: UN ECLA, Economic Survey of Latin America, 1972; quoting data
          from IMF, Balance of Payments Yearbooks

As can be seen in Table 5.II, during the period 1966-70, average net
non-compensatory flows of foreign exchange were positive; this increased the
monetary system's net international reserves, so that by December 1970 they
reached US $ 343 million - the best the country had achieved during the

whole decade (in former years, net international reserves were either negative or had a much smaller positive balance[14]).

One of the main reasons for this was the growth in exports during 1966-70, when their average level more than doubled those of 1960. This was mainly explained by the high average copper price on international markets. Imports also grew substantially, but more slowly than exports.

The other element which explained the rise in international reserves was the sharp increase in medium and long-term loans (which averaged over six times the 1960 level). This was mainly due to large credits granted by the United States Government to the Chilean Government via the Alliance for Progress. Short-term liabilities also grew quite rapidly. Even though these high inflows had a short-term positive effect on the Balance of Payments, they increased Chile's foreign debt substantially (Chile's total external debt grew from US$ 1,852 million in 1966 to US$ 3,123 million in 1970[15]); this implied a high future burden of repayment and servicing. In fact, already in the period 1966-70, the net inflow of external non-compensatory capital (including direct investment) was nearly all used up to pay for the large net remittances of profits and interests abroad, corresponding to investments and loans of former years (see Table 5.II).

2   Popular Unity's view of the Chilean economy before 1970

The main characteristics of the structure and functioning of the Chilean economy before 1970 as perceived by Popular Unity will be described; a critique of this diagnosis will follow.

Popular Unity's analysis of the Chilean economy was not only based on Marxist elements, but was enriched by the contributions of the 'structuralist' and 'dependency' schools, considered by many to be the first indigenous schools of economics in under-developed countries[16]. Popular Unity's diagnosis - and in particular, the emphasis on the distortions generated by the functioning of Chilean 'dependent state monopoly capitalism' - had a significant influence on the economic measures adopted[17].

The link between diagnosis of the Chilean economy and Popular Unity's economic strategy was made explicit in official documents. Thus, Pedro Vuskovic - the first Minister of Economic Affairs in Allende's government - stated in a Seminar on the 'Chilean Road to Socialism'[18]:

> The principal task in formulating our economic policy
> is that of translating the basic lines of Popular
> Unity's programme into concrete ways of running the
> economy. The programme emerged from an analysis of
> Chile's past experience.

There follows a characterization of the distortions created by Chile's development as a dependent state monopoly capitalist economy. Therefore, not only the programme of structural changes, but also short-term economic policy ('concrete ways of running the economy') were strongly influenced by Popular Unity's diagnosis.

Implicit in this diagnosis of the Chilean economy are elements which could have allowed the definition of more correct economic and financial policies than those followed[19]. A study of Popular Unity's characterization of the economy is therefore helpful to see how the Chilean Left failed to gain sufficient benefit from its own theoretical and practical knowledge of the Chilean economy; even more, it shows how it often took policy decisions which were contradictory to its own analysis. (One of the most complete diagnoses of the Chilean economy developed from a Popular Unity perspective

is found in Sergio Ramos' book[20,21]. Similar characterizations were
expressed by the Ministers of Finance, Américo Zorrilla, and of Economic
Affairs, Pedro Vuskovic, in their first public expositions[22]).

The structure of the Chilean economy was characterized by Popular Unity as a
dependent, monopolistic state capitalist one. The dependence of the Chilean
economy was seen to derive mainly from the growing dominance of foreign
capital over the whole country's economic structure. Strong ties arose
between the national bourgeoisie and the dominant centre. The former lost
its identity as its interests became increasingly identified with those of
international capital. The alliance between the centre and the internal
dominant classes was seen as the political condition for a further deepening
of dependence relations[23].

In the 1960s, the penetration of foreign capital was increasing,
particularly in the industrial sector. In 1968/69, foreign capital had some
degree of participation in 26 per cent of industrial corporations which
owned 60 per cent of the total capital in the industrial sector. The
proportions were much higher in the strata of the largest enterprises with
greater influence on industrial development[24].

Of particular significance for our analysis was financial dependence. As
described above, the high level of official borrowing and private credits
obtained in the 1960s led to an increase in the foreign debt; this implied
the need to devote a growing part of foreign exchange earnings to finance
debt repayment and servicing. Due to the debt structure, a large part of
this payment was concentrated in 1971 and 1972. At the same time, the high
level of foreign investment of former years implied high net remittances of
profits abroad.

The type of capitalist development followed by Chile was seen in Popular
Unity's diagnosis as leading to growing concentration of ownership of the
means of production. Towards the end of the 1960s, it was estimated that
284 enterprises controlled all sectors and sub-sectors of industry and 17
per cent of corporations concentrated 78 per cent of the total assets in the
economy. Furthermore, in the 161 largest corporations, the ten largest
shareholders controlled over 90 per cent of their capital[25].

Concentration of property was particularly high in banking (the groups which
owned the banks often coincided with those who controlled the rest of the
dominant enterprises). This led to very high credit concentration; in 1969,
1.3 per cent of the debtors used nearly half of total banking credit.

The high concentration of capital naturally affected other variables. Thus
three per cent of the industrial enterprises concentrated 52 per cent of the
gross surplus of the industrial sector[26]. As we shall see below, great
importance was attached by Popular Unity analysts to the large potential
surplus, which was to be captured by the nationalization of heavy industry;
this was expected to help control inflation and provide new financing for
public expenditure expansion.

The Chilean economy at the time was defined by Popular Unity analysts as a
system of state monopoly capitalism, which 'gives to the state apparatus a
power of intervention and regulation over the economy oriented towards
diminishing the contradictions within the system, while always favouring
large capital and its fundamental interest'[27]. The state apparatus had a
large and increasing role in Chile. Government expenditure, which by 1964
represented 36 per cent GNP in 1970, represented 47 per cent of GNP.

The 'modus operandi' of the Chilean state apparatus was to a great extent
derived from the fact that it favoured large capital and its interests.
Some aspects of this orientation influenced the state apparatus during the

Popular Unity Government. The state played a crucial and growing role in capital accumulation; public investment grew from 54 per cent of Total Gross Investment in 1964 to 75 per cent by 1969. An important and growing part of this public investment remained under the control of the private sector; the part of private investment financed (via long-term loans and grants) with public resources grew from 12.4 per cent in 1961 to 50.3 per cent in 1969[28].

The state tended to transfer financial resources to the private sector for directly productive investments, whereas investment remaining under its control was oriented largely towards indirectly productive investment, i.e. transport or basic services. As these were considered priority sectors, their services were sold at subsidized prices; this implied that profit margins in these sectors were much lower than in those which produce goods.

In fact, it became implicitly accepted that state enterprises were mainly for 'public benefit' and that profitability in them was somewhat unacceptable; if profits did or could occur in state enterprises, they should rapidly be transferred to the private sector. This was illustrated with two policies:

Discriminatory price policy; for example, traditionally, the state's price policy would allow very low profit margins to the public producers; the private distributors of these same goods or services would be allowed much higher profit margins[29]; and transfer of enterprises. Once enterprises created by the state had overcome their initial difficulties and risks, and their activity became profitable, they were transferred from the public to the private sector. Loss-making private enterprises were often bought by the state to save them from bankruptcy. There was, therefore, a tradition of non-profitability in state enterprises. Whenever profitability - or its possibility - appeared, these profits were soon transferred to the private sector.

One of the problems of Popular Unity's policy was that it continued and even extended the management style of the preceding state apparatus. Many of the policies which the Left implemented were correct and functional when the government was basically an instrument serving the interests of large capital enterprises; however, they were very often incorrect and contradictory to the aims of Popular Unity. Due to its structural changes, the Left weakened both foreign and national monopolistic groups by expropriating much of their property; however, due to its short-term and financial policy, it greatly accentuated the historic tendency of the state to transfer surplus to the private sector[30].

The previously very large and increasing role of the state in the Chilean economy implied, however, several important advantages for Popular Unity. As Bitar, op.cit. points out, the increasing presence of the state in the economy, as well as its direct participation in the ownership of the means of production, had become acceptable to large sections of the population. Furthermore, it implied the development of institutions such as Corporacion de Fomento, in charge of industrial planning and financing, with important potential for managing and planning the newly nationalized enterprises in that sector. Finally, as Vuskovic points out ('Politica economica y poder politico', in El Gobierno de Allende y la lucha por el socialismo en Chile Universidad Nacional Autonoma de Mejico, Mejico 1976,) institutions such as the Corporacion de Fomento had important legal powers largely unused till 1970, which allowed Popular Unity to nationalize enterprises without any need for legislation. A particularly interesting example was the use of the Corporacion de Fomento to nationalize the banks (for a detailed description of this process, see A. Inostroza, 'Nationalisation of the Banking System in Chile', in S. Sideri (ed.), op.cit.) Similarly, the existence of a law of agrarian reform (approved during the Frei Government) and of the Corporacion de Reforma Agraria later allowed Popular Unity to complete the expropriation of the latifundia without new legislation.

The characterisation of the economic structure was considered by Popular Unity analysts as necessary, but not sufficient for the study of a precise historical conjuncture. The main link between structure and function was seen to be income distribution. The structural characteristics of the Chilean economy just described, as well as the political structure within the society, were seen to lead to high levels of exploitation of the labour force, and of small and middle entrepreneurs. The economic structure was seen to function 'on the basis of growing inequality in income distribution'. The dynamism of the economy was perceived as increasingly oriented to satisfying the demand of a small sector of the population, leading to a demand structure which was both very diversified and of a restricted volume[31].

In fact, in 1968, the wealthiest one per cent of the population concentrated 10 per cent of national income, which implied an average per capita income for that group equal to 69 times the average for the lowest 10 per cent income-bracket group[32].

The existence of spare capacity in the Chilean economy was greatly emphasized in Popular Unity's diagnosis. It was attributed to the limited size of the market (greatly influenced by an unequal income distribution), the use of foreign technology, monopolistic manipulation of the volumes of production, and the existence of bottlenecks in certain sectors. In 1970, it was estimated that 25 per cent of industrial productive capacity was unutilized[33]. Popular Unity analysts did not sufficiently stress the fact that spare capacity was not merely a result of structural problems, but was accentuated by the short term recession at the end of the 1960s.

Unemployment was a further negative feature of the functioning of the Chilean economy which was worsened by the recession. Open unemployment averaged 6.6 per cent of the work force during the 1960s; if involuntary unemployment among the non-active population and equivalent unemployment (derived from under-employment) were added, then estimates of average unemployment would reach over 15 per cent of the total active population[34].

According to Popular Unity analysts, inflation was another distortion in the functioning of the Chilean economy which basically derived from its structure. Here in particular Popular Unity borrowed from the tradition of the ECLA 'structuralist' school, and often from rather simplistic or vulgarized versions of it.

A final characteristic of the Chilean economy as seen by Popular Unity as derived from its structure, was slow growth of output.

We shall examine here one of the more general problems posed by Popular Unity's diagnosis; the more specific problems presented by it and their implications for their short-term policy will be examined below.

Popular Unity analysts correctly saw and stressed the link between structural reforms and long-term changes in the functioning of the economy[35]. However, they exaggerated both the speed and the scope of the effects which structural changes would have on the functioning of the economy. This seems to be derived mainly from their mechanistic interpretation of the link between structure and functioning.

In fact, structural changes often accentuate short-term macro-economic financial disequilibria, and restrict short-term growth. There are several reasons for this, well illustrated by the Chilean experience. Structural reforms are frequently accompanied by economic measures which accentuate financial disequilibria (such as high wage increases and price freezes often linked with the nationalization process). Furthermore, initially they generate additional problems due to lack of expertise in management, lack of planning apparatus, unclearly defined rules for the rapidly growing state sector, etc. Finally, emphasis on structural changes deflects attention and operative capacity from short-term policy issues. This can be illustrated by the management of the Central Bank of Chile, during the Popular Unity Government. Much time and attention was directed - both by top officials and by its general staff - to the structural reforms in the sector: bank nationalization and re-structuring of the banking system. Concern with these structural changes (which would do relatively little to help solve short-term macro-economic disequilibria), often diverted attention from decisions on monetary and credit policy, with a direct bearing on short-term disequilibria[36,37].

In Popular Unity's analysis of inflation and the policies required to tackle it, we can find a good example of its relatively simplistic view of the link between structure and functioning, between structural reforms and short-term solutions to economic distortions.

Thus, in Popular Unity's Programme, it was stated that: 'The struggle against inflation is basically resolved by structural changes'... and the promise was made that....'We will control prices and stop inflation by immediately setting up the new economic structure'. The same basic view, though expressed in a more realistic form, was put forward in technical documents[38]: 'Public control of the greater part of the productive apparatus and marketing will at the same time lay the foundations necessary to end inflation'. When Popular Unity came to power, top government officials in charge of financial policies made similar statements.

Explicit in these statements was the view that structural reforms would very rapidly and easily allow the elimination of inflation. This was openly expressed by the Finance Minister in a newspaper article[39]. He wrote:

> Till the 3rd of November, galloping inflation plagued Chile. From that day, this process began to slow down.... During 1971, the new economic measures will have their effect, and with that price increases will disappear, they will be remembered in the future as a nightmare which existed in periods when the Government served large capital.

This newspaper quote shows a naive enthusiasm, perhaps mainly serving journalistic purposes. Government documents, some of them prepared by the same Minister of Finance, followed a more correct analysis[40]. However, statements like that above reflect the exaggerated optimism of many government officials. Furthermore, they misinformed the public, leading it to believe in a semi-effortless and semi-automatic solution to inflation, once structural reforms were carried out; this was counter-productive for government, as it unnecessarily committed it to the achievement of difficult goals.

It would seem that the insufficient importance given to short-term and financial management, as well as some of the incorrect policies pursued in this area (which are somewhat reluctantly recognised even by Vuskovic in his ex-post article, 'Política económica y poder político', op.cit.) were at least partly related to two specific influences on senior Popular Unity policy-makers. Bitar (former Minister of Mining and former member of the Economic Council of Ministers) shares the view put forward here that one of

these influences was 'structuralist' analysis, particularly in its more
sophisticated forms.   As Fitzgerald (in Thorpe and Whitehead, op.cit.)
points out, the problem is that 'structuralist' economists tend to minimize
the importance and even the relevance of monetary and financial problems.
Bitar stresses also the influence of the Cuban experience, because several
senior Popular Unity economists had worked in that country, in a context
which emphasized almost exclusively administrative measures and physical
planning.   This was particularly inapplicable to the Chilean context, given
the different power situation.

However important these influences were, the main problems of financial and
short-term policy seem to have arisen from their inconsistency with the
political strategy pursued, as well as the lack of unified economic and
political direction. We shall return to these problems later.

3   Political and economic objectives and strategy of Popular Unity

The key political objective which Popular Unity pursued was the conquest and
consolidation of political power for the working class and its allies; all
other objectives were derived from this central political aim.   The
distinctive element in the Chilean process was that only part of the state
apparatus - the Executive - was controlled by the parties of the Left, as a
result of the 1970 Presidential elections[41].

The political strategy followed was based on the concept of 'class
alliance'.   This supposed achieving the unity of the vast majority of the
population, including the working class and certain sectors of the middle
class, so that they would obtain power.   The purpose of this alliance was
made explicit in the Popular Unity Programme:

> The central policy objective of the united popular
> forces will be the search for a replacement of the
> present economic structure, doing away with the power
> of foreign and national monopoly capital and of the
> latifundio in order to initiate the construction of
> socialism.

This political strategy implied: (a) the need to attack the power base of
those social groups whose interests were menaced by the political project;
(b) broadening the popular base of the government; (c) neutralizing sectors
whose complete support could not be won, but who were not its main obstacle.
The main economic targets were derived from the political aims and strategy.

(a)   First priority was given to rapid advance in structural reforms. This
was consistent with the structural diagnosis of the economy and with the
political strategy adopted.   These reforms were expected to destroy the
power base of the dominant classes[42].   They were also to lay the base for
a future socialist economy, which would allow a new development pattern to
emerge.

(b)   The actions necessary to broaden Popular Unity's base were oriented in
two directions: (i) improvement in the living standards of the majority;
(ii) increase of workers' participation in the control of the economic
apparatus.

(c)   A third task was the design of policies to separate the small and
medium entrepreneurs' interests, as well as those of the self-employed from
those of the monopolistic groups.   Their neutrality (or even support) was to
be obtained by maintaining or increasing their profits, as a result of the
general short-term policy and through economic concessions to them.

The role of the middle classes in the transition to socialism is an area in which insufficient theoretical work has been done; Popular Unity's own approach was too aggregate, and emphasized the economic aspects excessively. Furthermore, there were important disagreements within the coalition about the role of the middle classes in the process.

The dominant view within Popular Unity clearly attached insufficient importance to ideological and political elements in the alliance with the middle classes. Castells' 'Comentario: la teoría marxista de los clases sociales y la lucha de clases en América Latina' (in <u>Las clases sociales en América Latina</u>, Siglo <u>XXI</u>, 1973) comment that, 'if the bourgeoisie and the proletariat are undoubtedly defined at the three levels (economic, political and ideological), other classes less clearly defined in the economic sphere are defined above all by political and ideological contradictions', seems particularly relevant to the Chilean middle classes.

Popular Unity tended to treat the 'middle class' as 'tactical allies', which implicitly assumed that this alliance could be temporary. No effort was made to conceive a strategic alliance with the middle classes, which would have implied including their long-term interests in the Popular Unity project, and not merely granting them temporary economic concessions (however, this would have been difficult to implement as important sectors within Popular Unity would have, and in fact did resist such long-term commitments).

As regards the small and medium entrepreneurs, they tended to oppose a government which did not define clearly the future limits of state property, as well as the nature of workers' participation in the remaining private sector. The fear of possible future loss of their property or limited ability to manage it overshadowed the initial increase in their profits and the economic concessions granted to them. Such fears were clearly increased by the right-wing opposition and media, and the government was unable to counteract these influences.

Important sectors of the self-employed (particularly those in the transport and commercial sector) were also fearful of losing their property. Of greater significance in their growing opposition to the government was the increasing disruption of the market, which we shall discuss below.

Finally, it should be stressed that not all sectors of Popular Unity gave support even to the limited concept of 'alliance with the middle groups', prevalent in the governing coalition. To the concept of a policy of alliances, was opposed the view of a policy of 'working class mobilization'[43].

Even though there was general agreement within Popular Unity about the central political objective of conquering power, there were important disagreements within the Left coalition about the concrete political strategy to be pursued. The conflict was mainly between Communists and Socialists; each party had a basically different strategy for the timing and methods of gaining power.

The Communists envisaged the Chilean revolution as passing through two distinct phases, the first one being limited to the fulfilment of 'bourgeois-democratic' goals (such as agrarian reform, nationalization of foreign and domestic monopolies and a general democratization of society). Once these tasks had been performed and consolidated, the strengthened working class, in close alliance with peasants and other progressive groups whose objective interests coincided with those of the working class, would be prepared to proceed to the second, socialist stage. A victory for the Popular Unity coalition in Chile would, according to the Communists' analysis, merely signify the initiation of the first of these two stages.

This 'longer view' on the construction of socialism was not shared by the Socialist Party, least of all by its leadership. Referring to the discussion within the Popular Unity held immediately after Allende's electoral triumph, the Central Committee of the Socialist Party declared in an internal party document: 'The difference between our opinion and that of the rest was that we Socialists demanded that the initiation of Socialism should be a task of this government and not only a historical perspective'. The two-stage revolution was described as highly unrealistic; the Opposition would never permit an armistice, letting the Left consolidate the conquests of the 'first stage'. Once initiated, the Socialist Party argued, the revolutionary proces would generate a struggle for power, and the outcome of this struggle could only be victory or defeat, socialism or counter-revolution.

Many contradictions (including those related to the 'middle groups' briefly discussed above) arose within Popular Unity due to these discrepancies between Communists and Socialists. One crucial contradiction – the concrete political strategy to be followed during the first two years of government – will be discussed here[44].

Certain sectors within Popular Unity – basically the Socialist and Mapu parties – advocated what will be called here the 'road of rapid institutional changes within the existing legal framework'. Concretely, when in April 1971 Popular Unity obtained 50 per cent of the popular vote in municipal elections, this group strongly advocated calling a plebiscite. This plebiscite was to be centred on the question of dissolving the Congress, asking the citizens to elect new representatives to the 'People's Assembly'. Had this plebiscite been favourable to Popular Unity, it would have brought a significant increase in state power[45].

The Communists, Radicals and President Allende himself turned down the Socialist proposal, fearing that a plebiscite would immediately force the Opposition to unite and hoping that the political gains of the UP could be consolidated during the period to come. Thus, an alternative strategy to the Socialist one – the gradual way – was de facto implicitly adopted. This strategy basically postponed confrontation with the opposition till elections were scheduled. In former experiences of transition to socialism it is relatively easy to deduce the political strategy from official Communist Party documents. Due to divisions within Popular Unity, the political strategy was never made explicit. Therefore, to detect the political strategy effectively chosen, one is obliged to look at the one adopted de facto. Although possibilities of plebiscite (as well as changes within the Army) were amply discussed, no concrete measures were taken in this direction. Therefore, a decision to follow the gradual way was implicitly adopted. The important implications for economic policy of following either political strategy will be discussed below.

4.   Design of short-term economic policy

a)   Brief description of the short-term policy

The short-term policy will be briefly examined, as well as its justification by Popular Unity analysts. Then, this policy will be evaluated in terms of the two different implicit political strategies described above.

Before examining the short-term policy, a reservation must be made. Popular Unity gave first priority within its programme to structural reforms. Due to the nature of this study, structural reforms will be analyzed here only insofar as they affect short-term economic policy and the short-term evolution of the economy[46]. Popular Unity analysts visualized both elements of the economic programme – short-term policy and structural reforms – as taking place simultaneously, supporting each other and the fundamental objective of Popular Unity to 'take power' in the society as a whole. Here we shall analyze only the short-term policy followed and its effects on the power struggle. Short-term economic policy objectives were determined by the existing framework. The main determining factors were: (i) the Popular Unity diagnosis; (ii) the political and economic conjuncture towards the end of 1970, and (iii) the aims of Popular Unity's general political strategy.

Several elements determined that rapid economic recovery and increase in employment should be important short-term policy targets. This decision was based on the chronic depression and the structural tendency towards unused productive capacity, and was strengthened by the need to face the recession towards the end of 1970, with its potentially serious political consequences. Given the political strategy, it also seemed necessary to ensure a climate of economic recovery so as to impede the identification of the majority of the entrepreneurs with the monopolistic groups. Rapid income redistribution was not only a priority target in itself, but was regarded as essential to broadening Popular Unity's political base.

We shall summarize briefly the economic conditions which Popular Unity stressed most when it took over the government. Elements not sufficiently emphasized by Popular Unity - though implicit in its own diagnosis - will also be examined.

Stress on the existence of spare productive capacity and of unemployment constituted the base for the design of Popular Unity's short-term policy. For this short-term economic policy 'the objective basis is found in the productive potential which the economy already has, and which the system has not been able to make use of due to institutional limitations, and its subjection to the interests of national and foreign monopolies'[47].

The base for Popular Unity's short-term economic policy was not just idle industrial capacity and unemployment - which, as we have seen, were in 1970 among the highest recorded in that decade - but also exceptionally high levels of foreign exchange reseves and industrial stocks. In December 1970, the Central Bank's net foreign exchange reserves reached their peak for that decade (US$ 343 million), and were equivalent to over three months' imports of goods and services.

It seems however that when the short-term policy was designed, not enough emphasis was laid on the limits of these idle resources, as well as the constraints which should be applied in their use. On the one hand, little stress was laid on the fact that there were definite global and sectoral limits to spare industrial capacity, as well as to unemployed labour[48]. Furthermore, the 'once-for-all' effect of exhausting foreign exchange reserves and industrial stocks was not sufficiently stressed.

Some resources, i.e. unemployment, will allow a permanent, even if limited, expansion of production (if there are no bottlenecks in the economy). Other resources - i.e. high level of industrial stocks and foreign exchange reserves - will allow a 'once-for-all' temporary expansion of sales. In the initially enthusiastic evaluation of the results of the 1971 short-term policy, this distinction was not sufficiently considered. Also, the analysis was centred on the industrial sector; in agriculture - especially in a period of rapid Agrarian Reform - it could not be expected to achieve significant production increases. The problem seems to be one of emphasis. Due to the nature of its diagnosis, Popular Unity stressed the existence of idle resources; however, not enough attention was put on their limits.

On the other hand, its diagnosis should have shown Popular Unity an important constraint in the use of the economy's idle resources. As Popular Unity analysts correctly emphasized, Chile was a dependent economy, clearly within the American sphere of influence. Financial dependence on the United States was particularly marked; the high level of official borrowing and private credits obtained in the 1960s had created a heavy burden of foreign exchange payments for the 1970s, a large part of which was concentrated on debt to the US Government and banks. As the Popular Unity's political and economic project clearly challenged US interests, it was to be expected that this country would respond by curtailing credits and aid. On the other hand, it was also to be expected that the Soviet Union and other socialist countries could not (due to their relatively low levels of foreign exchange reserves), and perhaps would not, wish to provide levels of credits and aid sufficient to compensate for those curtailed.

Under these circumstances (of a project of 'transition to socialism' in a country so dependent financially on its hegemonic power, with no abundant alternative sources of foreign finance) the only defence would have been to maintain a relatively high floor of foreign exchange reserves. The crucial importance of this point was clearly under-estimated by Popular Unity Government officials, as well as by the political leadership. It is noteworthy that Vuskovic, in his ex-post analysis, ('Politica economica y poder politico', op.cit. p.159) somewhat grudgingly accepts that 'foreign exchange reserves should have been used more cautiously, to counteract the financial blockade which imperialism would carry out'.

Therefore, it can be concluded that in the conjuncture faced, there existed some room for manoeuvre in using economic and financial policies for the pursuit of Popular Unity's central objection : increasing political power. (In comparison with other experiences of transition to socialism, e.g. the Soviet Union, there was the additional advantage that Popular Unity inherited an economy with no substantial financial disequilibira, even though there were some accumulated inflationary pressures.) However, manoeuvre was limited and its use should have been constrained due to the elements described above.

Popular Unity's initial short-term policy design suffered from two basic problems. First insufficient emphasis was laid on the limited availability of idle resources, and therefore on the limited room for manoeuvre. Second, as there was no clear concrete political strategy, there was no clarity either in how to use this limited flexibility in the pursuit of Popular Unity's objective of increasing political power. This point will be examined once the short-term policy is described.

To achieve the dual aims of economic recovery and income redistribution, the 1971 short-term economic policy was directed towards an increase in production aimed mainly at wage goods. Growth in production was to be provoked by an increase in demand. This would be achieved by: (a) increasing the real income of workers and (b) deficit expansion of public expenditure. In both aspects, the original aims set forth by Popular Unity policy-makers were widely surpassed.

One of the cornerstones of the reactivation programme was its incomes policy. Immediately after taking office the government took up negotiations with the Central Workers' Union (CUT) in order to sign an agreement which would establish criteria for private and public renumerations in 1971.

This agreement guaranteed a minimal increase in wages and salaries for all workers and employees equal to the retail price increase of 1970 (that is, 34.9 per cent). Above this across the board increase, the low income stratas received additional allowances, which reached a 66 per cent increase for the lowest income level. Finally, a process of standardization and levelling of all social benefits, such as pensions and family allowances, was begun.

The final result of the incomes policy implied an average increase of labour incomes which was far beyond the target set up in the CUT - government agreement. When negotiations had been concluded, average income per employed person had grown by 54.9 per cent, as against the 40 per cent originally envisaged by the government[49].

This incomes policy was combined with strict price control. For the private sector, this was based on the concept that profit margins were excessive; for the state and recently nationalized enterprises, prices were frozen. During the first year, this policy was successful. Retail prices rose by only 22.1 per cent. Therefore, real wages increased substantially during 1971.

Average real income per person employed grew by 27 per cent. As employment grew by 4.8 per cent, the total wages and salaries bill (in real terms) grew by 33.1 per cent. During the first half of 1972, real wages and salaries continued to rise. However, after July 1972, this tendency was reversed, even though real incomes were still far above 1970 levels.

The other cornerstone of the reactivation policy was the deficitary expansion of public sector expenditure. Thus, in 1971, public expenditure increased by 75 per cent in nominal terms. This rapid growth was not accompanied by an increase in public sector revenues[50]. The total state deficit grew at an amazing rate; it increased - in real terms - by 145.3 per cent in 1971 and by 76.0 per cent in 1972[51].

In both 1971 and 1972, the total state budget deficit was much larger than that originally programmed by the government. This was because the effective fiscal deficit more than doubled the size of the programmed one in both years, and because there was a large non-programmed deficit in the rest of the state sector. (This includes the decentralized institutions, the state enterprises and the growing sector of newly nationalized enterprises.)

The large state deficit was financed mainly by credit from the monetary system to the government. Thus, credits from the monetary system (which include the Central Bank and the banking system) covered most of the total public deficit. During 1971, these credits were six times larger (in real terms) than those of 1969-70[52].

The increase in public deficit, and the form of its financing, led to high growth of the money supply. In 1971, money held by the private sector increased by 119 per cent. It is interesting to note that the initial monetary programme of the Central Bank had projected for 1971 an increase of money held by the private sector of under 54 per cent[53]. In 1972, money held by the private sector grew even more rapidly - by 138 per cent over 1971 levels.

b)   Evaluation of the functionality of the short-term policy

Given Popular Unity's lack of emphasis on short-term economic policy and management, no explicit detailed theoretical or analytical framework was elaborated; furthermore, there was no realistic, quantitative framework, which integrated the real and the financial sector, and which attempted to achieve compatibility between global and sectoral demand and supply. ODEPLAN (the planning office) either did not quantify some of these crucial aspects, or produced unrealistic estimates, based on unrealistic asumptions, (See, ODEPLAN, Resumen del Plan de la Economía Nacional, 1971-76, Santiago, 1971, as well as a comparison with the real results for 1971, in Bitar, op.cit. pp. 252-54).

Although some observers and participants (e.g. Bitar, op.cit.) claim that Popular Unity's short-term policy had a Keynesian 'inspiration', it seems more correct to attribute to it a Kaleckian origin. As we have seen, Popular Unity's short-term policy not only stressed economic expansion based on idle capacity, but also income redistribution and an increase in the production of wage goods (these two latter points are a more central concern in Kalecki's works than in those of Keynes). Furthermore, several of the main designers of Popular Unity's short-term economic policy, and particularly its main architect, Pedro Vuskovic, continuously stressed as crucial in their description of this policy, a mechanism often repeated in Kalecki's writings. This was the concept that, given price controls, prices would increase less than wages, leading to a reduced unit profit rate; assuming spare capacity of wage goods production, an increase in production and sales in this sector would compensate for the decline in unit profits, maintaining the absolute level of profits. For example, Vuskovic in one of his main and often quoted policy statements, his speech to the Inter-American Committee for the Alliance for Progress (CIAP) in February 1971, (reproduced in El pensamiento económico de Allende, op.cit. in (22)) stated that:

> The short-term economic policy responds to the aims made explicit in our programme. One of their main concrete expressions is the Popular Government's line on wages, salaries and prices....
>
> The wage, salary and price policies of the Popular Government clearly imply a decline in the unit profit rate, which will affect the income of capital; these will be compensated only to the extent that production and productivity will increase simultaneously, based precisely on the increased purchasing power of the workers.

Very similar quotations and analysis can be found in other statements and articles on Popular Unity's short-term economic policy by Vuskovic and others (see, for example, P. Vuskovic, 'Distribución del ingreso y opciones de desarrollo', Cuadernos de la Realidad Nacional, September 1970; P. Vuskovic, 'The Economic Policy of the Popular Unity Government' particularly p. 52 in The Chilean Road to Socialism, op.cit. P. Vuskovic, 'Política económica y poder político', op.cit. particularly p.7, and Ramos op.cit.

The most formalized analysis of Popular Unity's national short-term economic policy, explicitly based on a Kaleckian framework, was written by Julio Lopez, advisor to the Minister of Economics; this analysis was published in the September 1971 issue of the journal Cuadernos de la Realidad Nacional, where, as Zammit and Palma point out, the most significant debate on Chile's road to socialism took place[54].

A Kaleckian framework assumes the existence of excess capacity within the economy and the technological feasibility of short-term changes in the level of output. Furthermore, it supposes that there is imperfect competition and that profit margins depend on the degree of monopoly in the economy and on trade-union power. Thus, prices are cost-determined. As demand expands, the response of the productive system to this increase is via an expansion of output (and not of prices and profit margins). Given these assumptions, the effects of an expansion of demand will be examined. For purposes of analysis, the increase in real wages and the expansion of public expenditure are discussed separately.

The increase in real wages was expected to have several effects, all of which were desirable for Popular Unity, and contributed towards the achievement of its aims. It was expected that an increase in real wages would stimulate growth of production and employment; even though it would improve income distribution[55], profit levels would be maintained.

The increase in real wages would not reduce the level of profits realised by the capitalists. The fall in the profit margin (profit per unit sold), due to the increase in wages, would be exactly compensated by the growth in the number of units sold. The growth in the volume of sales corresponds to the expansion of wage-earners' consumption, provoked by the wages increase. The operation of this mechanism implies some assumptions about the evolution of demand. The level of demand depends on private expenditure, that is, on expenditure of capitalists and wage-earners[56]. In any short period, it can be assumed that capitalists' expenditure on investment and consumption results from their decisions in former periods; it is improbable that their decisions will be modified due to a wage increase[57].

On the other hand, the increase in wages will provide an immediate growth in wage-earners' consumption, of the same volume as the wages increase, (assuming that workers do not save). In absolute terms, the growth in the volume of sales would exactly equal the growth in wages, and hence equal the increase in total costs. Obviously, the level of profits – which equals the difference between volume of sales and total costs – would not change, as both items increase by the same absolute magnitude. Thus, the fall in unit profit margin would be exactly compensated for by the growth in units sold.

The same positive effects would be achieved by an increase in public expenditure, financed by taxation of the capitalist class. It is again assumed that capitalists' expenditure during a certain period results from decisions taken in former periods, and would not be modified immediately by a change in disposable income.

Let us examine the effects of a tax on profits, used to finance an increase in government expenditure. As the capitalists' expenditure would not be modified in the period considered, growth in public expenditure would increase total demand, causing sales, output and employment to increase. The growth in aggregate demand would be equal to the taxation increase. As the ratio of prices/cost is given, total profits before taxes would increase in such magnitude that after tax profits would remain constant. Therefore, this measure – like that of increasing real wages – would increase output and employment, improve income distribution (as the share of profits in total income falls), while maintaining the absolute level of profits.

The effects on income distribution would be less desirable – given Popular Unity's aims – if the growth of public expenditure were financed by budget deficit. In this case, increasing expenditure would provoke a growth of sales, output, employment and profits. As sales and output grew, and the profit margin remained constant, the absolute level of profits would increase. Income distribution would remain unchanged.

In evaluating this framework, it is important to emphasize that once full capacity is reached, Kalecki's theory and policy conclusions are no longer valid. This was not explicit in Popular Unity's analysis, which stressed the existence of idle capacity, and not its limits and exhaustibility.

Once full capacity is reached, the behaviour of the economy can be more appropriately interpreted by a 'Kaldorian' framework of analysis. (The distinction between a 'Kaleckian range' and a 'Kaldorian range' was suggested to me by R.E. Rowthorn's mimeographed paper, 'Income Distribution and Taxation', Cambridge, 1975)[58]. Contrary to Kalecki, Kaldor regards full capacity utilization as the norm.

When the economy is at full employment, increases in aggregate demand do not generate growth of output, but of the profit share. Thus profit margins are not determined by market structure and trade union power (as in the Kaleckian range) but by the level of aggregate demand. In this case, the effects of an expansion in public expenditure will be basically different from those when the economy is within the 'Kaleckian range'.

If public expenditure growth were completely financed by a tax on profits, the expansion of demand would naturally not generate growth of output. It would increase pre-tax profits by the same amount as the tax on profits would grow. The effect on income distribution would thus be neutral.

Furthermore, deficitary expansion of public expenditure would have effects completely disfunctional to Popular Unity's aims. It could increase neither output nor employment. The gap between aggregate demand and supply would have to be bridged by inflation and/or scarcity and/or imports[59]. If these reach excessively high levels, they have negative effects, particularly harmful in a context of transition to socialism.

If inflation were the mechanism chosen to bridge the gap between demand and supply, then it would imply a worsening of income distribution, as the share of profits rose.

If fixed prices and scarcity were the mechanism chosen, then goods and services would be erratically distributed, favouring those more influential in the society and/or able to pay higher prices on the black market. This would also imply a more unequal distribution of goods and services. Furthermore, the inevitable appearance of black markets would generate an atmosphere of corruption and speculation, particularly undesirable during transition to socialism. There would come a point when it became more profitable to speculate than to engage in productive activities; this would naturally have an adverse effect on productivity and production. When people invest in all kinds of products and sell them weeks or months later for higher prices, scarcity is artificially exacerbated.

The negative effects of scarcity and black markets could be eliminated if rationing were introduced. However, for reasons that we shall detail below in Section 5.IV, it should have been clear to the Popular Unity Government that effective rationing was not feasible during its first years in power.

Inflation generates other undesirable effects. With high inflation, neither general nor financial planning can be carried out with any precision. The difficulty in planning, control and accounting makes the management of the newly-nationalized units, as well as of the rest of the state sector, even more complex. This effect could be restricted if physical planning were functioning properly. However, in Chile, as in any experience of transition to socialism, in the early stages there was insufficient time to set up an effective physical planning apparatus[60].

Furthermore, high levels of inflation and/or scarcity could be expected to provoke a negative reaction among 'the middle groups', turning them against the Popular Unity Government. In other experiences, 'the middle groups' have always been frightened of hyperinflation and scarcity, and opposed strongly those governments under which these phenomena occurred. This would become particularly true in the case of Chile, as the Opposition's ideological apparatus efficiently exploited these problems.

If imports were the mechanism chosen, this would hit foreign trade and foreign exchange reserves. As was explained, this would be specially damaging in the case of Chile as it was a dependent country in transition to socialism.

Unless import controls were established, the expansion of demand via public deficit would imply higher levels of imports[61]. In the Kaleckian range, as output increases, this would imply higher imports of inputs. However, in the Kaldorian range, this would imply increasing imports of consumer and investment goods[62]. This effect would operate with greater strength if, under inflationary conditions, exchange rates were fixed.

If exports did not grow as rapidly as imports, foreign reserves would begin to fall, so that first, imports of consumer goods, and then, imports of inputs would have to be curtailed. The first would limit availability of total goods, whereas the second would also reduce internal production.

When this situation was reached, scarcity would reflect not only increases in demand, but also a fall in supply. Real consumption would thus be falling. If the economy were at this stage when the power confrontation began, it would be a particularly unfavourable situation for the government. The past increases in real consumption (achieved while the economy was in the 'Kaleckian range') would by now be forgotten and the present fall in consumption would be felt more immediately, and naturally stressed more by the opposition media.

From this analysis, it can be seen that policy conclusions are completely different in the 'Kaleckian' and in the 'Kaldorian' range. While the economy is within the 'Kaleckian' range, the optimum policy to follow is to increase real wages and/or increase government expenditure financed by a tax on profits; this would provoke effects, all of which are functional to Popular Unity's aims[63]. Within this range, if the increase in government expenditure is financed by deficit, its effects are positive as regards recovery of the economy, and neutral as regards income distribution.

Policy conclusions are quite different within the 'Kaldorian range'. Once full capacity is reached, deficit financed increases in government expenditure have effects completely disfunctional to Popular Unity's aims. A policy conclusion, crucial for Popular Unity, can be derived from this analysis. If for some reason, it is not feasible to finance the increases in taxation, it is necessary to use alternative means which reduce the private sector's buying power, so as to avoid the negative effects of a deficitary expansion in government expenditure[64]. The alternative measures to be adopted should depend largely on the institutional set-up and the margin of manoeuvre which the government has with different policy instruments. In the case of Popular Unity, the best alternative to increases in taxation seemed to be increases in prices of state and nationalized enterprises.

The above economic analysis must be linked to political strategy, to allow us to define the link between economic policy and political strategy. We will attempt to deduce some general conclusions about the timing and magnitude of the required expansion of demand for alternative political strategies.

The basic idea is that, when the moment or moments of crucial definition of power are expected to occur, the economy should be within (or have just surpassed) the Kaleckian range, so that the positive effects of the expansion of demand result in maximum political capital being obtained.

As was described above, one political alternative was that of rapid institutional changes. This implied that, during the first year of Popular Unity's government, moments of crucial definition of power (i.e. plebiscite to change the composition of Congress, or perhaps even changes in the Army) would begin to occur. If this road were followed, then the expansion of demand should be rapid, so as to achieve the maximum positive effects (within the Kaleckian range) before the crucial moment of confrontation came. Rapid improvement in income distribution, quick increases in production and consumption would doubtless have contributed to increase mass support for the government, essential to winning a plebiscite[65]. Were it necessary to make some sacrifice of exhaustible resources (such as foreign exchange or stocks) and/or provoke financial disequilibria this would be justified in terms of its functionality towards the achievement of power. Furthermore, once a stronger power position were assumed, measures could be taken to compensate for former loss of resources and to control the financial disequilibria (i.e. stricter wage controls, rationing, monetary reform).

If a gradual political strategy were followed, the expansion of demand should be both much smaller and slower than in the former case, so as to maintain the economy within the Kaleckian range for a long time. In Chile, important elections (that is, those which could have implied fundamental gains for Popular Unity) were to be held in March 1973 (for the replacement of an important part of Congress) and in September 1976 (Presidential elections)[66]. Thus, when the crucial moments of confrontation came, popular support for Popular Unity would be increased by the continuous positive effects of demand expansion still prevailing in the economy. It could be concluded that a gradual economic policy would be the one most helpful in achieving the goals of a gradual political strategy. Therefore, once this political strategy were in fact chosen, a key policy objective should have been to control the growth of aggregate demand within certain limits and to time this growth adequately.

However, as was briefly described, the economic policy followed implied a very strong expansion of aggregate demand during both 1971 and 1972. This policy was clearly disfunctional to the gradual political strategy de facto chosen; it tended to exhaust the full range of positive effects during the first year[67]. During this period, there were no important elections. The short-term economic policy did contribute to the increase in popular support for Popular Unity during its first year of government. This was reflected in the results of the April 1971 municipal elections, when Popular Unity increased its support from the 36.4 per cent it had obtained in the Presidential elections to slightly over 50 per cent of all votes. However, in terms of increasing state power, this was not significant at all, as municipal institutions have no importance within the Chilean power structure. Due to the political strategy adopted, in fact, no real political capital was made of the significant increase in mass support.

When the much more crucial electoral confrontation – Congress elections – occurred in March 1973, the economy was clearly within the 'Kaldorian range'; all the negative effects of excessive demand growth had openly manifested themselves (see description below, section IV). The relatively favourable results for Popular Unity (44 per cent of the popular vote) were achieved in spite of the deterioration in the economic situation. Due to successes in both nationalization and workers' participation, and in the face of growing aggressiveness from the external and internal opposition, the workers rallied around a government which they felt represented most clearly their long-term interest, in spite of the existing economic problems. Had the economic policy been more gradual, and were its positive effects still prevailing in the economy, perhaps Popular Unity could have achieved the required 50 per cent in the Congress elections, which would have meant a decisive increase in its share of state power. It is naturally impossible to determine the exact effects which an alternative economic policy would have had on the electoral results. However, one can say that an alternative policy would have had much more favourable economic effects during 1973; this would have undoubtedly increased mass support (and decreased opposition) of different strata.

We will attempt to explain some of the reasons for the disfunctionality between the economic policy and the political strategy adopted. One factor was that those in charge of the design and implementation of the short-term policy[68] had in mind an implicit political strategy (that of rapid

institutional changes) different from that <u>de facto</u> adopted by the political
leadership.   To a great extent, this was because those in charge of
designing   the   short-term   economic   policy   were   mainly   militants   or
sympathizers   of   the   Socialist   and   Mapu   parties,   which   advocated   rapid
institutional changes, i.e. plebiscite.   However, President Allende himself,
influenced strongly by the Communist Party, chose implicitly the gradual way
when, after the spectacular electoral success in April 1971, he refused to
call a plebiscite.   The discrepancy between economic policy and political
strategy became more blatant after April 1971 when the gradual political
strategy was implicitly adopted and the policy of rapid expansion of demand
was not modified.

One can criticise the role which many economists played (particularly after
April 1971).   Many of the divisions among economists were based on political
or institutional loyalties; often this brought unnecessary sectarianism, as
many of the issues could have been resolved so that different political
parties and government institutions would have agreed.   Other economists
acted more as politicians, often hoping that their actions within the
economic sphere would help impose one political strategy[69].

The Popular Unity economists did not carry out their main role thoroughly,
given the situation of an ill-defined political strategy.   This was first,
to show the political leadership the limits and exhaustibility of the idle
resources available in the economy; second, to impress upon the political
leadership the need to use the limited room for economic manoeuvre available
in such a way as to obtain maximum political capital.

It could be argued that it is easy to make these comments with the hindsight
of   academic   research,   but   that   given   the   heat   and   complexity   of   the
situation, it was practically impossible to visualize these problems clearly
at the time.   However, there were Popular Unity economists – mainly within
the financial sphere – who clearly pointed out the first aspect mentioned
above.   The   most   important   of   these   reports,   'Situacion   actual   y
perspectivas de la politica financiera', (op.cit.) was written as early as
April 1971; it forecast with remarkable accuracy the 1971 increase in the
money supply and the Balance of Payments Deficit, and pointed out some of
its negative effects.   By forecasting financial disequilibria, this report
clearly detected the limits of the short-term policy; it also suggested some
counter measures.   Not enough attention was paid to these financial reports
by the political leadership.   This may have been partly because the reports
did   not   stress   some   of   the   medium-term   adverse   effects   of   the   policy
followed – including on income distribution and the centralised management
of the economy – which might have made a greater impact on the Popular Unity
leadership than mere financial variables[70].   Furthermore,   the   political
leadership was in closer contact with economists concerned basically with
topics other than financial disequilibrium, such as structural reforms.

Clarification by economists of the importance of these issues to the
political leadership could have forced – one way or another – a decision
such   that   economic   policy   and   political   strategy   could   have   been
functionally linked.   Once the economic policy of rapid demand expansion was
launched, clarity about the very short-term and reversible nature of its
positive effects might have moved the political leadership to adopt the
political   strategy   which   capitalised   best   on   these   positive   effects
(plebiscite)[71] .   Given   the   political   reasons   for   not   adopting   this
strategy (in spite of the economic considerations), then the economists
should have accepted this political decision, and modified economic policy
to make it suit the political strategy.

It is interesting to quote here the ex-post perception of these issues by
one of the main actors in the process, Pedro Vuskovic.   In 'Política
económica y poder político' (op.cit. pp.174-8) Vuskovic writes:

Since the beginning of the Government, a transfer of
responsibility from the political direction to the
'technical teams' became evident, independently of
parties. This separation, which was particularly
noticeable during the first stage, had important
consequences at several levels. First, it deprived
the political leadership of a permanent and up-dated
evaluation of the economic situation and its
perspectives, as a base for adopting crucial policies
in other fields. The political leadership (of the
different parties) did not participate systematically
in the economic analysis and those in charge of
economic policy did not attend regularly the debates
on political decisions, nor did they make sufficient
effort to spell out the general implications of the
economy's evolution. An important consequence was
that it was not made sufficiently clear at the
required time, that some of the positive and even
spectacular results of economic policy during this
first stage were inevitably transitory and that they
offered an objective favourable base – but not
necessarily a lasting one – to advances in the
consolidation of political power....It is clear that
these were not merely formal matters, but were
influenced mainly by those aspects which, within the
broad Popular Unity agreement, remained as
controversial points. However, we should not dismiss
the influence of organization and administrative
factors within the direction of the process, which
weakened the necessarily permanent relationship
between the political and economic direction, and
which caused responses more to crystallized situations
than to timely and adequate projections.

A second level of explanation is that an important part of the rapid
expansion of demand was not caused by deliberate government action but was
provoked by other causes, mainly determined by moves on the part of the
Opposition.

On the one hand, average wage increases surpassed by far the limits set in
the CUT – Government agreement. This element to a great extent escaped
Popular Unity's control, in spite of the fact that the Left was strongly
represented among the CUT Councillors[72]. The long-term tradition of all
Chilean trade-union leaders (clearly including the Socialist and Communist
ones) was to concentrate on maximizing economic demands in their own trade
union. When Popular Unity won the presidential elections, the Christian
Democrat (Opposition) trade union leaders increased their pressure for wage
increases so as to gain popularity and create contradictions for the
government. Competition among parties for trade union support was increased
because of CUT elections in May 1972. Within this context, the Left
trade-unionists could not afford politically – and did not wish – to
restrict wage demands[73].

Another important instance when demand expansion was far quicker than
programmed by the Popular Unity Government was in the case of the state
budget deficit. As will be described below, the much larger deficit than
programmed was to a great extent due to the opposition's action in blocking
taxation bills.

The key criticism of Popular Unity's short-term policy can now be briefly
outlined at a more concrete level, taking into account the elements
discussed above. This criticism accepts as a given political decision that

the electoral road was the one de facto adopted, and that the opposition
generated certain actions which implied an expansion of demand larger than
the programmed one. Why did Popular Unity not take other measures, which
were institutionally feasible, to limit the increase in the private sector's
buying power? If nominal wages could not be controlled, why did Popular
Unity not allow prices to rise more, so as to restrict the growth of real
wages? If it was impossible to increase taxation, why not use alternative
methods to reduce the private sector's buying power, such as increases in
prices of nationalized enterprises? Why transfer even more surplus to the
private sector by granting it credits via the recently-nationalized banks at
heavily subsidised (very negative in real terms) interest rate? We shall
return to these questions in section V.

II   Causes of financial and monetary disequilibria. Analysis of political and economic forces which affect it

The causes of the monetary disequilibria during Popular Unity's Government
will be studied. After describing the evolution of the financial variables,
we shall analyze the forces and policies conditioning or determining these
financial variables. We shall attempt to distinguish, particularly for
1971, between those elements determined by the opposition's actions and
those originating in Popular Unity's policy; this will be important for
determining Popular Unity's range of manoeuvre for diminishing the volume of
the financial disequilibria. We shall concentrate on the first two years of
the government period during which there was a larger margin for the design
of economic policy.

1   Evolution of the state sector's deficit

We shall start by giving an overall view of the evolution of the state
sector's total deficit and its composition; then we shall examine its
components.

As can be seen in Table 5.III, the total deficit of the state sector
expanded at a very rapid rate (by 145.3 per cent in 1971 and by 76.0 per
cent in 1972, in real terms). The 1972 total deficit of the state in 1972
was more than four times the 1970 level (in real terms). In fact, the 1972
total deficit of the state sector was equivalent to approximately 20 per
cent of total Gross Domestic Product that year.

The 1971 rise in the state deficit was due mainly to the increase in the
central government's fiscal deficit; it should be noted, however, that as
this classification reflects the accounting definition, an important part of
the fiscal deficit goes to transfers to decentralized entities and
traditional state enterprises. Over 55 per cent of the increase in the
state deficit in 1972 is explained by the deficit of the recently acquired
social property enterprises.

2   The Fiscal Sector

(i)   Larger Fiscal Deficit than Programmed

We shall first examine the main factors which explain the fact that the
effective fiscal deficit was so much larger than programmed, trying to
distinguish between those elements determined by opposition action, those
determined by the government's actions, and those dependent on other
factors.

To understand Table 5.IV, certain information about the budgetary process is
necessary.

There are two types of expenditure bills which the executive presents to

TABLE 5.III

TOTAL DEFICIT OF THE STATE SECTOR

		Millions of 1972 Escudos			Real growth rates	
		1970	1971	1972	1971/70	1972/71
I	Central Government (Fiscal Deficit)	6,152.7	22,283.5	26,575.4	262.2%	19.3%
II	Decentralized agencies and Traditional State Enterprises Deficit	6,570.5	8,994.7	15,047.8	35.8%	68.6%
III	Total Public Sector Deficit (a)	12,723.2	31,208.2	41,523.2	145.3%	33.1%
	Social Property Enterprises Deficit (b)	-	-	13,400.2	-	-
IV	Total State Sector Deficit (c)	12,723.2	31,208.2	54,923.4	145.3%	76.0%

(a) These data reflect the accounting deficits; it follows the categories with which the Executive presented each year the Central Government's Budget to Congress for its approval, the yearly reports of the Ministry of Finance used the same categories.

The deficits or surpluses effectively generated in the "Central Government Sector" and the "Decentralized Entities and State Enterprises" were estimated to reach the following levels:

	Millions of 1972 Escudos		
Surplus or Deficit ( )	1970	1971	1972
Central Government Surplus	12,196.3	6,824.3	1,864.2
Decentralized Entities and State Enterprises Deficit	(24,919.5)	(38,033.0)	(43,388.1)
Total Public Sector Deficit	(12,723.2)	(31,208.2)	(41,523.2)

In these figures, the Central Government result is a Surplus, as it excludes the Transfers to Decentralized Entities and State Enterprises Deficit.

(b) Social Property Enteprises refers to those enterprises nationalized during the Popular Unity Government; they include the large copper companies. Traditional State Enterprises refers to those belonging to the State, before 1970.

(c) The term "State Sector" was coined here for analytical purposes; it includes some enterprises, classified as Social Property Enterprises, which legally were not owned by the State. The size of the "State Sector" varies for each year as new Social Property Enterprises were incorporated into it.

Sources: Balance Consolidado del Sector Público de Chile, Años 71-72 - Enero - Sept. 1972 y Período 1970 - Sept. 1973. Ministerio de Hacienda. Santiago de Chile, 1975 and Exposición sotre el Estado de la Hacienda Pública presentado por el Ministro de Hacienda Contralmirante don Lorenzo Gotuzzo. Octubre 1973. Ministerio de Hacienda and International Monetary Fund. Chile - Recent Economic Developments. March, 1975. (This latter document provided the date for the Social Property Enterprises, which is unavailable or unclear in the Chilean sources quoted above.)

TABLE 5.IV

FISCAL RESULTS - PROGRAMMED AND EFFECTIVE, 1970-72

(Millions of 1972 Escudas)

	1970		1971		1972	
	Budgeted (1)	Effective (2)	Budgeted (3)	Effective (4)	Budgeted (5)	Effective (6)
Total Fiscal Incomes	40,409.3	41,219.3	53,005.3	42,540.0	39,447.8	38,375.1
Total Fiscal Expenditure (a)	42,216.2	47,372.0	63,731.6	64,823.5	51,758.2	64,950.5
Total Deficit	1,806.9	6,152.7	10,726.3	22,283.5	12,310.4	26,575.4

Larger Deficit than Programmed (Percentual Composition)

	1971 (b) (7)	1972 (c) (8)
Lower Incomes than Programmed	91.0	9.0
Larger Expenditure than Programmed	9.0	91.0
Total Larger Deficit	100.0	100.0

Sources: Exposición sobre el Estado de la Hacienda Publica. Presentada por el Ministro de Hacienda Contralmirante don Lorenzo Gotuzzo Borlando Oct. 1973, op.cit. above. The data (presented in millions of Escudos of each year) have been converted to 1972 millions with the same deflator indexes used in Balance Consolidado del Sector Publico, op.cit.

(a) Total Fiscal Expenditure includes both Current and Capital Expenditure.

(b) Based on columns (3) and (4).

(c) Based on columns (5) and (6).

Congress.   One of them is the budget law itself; the expenditures and
revenues presented by the Executive have to be approved by Congress. If the
Congress does not approve in time the proposal of the Executive, this
proposal automatically becomes law.   Therefore, the resulting deficits are
those programmed by the Executive.

There is another type of Expenditure Bill, called Re-adjustment Law, which
is devoted to financing wage and salary increases, which compensate for
inflation. The executive has no legal power to impose the financing of this
project. Congress may use different mechanisms, described below, to reduce
the financing of these re-adjustment laws.   As inflation accelerated in
1972, an additional re-adjustment law had to be passed towards the end of
the year.   This explains the fact that effective expenditure is so much
higher than budgeted expenditure.

In both 1971 and 1972, the budget or programmed deficit was less than half
the effective fiscal deficit.   In 1971, the budgeted fiscal deficit
accounted for only 48 per cent the effective deficit. As will be discussed
later, this budgeted deficit would not have caused large monetary
disequilibria.

As can be seen in Table 5.IV, 91 per cent of the 'Larger Deficit than
Programmed' occurred because effective revenues were substantially smaller
than those budgeted by the Executive; these smaller revenues (78 per cent)
were explained mainly by the fact that taxes yielded less than expected by
the Executive; the rest (22 per cent) was caused by Congress's refusal to
finance a significant part of the re-adjustment law[74].

We shall examine which taxes yielded less than programmed by the Executive,
and the reasons for this lower yield. Copper taxation fell far below its
programmed level. As there was no repatriation of profits by the foreign
copper companies, the Treasury received no taxation for this item. The main
reason for this was the sharp fall in the price of copper[75].

The tax on tax debtors also gave a far lower yield than had been budgeted.
The yield of this tax was over-estimated, mainly because the Treasury
officials who projected it did not realize that the number of tax inspectors
available was insufficient for the magnitude of the task attempted.
(Information based on interview material.)

Even though some taxes yielded less than programmed, due partly to the
errors of projection and decisions mentioned above, some successful efforts
were made by the Executive to increase taxation. These initiatives were
taken mainly in direct taxation; higher rates in business income tax and on
property tax were introduced and a new tax on the capital of incorporated
companies was established[76].   In the field of indirect taxation, efforts
centred on reducing evasion. No precise estimate was made of the net effect
on tax increases of these modifications. However, most of the increases
which occurred in direct taxation can be attributed to them[77]. The sharp
growth in indirect taxation can only be partly attributed to the efforts
made by the Treasury, being mainly explained by the increase in the level of
economic activity.

TABLE 5.V

TAXATION REVENUES

Millions of 1972 Escudos

Taxation Revenue		1970	1971	1972
1.	Direct Taxes	16,361.2	13,964.7	10,047.6
(a)	Income	8,037.6	10,835.4	8,257.4
	(i) Business	(4,547.6)	(4,433.9)	(2,779.3)
	(ii) Personal	(3,590.0)	(6,401.5)	(5,478.1)
(b)	Property	1,704.5	2,280.3	1,605.9
(c)	Copper	6,619.1	849.0	120.2
2.	Indirect Taxes	22,739.7	26,320.3	26,097.7
(a)	Sales taxes	10,129.2	13,602.8	13,325.1
(b)	Excise tax	2,952.9	3,417.3	4,442.3
(c)	Service turnover tax	2,883.1	2,906.1	2,665.4
(d)	Stamp tax	2,116.8	2,226.0	1,878.4
(e)	Import duties	4,371.0	4,153.8	3,776.3
(f)	Others	286.7	14.3	10.2
Total Taxation		39,100.9	40,285.0	36,145.3

Source: Balance Consolidado del Sector Público, op.cit.

Some sources claim that further efforts could have been made by the Executive to increase taxation by using existing laws[78]. The most important example given is that Inland Revenue should have used its legal faculty to revalue all territorial property. These criticisms are not valid, as it was not feasible to carry out this general revaluation; according to the existing law, the revaluation could not be carried out for all territorial property, but had to be done case by case. The team available could not have advanced at a much quicker pace than that actually achieved during 1971[79]. It was therefore difficult to increase tax revenue by this mechanism; any additional increase would have been very marginal.

As mentioned, 22 per cent of the 'Lower Revenue than Programmed' was explained by the fact that Congress refused to finance a significant part of the readjustment law. The opposition used different mechanisms to reduce the revenues approved. One was delaying the approval of the law and its financing; this caused loss of revenues in those taxes without retroactive effect (particularly indirect taxes). Another mechanism used was the rejection of certain taxation proposals presented by the Executive to Congress; sometimes these proposals were replaced by fictitious financing (that is, by sources of finance which could not and did not yield what Congress estimated).

Nine per cent of the 'Larger Deficit than Programmed' is explained by larger expenditure than programmed (see Table 5.IV). As will be detailed below, this larger expenditure was basically determined by higher wage increases than initially agreed upon.

As the government saw that taxation was yielding less revenue than programmed, it attempted to launch a programme for curtailing fiscal spending. These attempts were unsuccessful as public expenditure decisions were very decentralized, making it extremely difficult to reverse a tendency which had been so vigorously followed. Furthermore, not enough political support and priority was given to this task by the government as a whole.

We shall summarize the elements which in 1971 caused the effective fiscal deficit to more than double the programmed one. The main reason was that taxes yielded less than programmed, basically as a result of an accidental element (the fall in the price of copper), of policy decisions (i.e. non-devaluation and policy in relation to copper companies) and of errors of projection. A relatively small part of the explanation lies in the Congress's refusal to finance the readjustment bills.

The Executive made some relatively fruitful efforts to increase taxation. There seems to have been little margin left for additional taxation initiatives within the existing legislation and given staff limitations. However, the Executive did not display great initiative in presenting taxation bills to Congress, nor did it make a political issue of the fact that the opposition in Congress rejected or delayed the approval of some of its proposals.

Thus, even though relatively efficient, the Executive did not do all that it could have done, given that it had programmed such high levels of expenditure and that revenue was falling behind the projected levels. Probably the main explanation for this lies in the fact that at the time the government was not giving high priority to financial issues, as its main efforts were focused elsewhere, particularly on structural reforms. Lack of experience in dealing with problems in the financial sphere both at the executive and technical level provide a secondary explanation.

We shall now examine why in 1972 the effective deficit again more than doubled the programmed fiscal deficit.

A minor part of the 'Larger Deficit than Programmed' was caused by the fact that fiscal incomes were smaller than programmed. In fact, 1972 total fiscal income, in real terms, was below the 1971 level (see Table 5.IV.)[80] This fall is attributable in part to the financial policies followed both in 1971 and in 1972.

Accelerating inflation had a negative effect on direct taxation revenue. Income tax in Chile was applied on the former year's income readjusted by that year's inflation. As inflation accelerated sharply, taxation yield in real terms fell., In relation to property taxes the problem was even more serious. In Chile rateable values were not readjusted periodically, but once every five years. In periods of sharp inflation, these rateable values became much lower than the real value. Furthermore, there was a sharp fall in the direct taxation paid by the recently nationalized enterprises. As the effects of the price policy and of the sharp increases in wages were felt (for details, see below), profits - and the tax on profits - fell drastically.

The increasing importance of black markets affected indirect taxation yield. Even though in 1972, production of goods and services was increasing, the yield of sales tax and services turnover tax fell (see Table 5.V).

Finally, there was an 'extra-economic' or 'purely political' reason for the fall in taxation: the bosses' strike, organized by the opposition. The smaller taxation yield due to the direct effect of the bosses' strike was estimated by the Minister of Finance to have been E. 1,000 million[81] (this would be equal to the lower income than programmed for that year - see Table

5.IV).

The main part of the 1972 'Larger Deficit than Programmed' is attributable
to the fact that the readjustment bills were passed by Congress with huge
deficits. Congress refused to finance 72 per cent of the initial Law of
Readjustment[82]. As inflation accelerated (an effect of the disequilibria
which began in 1971), the government introduced extraordinary readjustment
laws to finance new wage increases, which would compensate the loss of
workers' real incomes[83].   Over 90 per cent of the expenditure resulting
from these additional readjustment laws was not financed by taxes[84].
Practically all the taxation initiatives presented by the Executive to
finance these bills were rejected by Congress. Several of these rejected
initiatives - such as modifications proposed on the territorial tax and
readjustment of property values - would have given a high yield;
furthermore, they had the advantage (from Popular Unity's point of view) of
being strongly progressive, affecting mainly the wealthiest strata.

Given that the political contradictions and the level of class struggle were
increasing sharply during 1972, the opposition's attitude in Congress was
functional to its interests.   On the one hand, it was defending the
interests of the wealthier groups; however, more significantly, it was
helping increase financial disequilibria, which weakened the government.

It seems that Popular Unity should have reacted more strongly to the
Opposition's attitude in Congress. It should have shown - by campaigns in
the media and amongst the trades unions - the clear class content of the
opposition's attitudes.   Even if this had not provoked changes in the
Congress' taxation decisions, it would have had an important pedagogic and
mobilizing effect among the workers and certain sectors of the middle class.
This kind of issue would have perhaps helped Popular Unity in regaining the
initiative of mass mobilization, which it was losing at the time.

It could be concluded that in 1972 a very substantial part of the 'Larger
Deficit than Programmed' was a reflection in the financial sphere of the
fact that the class struggle had become more intense and the opposition's
actions more aggressive.   Even though the larger deficit than programmed
occurred mainly as a direct effect of the opposition's actions in Congress,
the original cause was a large growth in public employees' nominal incomes,
due mainly to high inflation and, to a lesser extent, to the increase in
their real incomes.   Furthermore, it is not certain that, had the
Executive's taxation initiatives been completely approved, they would have
yielded enough to cover the whole additional increase in expenditure.

We saw that in 1971 Popular Unity did not take all the taxation initiatives
which were viable. Popular Unity did display abundant taxation initiatives
in 1972, but all were rejected by Congress. It was therefore relatively
wasteful to have spent so much technical effort in the field of taxation
initiatives in 1972.

To diminish financial disequilibria, the Executive should have concentrated
- even more in 1972 - on the use of policy instruments, which it could
manage without needing to obtain the opposition's approval in Congress (i.e.
price and interest rate policies).

(ii) Rapid growth of Fiscal Deficit and of Fiscal Expenditure

Having examined why the fiscal deficit more than doubled the programmed one,
we shall now examine the elements which determined its rapid growth.

The rapid growth in the fiscal deficit was caused by the fact that while
fiscal current revenue fell somewhat between 1970 and 1972, (for reasons
described above) fiscal expenditure grew sharply (see Table 5.VI).   The

growth in real total fiscal expenditure was caused by the increase in current expenditure, which grew by 43.1 per cent in 1971 and by 8.2 per cent in 1972. Real capital expenditure grew in 1971, but fell in 1972 to slightly below its 1970 level.

The growth in current fiscal expenditure is explained basically by increases in payments to public employees. As can be seen in Table 5.VI, during 1971 real wages and salaries grew by 25.4 per cent. Payments to Social Security and Family Allowances in real terms grew much faster, at 75.2 per cent. The agreement between the Central Unica de Trabajadores (the Chilean TUC) and the government included very high increases in the family allowances of state employees, particularly for the lower paid ones (for example, manual workers in the state sector had their family allowances doubled).

If we add the growth of wages, social security and family allowances and the part of the increase in transfers to public and private sector which goes to increases in payments to labour[85], these items total 65 per cent of the increase in total fiscal expenditure.

Furthermore, these figures show that total real income paid to public employees increased in real terms during 1971 by 48 per cent. As employment grew by approximately four per cent per public employee, real income increased by 44 per cent.

It can be concluded that the wages policy applied in 1971 to the public sector was a) the main element which explained the rapid growth of fiscal expenditure, and b) implied a very significant increase in public employees' real income.

In 1972, even though total real fiscal expenditure remained constant, payments to public employees increased again. Wages and salaries grew by 11.7 per cent. If one includes family allowances, social security payments and transfers to the public and private sector, incomes paid to public employees grew by 12.5 per cent[86,87]. As employment did not grow, this means that real income per public employee increased by the same percentage.

It is noteworthy that even though there was such a large state deficit in 1972 and fiscal incomes were falling, real incomes paid per public employee were still growing at a significant rate.

The main part of these high increases in wages and salaries correspond to the re-adjustments agreed upon by the Central Unica de Trabajadores and the government. However, the effective increases greatly exceeded the original agreements. In 1971 the wage and salaries re-adjustment initially agreed upon implied an average increase of 35 per cent; the effective increase reached approximately 48 per cent (both percentages are in nominal terms)[88]. Therefore 25 per cent of the wage and salary increase and 16 per cent of the increase in fiscal expenditure are explained by the amount by which effective payments to public employees exceeded the rates initially agreed[89].

Thus, the wage policy pursued in the public sector can be criticized on the following grounds:

(a) The initial increase granted by the government in its agreement with the Central Única de Trabajadores seems excessive (it implied a very high real growth of income per public employee for 1971). The aims of economic recovery, income redistribution and widening political support could have been attained with lower increases in workers' incomes. The government should at least have attempted to impose less ambitious targets in its negotiations with the workers.

TABLE 5.VI

FISCAL INCOMES AND EXPENDITURE — ORIGIN OF THE FISCAL DEFICIT, 1970-72 (a)

	Millions of Escudos of 1972			% of variation (in 1972 Escudos)		
	1970	1971	1972	1971/70	1972/71	1972/70
I Current Revenue	41,219.3	42,540.0	38,375.1	3.2	-9.8	-6.9
1. Tax revenue	39,100.7	40,285.0	36,145.3	3.0	-10.3	-7.6
2. Non-tax revenue	2,118.4	2,255.0	2,229.8	6.4	-1.1	5.3
II Current Expenditure	32,789.4	46,934.2	50,799.9	43.1	8.2	54.9
1. Wages and salaries	12,771.3	16,016.6	17,884.7	25.4	11.7	40.0
2. Purchases of goods and services	2,317.2	2,679.9	2,890.9	15.7	7.9	24.8
3. Social Security and Family Allowances (b)	5,776.3	10,122.1	10,079.6	75.2	-0.4	74.5
4. Transfer to Public and Private Sector	10,764.8	17,020.8	19,588.3	58.1	15.0	81.9
5. Interests of the Public Debt	1,159.8	1,094.8	356.4	-5.6	-67.4	-69.3
III Current account deficit (-) or surplus	8,429.9	-4,394.2	-12,424.8			
IV Capital expenditure (c)	14,582.6	17,889.3	14,150.6	22.7	-20.9	-3.0
Fiscal investment	11,508.8	14,518.2	12,924.7	26.1	-11.0	12.3
Debt amortization	3,073.8	3,371.1	1,225.9			
V Total expenditure (II + IV)	47,372.0	64,823.5	64,950.5	36.8	0.2	37.1
VI Total deficit (-) or surplus (III + IV)	-6,152.7	-22,283.5	-26,575.4			
VII Financing	5,994.7	22,371.7	28,675.5	273.2	28.2	378.3
1. Internal Borrowing	5,207.0	21,110.7	27,560.2	305.4	30.6	429.3
2. External Borrowing	267.7	352.9	97.5	31.8	-72.4	-63.6
3. Others	520.0	908.1	1,017.8	174.6	11.2	195.7
VIII Cash Variations	158.0	-88.2	-2,100.1			

(a)   Primary information taken from <u>Balance Consolidado del Sector Público
      de Chile, Años 71-72 Enero-Sept. 1973 y Período 1970 - Sept. 1973</u>
      op.cit. above.

(b)   The item social security includes both contributions to the social
      security system (of the State as employer) and payments to private
      recipients.   It includes the contributions which the Central
      Government pays for the Decentralized Entities and State Enterprises.

(c)   Includes part of the capital expenditure carried out in the
      Decentralized Entities and State Enterprises.

(b)   When these high levels of re-adjustment had been agreed upon, they
should have been linked to a commitment by the Central Unica de Trabajadores
that there would be no further demands during the year. No reference at all
was made to wage restraint in the above-mentioned agreement.

An alternative (or additional) clause could have accepted further wage and
salary increases to public employees only if additional taxation were
approved to finance it. This would have limited the inflationary potential
of further wage increases.   Were the opposition to have rejected these
higher taxes (as probably would have occurred), the burden of political
responsibility in limiting wage increases would have been transferred to the
opposition.

It seems evident that Popular Unity should have used more influence on the
trade union movement in attempting to achieve wage restraint, particularly
for the public sector.

There were elements which would have made this feasible. The Left had a
strong representation amongst the Councillors of the Central Única de
Trabajadores[90]. At the beginning of 1971, the two main Marxist parties -
Communists and Socialists - controlled 75 per cent of the Councillors. If
the Radicals (most of whom supported Popular Unity) and other Left-wing
parties were added, then this 'Broad Front' would have controlled 89 per
cent of the Councillors[91].

However, no serious attempt to impose restraint on wage demands was made by
the Popular Unity political leadership.   Both during the presidential
campaign and in the first year of government, emphasis was mainly on income
redistribution and income increases for the workers, rarely on the limits
which these increases should have. It was only later - in 1972 - that the
government and the Popular Unity political leadership made more attempts to
emphasize wage restraint[92].   However, as we saw, at that time workers'
incomes had already grown substantially.

It should be pointed out that had Popular Unity seriously attempted to
control increases in public employees' real income, the effectiveness of
such an attempt would have been limited by several factors. One was the
date at which elections were to be held for the new Central Única de
Trabajadores (May 1972). The traditional economicism of trade union leaders
- shared by those adhering both to the Popular Unity and Opposition parties
- tended to be exacerbated before such elections. Furthermore, there were
features which made it particularly difficult to control wage and salary
increases amongst public employees. In the Chilean public sector, many
public agencies are autonomous and can defeat government wage policies by
such tactics as increasing the number and type of promotions granted, the
amount of overtime allowed, and the attainment of additional benefits.
Furthermore, income differentials between institutions had traditionally
created competition between them (to increase, diminish or maintain these

differentials) which inevitably led to increases beyond those fixed by government policy[93].

Also, the nature of the workers' organization in the public sector made it more difficult for the Popular Unity government to impose a policy of wage restraint.   There was the curious paradox that as trade unions were not legal in the state sector, the 'associations' which performed their functions were not subject to the manifold restrictions of the labour code. A very high percentage (approximately 90) of public employees belonged to these union-like organizations.   Many of them had constituted large and powerful federations, which had the advantage, denied to other Chilean workers, of one employer with whom to negotiate - an employer used to spending more than he received.

Finally, the political affiliations of public employees differed from those of the rest of the workers. In the public sector, the two strongest parties were the Radicals and the Christian Democrats.   Naturally the Opposition Christian Democrat trade union leaders wished to increase their popularity by demanding high wage increases, which would surpass the limits set by the government.   The majority of the Radical Party supported the Popular Unity alliance; however, it probably would not have been eager to impose curbs on wage demands.   The Radical Party did not have as much discipline as other parties (i.e. Communists).   Furthermore, radical unionists were not very ideologically motivated; much of the public employees' support of the Radicals was based on the wish to maintain an income differential with workers from other sectors of the population, a wish which the Radicals had traditionally supported.

3   Decentralized Entities and Traditional State Enterprises

The tendencies in this sector follow a similar pattern - and as was explained above are to a great extent included - in the trends analyzed for the fiscal sector; for data, see Table 5.VII, main figures and those in note (a).

We shall analyze briefly the evolution of the traditional state enterprises' finance. This analysis throws light not only on the financial situation of the traditional state enterprises, but also on the nationalized enterprises, as the financial policies applied in the recently nationalized sector follow a similar pattern to those of the former. The advantage in analyzing state enterprises is that they have the same coverage during the whole period 1970-72.   In the case of nationalized enterprises, the coverage varies substantially as the sector grew drastically during the period; this makes a comparative study of its financial evolution extremely difficult. Another element is that the information for state enterprises - traditionally compiled and published by the Studies Department of the Ministry of Finance - is more reliable than that available for the newly nationalized enterprises.

TABLE 5.VII

EVOLUTION OF SOME FINANCIAL VARIABLES FOR STATE ENTERPRISES, 1970-72[a]

	Millions of 1972 Escudos			Real growth rates	
	1970	1971	1972	1971/70	1972/71
Total payments to employees and workers[b]	5,012	7,026	7,383	40.2%	5.1%
Sales of goods and services	10,935	13,160	11,653	20.3%	-11.4%

(a)   Source: Primary information based on Balance Consolidado del Sector Público de Chile ......, op.cit.

(b)   Includes wages and salaries, payments for social security and family allowances.

An explanation of the growth in the state enterprises' deficit during the period 1970-72 can be seen clearly in Table 5.VII. In 1971, expenditure for payments to public employees and workers grew by 40.2 per cent in real terms; increases for sales of goods and services grew by a mere 20.3 per cent; in 1972, payments to workers and public employees grew by 5.1 per cent, whereas incomes for sales of goods and services fell by 11.4 per cent.

The growth in incomes from sales of goods and services which did occur in 1971 was mainly due to production increases. Output in state controlled enterprises grew by 14.9 per cent[94]. In 1972 incomes from sales of goods and services fell by 11.4 per cent even though output grew by at least four per cent[95]. This fall is explained by the sharp decline – in real terms – of state enterprises' prices. In 1972, inflation reached 163.4 per cent. Many prices of state controlled enterprises were frozen at the 1970 or 1971 level till July or September 1972; other prices in state-controlled enterprises grew at a much slower rate than the average price index for industrial goods.

A few examples of the evolution of prices for state enterprises are given in Table 5.VIII, which shows that the main factors which determined the growth of the deficit in state enterprises was an extremely rapid growth in nominal and real wages accompanied by a fall in real terms – of state enterprises' prices.

TABLE 5.VIII

PRICE INDEXES[a]

	1970	1971	1972
Oil products (ENAP)	100.0	100.9	142.6
Electricity (ENDESA)	100.0	105.5	122.6
General wholesale index for industrial products	100.0	113.9	189.3

(a)   Source: World Bank. Special Report on the Chilean Economic Outlook. Vol.III. Report No. 551-CH. Table 9.8. Washington, October, 1974.

4   Deficit of Social Property Enterprises

The deficit of the newly nationalized enterprises assumed rapidly growing importance in the total state deficit. As can be seen from data in Table 5.III, in 1972, growth in the nationalized enterprises' deficit accounted for over 55 per cent of the growth in the total state sector deficit. By 1973 the deficit of these enterprises represented over 35 per cent of the total deficit for the state sector[96].

The main factors which determine the deficit in nationalized industries are similar to those in state enterprises: the wage and price policies pursued. There are, however, other elements which contribute to explain the high deficits of the nationalized industries; one element is inefficiency – both at the level of the enterprise and at the level of the planning and financial institutions in charge of these enterprises. Another element was the initial need to replace the working capital which the capitalists had taken out of their enterprises before they were nationalized.

Payments to labour seem to have increased even more rapidly than in the rest
of the public sector, due to the excellent bargaining position of the
workers.   The government, anxious to avoid conflicts, offered little
resistance to the workers' demands.   These demands were stimulated by
Popular Unity trade union leaders eager to show their followers the
immediate benefits of nationalization.   They were fomented by the opposition
which supported virtually all wage claims presented in the social property
enterprises[97].   It was obviously politically convenient for the opposition
to press for higher wages.   If these were not granted, they could provoke
strikes, thus affecting the level of production and projecting a negative
image of the nationalized sector.   If these high wage demands were granted,
the opposition could later criticize the government for the decreasing
profits or increasing losses of nationalized industries.

Obviously Popular Unity should have attempted to exercize greater restraint
on wage increases.   At the same time, Popular Unity trade union leaders and
managers of nationalized enterprises should have stressed the great
non-economic advantages which workers were obtaining from nationalization,
such as participation in decision-making.   Instead, most of them preferred
to compete with each other or with the opposition for higher wages.   Some
managers of nationalized enterprises went as far as granting higher wage
increases than were demanded by the workers[98].

Managers and trade union leaders of nationalized enterprises also competed
with each other to grant a wide range of fringe benefits to their workers.
Child care, medical and dental centres were installed in many nationalized
industries; subsidized meals were served at the workplace.   These efforts to
achieve much needed improvements in working conditions naturally had a large
impact on the enterprises' costs.   It could be said that Popular Unity trade
union leaders and managers thought they could offer in _advance_ many of the
economic advantages, the real base for which could only be provided by
future sustained socialist development.

These high wage increases were accompanied by a policy of nearly complete
price freezing.   Most prices of nationalized enterprises did not increase at
all or grew very marginally from November 1970 till July 1972, whereas the
general price index grew by 51.2 per cent during that period.

The main reason why prices of state-controlled enterprises were not
increased before was linked to lack of political definition within Popular
Unity.   Unfortunately, discussions on prices in the newly nationalized and
traditional state enterprises were nearly always linked to broader political
discussions within Popular Unity, such as the speed and scope of the
nationalization process.   As the decisions on price policy were presented as
part of a broader discussion, the issue became political and not technical.
As there was no agreement about the general strategic issues, decisions were
not taken on more specific aspects, on which there was agreement amongst the
different groups.

After 1971, the group of economists headed by the Minister of Economic
Affairs, Pedro Vuskovic, proposed to increase prices of nationalized
enterprises so as to alter the relative prices between state controlled and
private industry.   This would strengthen the state enterprises and stop the
undesired transfer to surplus from the state to private industry.   Also
after 1971, the other group - headed by the Minister of Finance - proposed
to increase both prices for state-controlled enterprises and for the private
sector.   While this would imply a higher level of inflation in the meantime,
it was seen as reducing future inflationary pressures.   Therefore, both
groups agreed that it was correct, desirable and urgent to increase prices
in nationalized enterprises.   However, this important decision was delayed,
as the discussions between both groups were centred on broader, more
ideological issues; even non-ideological technical issues were discussed

with sectarianism.

The excessive deficits of - and the resulting credits to - nationalized
enterprises, were accepted without much difficulty due to the attitude and
behaviour of the monetary authorities.

Even though government officials established formal limits to global and
sectoral credit expansion, these limits had no true political support from
the government executives or from the political leadership. (This attitude
seems to have been influenced by the implicit belief amongst many government
officials that structural changes would easily allow the elimination of
inflation; this implied that monetary policy had secondary importance.
Furthermore, the emphasis on structural changes deflected attention and
operative capacity from the short-term policy centres and issues. As we saw
above, this was perhaps most serious in the case of the Central Bank, whose
executives were often more occupied with bank nationalization and
restructuring of the banking system than with credit and monetary policy.)
The limits to credit expansion were therefore being continuously exceeded as
a result of pressures from different sectors.

Thus, at the beginning of 1972, the Central Bank and the Ministry of Finance
agreed that a total of E 3,000 million would be granted during the year to
cover total deficit for Social Area Enterprises. By May 1972, it was
recognized that this limit would be widely exceeded; officials from the
Studies Department of the Central Bank proposed a limit for the year of
E 6,000 million. The effective level of credit granted was equivalent to
E 14,700 million[99].

It is true that part of the deficit in the social property enterprises was
an inevitable result of nationalization and of the financial policies
pursued by the government. However, had definite limits been set on credit
expansion, the enterprises would have been obliged to reduce inefficiency,
and above all to control excessive wage increases. Furthermore, the
nationalized enterprises would have demanded from the corresponding
government authorities an increase in prices; this might have forced the
government to change its price policy earlier.

Even if adequate political support to credit constraints had been given
there would have been great difficulties in establishing an adequate system
of financial evaluation at sectoral and enterprise level. First, there were
the inevitable problems of lack of information and technical skill, at both
enterprise and government level. This was made worse by a maze of
controlling institutions which did not work in a co-ordinated way[100].
Lack of co-ordination, even amongst financial institutions, is illustrated
by the fact that during the first half of 1972 the Central Bank granted
E 600 million less of credit to the Social Area than had been authorized by
the Ministry of Finance. The cuts were made by the Central Bank as it was
clear that there was an over-estimation of the enterprises' credit needs.
(Information based on personal experience, as Head of Department of Credit
to State and Nationalized Enterprises, at Central Bank.)

Second, it was practically impossible for the supervisory and planning
institutions - under the circumstances - to evaluate and control yearly
budgets. The enterprises could not elaborate precise budgets as they could
not predict the general level of inflation even approximately; neither were
prices or investments policy for the nationalized sector fixed in advance by
the government. By 1972, inflation was soaring and relative prices were
changing rapidly; it was virtually impossible to distinguish what part of
cost increases originated in growing inefficiency and what part in
inflation.

5   Brief summary

It can be concluded that financial disequilibria in the public sector are
explained by two basic elements.   One element is the form in which the
government was obliged to 'redistribute income'.   On the one hand, large
improvements were made in public employees' real incomes.   On the other, the
opposition had sufficient political power to block the taxation measures
which would have allowed for income to be transferred from the wealthy
groups to the workers.

A second element was the price policy pursued in state and nationalized
enterprises.   This was determined mainly by the lack of political clarity
within Popular Unity and by the form in which decisions were taken within
the government.   The policy of low prices in state and nationalized
enterprises basically implied a transfer of resources from the public to the
private sector.   Its redistributive effect – in terms of classes – was not
so clear.   It partly favoured consumers in general.   It seems to have
favoured most those private enterprises which bought goods and services
produced by the state sector as inputs or those which distributed
state-produced goods and services, and increased their prices rapidly in
response to the excessive demand prevalent since the end of 1971.

III   Evolution of money

We shall now describe how the financial disequilibria, which were borne
mainly in the public sector, influenced the evolution of money.   It should
be noted first that, as in most underdeveloped countries, in Chile fiscal
and monetary policy were much more directly linked than in developed
countries, due to the practical non-existence of a capital market where the
government could finance its deficit.   In Chile at the time, dealings by the
public in treasury bills, saving bonds and readily marketable securities
were virtually non-existent.   Mainly because there were no developed
financial markets, interest rates were fixed institutionally, bearing no or
little relationship to the evolution of the money supply.   These
circumstances have important consequences for the operation of the economy;
the demand for money is primarily a transactions demand and, moreover, where
the asset motives exist, they are usualy satisfied by investment in real as
opposed to financial assets.   This implies that in such economies, the
impact of increases in the money stock on increased expenditure of goods and
services and real assets is more certain and direct than in developed
economies, with sophisticated capital markets, where the effect seems to be
transmitted indirectly, basically via changes in the structure of interest
rates.   Naturally, this argument is reinforced for underdeveloped economies
with very high rates of inflation or hyperinflation, as any existent 'demand
for money for speculation' would immediately disappear as a result of the
high inflation.

As can be seen in Table 5.IX, during the period 1970-72, money issue and
money held by the private sector grew at an extraordinarily fast pace.

TABLE 5.IX

EVOLUTION OF MONETARY VARIABLES, 1970-73(a)

Annual growth rate of money issue (b)		Annual growth rate of money held by the private sector (c)	Annual % variation of banking multiplier
1970	70.3	51.8	-10.9
1971	132.7	119.0	-5.9
1972	174.4	138.8	-13.0

(a) Source: Ernesto Miranda, op.cit.

(b) This variable refers to the quantity of money issued by the Central Bank.

(c) This variable refers to notes and coins plus bank deposits; it was chosen because of its direct impact on the private sector's aggregate demand. Money in the hands of the public sector has a much slower rotation; furthermore, expenditure of the public sector is determined by variables other than the money in its account.

The growth of money in the hands of the private sector during 1971 more than doubled the 1970 growth rate[101]. During the period 1970-73 the quantity of money held by the private sector increased by 995 per cent.

The rapid growth in money issue was mainly caused by the public deficit. In 1971, 97 per cent of the money issue was oriented towards financing the public sector; in 1972, 99 per cent of the money issue went to this purpose.

We shall examine in some detail the monetary evolution during 1971 and 1972[102]. First, we shall describe the origins of adjusted money issue for 1971. As can be seen from Table 5.X, operations with Treasury account for 75 per cent of the adjusted money issue. The growth of internal credit explains 22 per cent[103] and foreign exchange operations three per cent. Fiscal deficit financing increased its importance significantly in relation to 1970.

Even though practically all the money issue was oriented towards financing the public sector, it is interesting to note that a large proportion of the Public Deficit (40 per cent) was covered by sources other than money issue (see Table 5.XI, third column). Had these sources not been available, then the impact of the public deficit on the money issue in 1971 would have been even greater[104].

TABLE 5.X

ORIGINS OF ADJUSTED MONEY ISSUE (PERCENTAGE COMPOSITION) (a)

	Adjusted Money Issue	Exchange Operations	Internal Credit (Net Credit to Private Sector and Rest of Public)	Operations with Treasury (Net Credit to Central Government)
1970	100.0	8.4	36.5	55.1
1971	100.0	3.3	22.1	74.6
1972	100.0	−26.9	53.4	73.5

(a)   Source: Ernesto Miranda, op.cit. data based on Sintesis Monetaria, Departamente de Estudios, Banco Central.

As can be seen in Table 5.XI, an important part of the fiscal deficit was financed by other sources, mainly increases in debts to suppliers; the banking system played a minor role. In the case of the nationalized and state enterprises and decentralized institutions, other sources refers to the reduction in refinancing by the Central Bank to the banking system, which compensated for the expansion of credit to this sector by the Central Bank. Also, the banking system contributed an important amount towards financing this sector without additional growth in the money issue. Due to the rapid growth in the money supply, the banks had a quick increase in their own liquid resources; the growth of credit granted to the private sector was small. Therefore, the banks could finance credit expansion with their own resources, and thus a large expansion of credit was accompanied by a fall in refinancing needs from the Central Bank.

TABLE 5.XI

PUBLIC DEFICIT AND ITS FINANCING 1971

(Millions of Escudos)

	Fiscal Deficit	Deficit of Nationalized and State Enterprises and De-centralized Institutions	Public Deficit
Central Bank Credit (Money Issue)	(8,610.4)	(2,953.3)	(11,563.7)
Banking System	(873.2)	(2,421.6)	(3,394.8)
Total Monetary System	9,483.6	5,374.9	14,858.5
Other sources	3,099.4	1,373.1	4,472.5
Total Financing	12,583.0	6,748.0	19,331.0

(1)   Information elaborated on the basis of primary data taken from Ernesto Miranda, op.cit.

The quantity of money in the hands of the private sector can be estimated as the product of the adjusted money issue times the banking multiplier. As can be seen in Table 5.IX, the banking multiplier fell by 5.9 per cent in 1971.

The only factor which acted in the direction of reducing the banking multiplier was the sharp rise in the rate of effective reserves. This rise was explained by the quantitative control exerted by the Central Bank on the commercial banks' credit expansion. The Central Bank could have limited credit expansion to the private sector even further, as this sector had large excess liquidity as a result of the public sector deficit. This would have reduced the multiplier more, and thus diminished the impact of the money issue on the quantity of money in the hands of the private sector. However, the effect of a stricter control on the private sector would have been relatively marginal in 1971, as credit expansion to this sector was a small fraction of the total expansion of the monetary system.

Monetary evolution during 1972 will now be examined. As can be seen in Table 5.X, the growth in the adjusted money issue had a strong compensatory effect from foreign exchange operations (caused by the large balance of trade deficit). If one eliminates the effect of these exchange operations, 41 per cent of the money issue is explained by internal credit and 59 per cent by operations with Treasury; the proportions return to ratios similar to those in 1970. The main reason for this is the increased importance of the deficit of state and nationalized enterprises and decentralized institutions.

Again in 1972 practically all the money issue was devoted to covering the public sector deficit. Furthermore, as can be seen in Table 5.XII, most of the public deficit (73 per cent) was covered by money issue, a higher proportion than in 1971. Thus, in 1972 the public deficit had a much more direct impact on money issue, as alternative sources of finance were drying up.

TABLE 5.XII

PUBLIC DEFICIT AND ITS FINANCING, 1972 (a)

	Net Central Bank Credit (Money Issue)	Other Sources (b)	Total
Fiscal Deficit	23,917.6	2,319.9	26,648.0
Deficit of State and newly Nationalized Enterprises and Decentralized Institutions	18,215.0	12,765.7	30,980.7
Public Deficit	42,132.6 (73%)	15,085.6 (27%)	57,628.7 (100%)

(a) Information elaborated on the base of primary data, taken from Ernesto Miranda, op.cit.

(b) Includes Banking Credit and Credit of Suppliers. The primary data do not provide enough information to enable us to separate both categories.

The banking multiplier in 1972 fell by 13 per cent, a decrease much sharper than that of 1971 (see Table 5.IX). This was basically a random result of different phenomena, and not a result of deliberate policy actions. The fall in the multiplier is explained mainly by the strong increase in the public's preferred cash/deposit ratio[105] and of the ratio of money in the hands of the public sector to money in the hands of the private sector.

The increase in the public's preferred cash/deposit is explained mainly by changes in commercial habits (disappearance of consumer credit and demand of payment in notes), in the growing supply difficulties and in the steady growth of black markets[106]. The growth in the rate of effective reserves is explained by the measures of quantitative control of the banking sector's credit expansion. The increase in the money in the hands of the public sector is explained partly by the ease with which the Central Bank gave credit to the fiscal sector, which induced it to maintain a rather high level of deposits. Furthermore, due to the income redistribution measures already described, Social Security institutions were in a better financial position, allowing them to keep higher cash balances.

IV   Effects of the Short-term Economic Policy and
      Balance of Payments Evolution

The Chilean economy's initial response to the short-term economic policy launched by Popular Unity was extremely positive, both in terms of production growth and of improvement in income distribution.

As a result of the rapid expansion of aggregate demand, in 1971 production increased at a much higher rate than usual. Gross Domestic Product grew by 8.3 per cent (more than doubling the average growth rate of the previous five years, see Table 5.XIII.)

TABLE 5.XIII

EVOLUTION OF GROSS DOMESTIC PRODUCT, BY SECTOR.   ANNUAL GROWTH RATES

(percentages) (a)

Sector	1965-70	1971	1972	1973
Agriculture	3.0	5.1	-3.5	-14.6
Mining	4.9	1.7	-2.4	1.5
Manufacturing	3.6	12.9	3.5	-5.1
Construction	0.7	9.5	-9.7	-20.0
Sub-total goods	3.5	8.7	-1.0	-6.4
Sub-total basic services	3.8	4.8	2.5	-4.3
Sub-total other services	4.1	7.7	4.2	-0.7
Total	3.8	8.3	2.1	-4.1

(a)   Source: Economic Survey of Latin America 1973, United Nations, New York, 1975.

Manufacturing production grew even more rapidly — by 12.9 per cent responding to the high level of demand; construction also had a high growth rate (9.5 per cent), mainly due to public sector building. Unemployment fell rapidly; the rate of unemployment (for Gran Santiago) fell from 8.3 per cent in December 1970 to 3.8 per cent in December 1971.

Income distribution improved substantially. The share of payments to workers and employees in National Income increased from 52.3 per cent in 1970 to 61.7 per cent in 1971[107,108]. In the industrial sector, the improvement was even greater; the participation payments to labour increased from 41.6 per cent in 1970 to 54.8 per cent in 1971[109].

Even though in 1971 there was ample excessive aggregate demand, inflation in fact was reduced. The government was able to impose price controls on the private sector and to fix low or zero price increases for the state enterprises; the growth of wages and other costs was absorbed either by productivity increases and/or by a reduction of the profit margin.

TABLE 5.XIV

PERCENTAGE VARIATIONS OF PRICE INDEXES AND MONEY SUPPLY

(December to December variations) (a)

	1971	1972	1973
Retail price index	22.1	163.4	508.1 (b)
Wholesale price index	21.4	143.3	1,147.1
Money held by the private sector	134.3	151.8	362.9

(a)   Source: Banco Central de Chile. Boletín Mensual No. 599. Enero 1978.

(b)   According to most sources, the retail price index rose faster during 1973 than the one calculated by the National Statistical Institute, as this Institute did not incorporate properly the prices prevalent in the black markets. For example, the IMF Mission estimated that the retail price index during 1973 increased by 649.0 per cent. Source: Recent Economic Developments, IMF, Chile, March 1975 op.cit. The Inter-American Committee for the Alliance for Progress (CIAP) calculated an 'adjusted' index of consumer prices, which gave a 681.6 per cent increase for 1973. Source: El esfuerzo interno y las necesidades de financiamiento externo para el desarrollo de Chile CIAP/650, Jan. 1974.

In fact, in 1971, prices grew at a much slower pace than money supply (see Table 5.XIV). This can be explained by the sharp increase in the demand for money during 1971. Many of the factors which acted to increase the demand for money during 1971 had a 'once-for-all' effect. Other factors were completely reversible; while in 1971, they increased the demand for money, in later years they would decrease it.

In 1971, not only did output grow but also the aggregate supply of goods and services was temporarily further increased by a fall in industrial stocks and a growth of imports in consumer and intermediate goods (both had a 'once-for-all' effect).

There were additional factors which increased the demand for money during 1971. First, as the money supply grew, private credit contracted; during 1971 there was a gradual disappearance of credit to consumers and of suppliers' credit[110]. As the liquidity formerly created by the private sector disappeared, part of the increase in the money supply was absorbed without creating pressure on aggregate demand. This element had a 'once-for-all' effect; it was exhausted as soon as private credit disappeared (at the beginning of 1972).

Second, there was a change in the preferred ratio between liquid assets and fixed capital. Due to the uncertainty arising among the propertied class during and after the Presidential election[111], and as a result of the nationalization process, the preference for holding liquid assets in relation to fixed assets increased. As will be seen below, this factor acted only temporarily; as inflation and the cost of holding money increased, the demand for money caused by this factor was transformed to demand for other assets.

Furthermore, much of the potential inflationary pressure did not manifest itself in 1971 due to the lag between monetary fluctuations and their manifestation in the markets. The lag in the impact of monetary variations on price fluctuations is larger when there are administrative controls - such as price fixing - which delay the 'natural' price increase. Finally, expectations of inflation seemed to decline, particularly at the beginning of 1971.

We shall now examine the only negative element manifesting itself in the economy's evolution during 1971 - the balance of payments. As can be seen in Table 5.XV, in 1971, to the negative high level in the current account balance was added a negative result in the net external non-compensatory capital flows; as a result, net international reserves of the monetary system fell substantially.

TABLE 5.XV

BALANCE OF PAYMENTS, 1970-72

(millions of dollars) (a)

		1970	1971	1972
Current account balance		-114.0	-236.0	-638.8
Export of goods and services		1,267.0	1,132.0	965.2
Imports of goods and services		-1,202.0	-1,231.0	-1,463.0
Net remittances of profit and interest abroad		-179.0	-137.0	-141.0
Capital account		114.0	236.0	638.8
(a)	Net external non-compensatory capital	235.0	-31.0	301.7
i)	Direct investment	19.0	-42.0	-
ii)	Long and medium-term loans	380.0	245.0	318.8
iii)	Amortization payments	-140.0	-192.0	-23.1
iv)	Short-term liabilities	-24.0	-42.0	-
v)	Official transfer payments	-	-	6.0
(b)	Domestic non-compensatory capital or assets	-7.0	25.0	
(c)	Errors and omissions	-46.0	-22.0	-0.1
(d)	Allocation of S.D.R's	21.0	17.0	18.5
(e)	Net compensatory capital (increase or improvement)	-89.0	247.0	318.7
i)	Balance of Payments loans, trade arrears, deferred payments, IMF position and other liabilities	5.0	102.0	222.4
ii)	Amortization payments	-73.0	-40.0	-1.6
iii)	Movements of foreign official reserves	-21.0	185.0	97.9

(a)   Source: Economic Survey of Latin America, 1972, UN, New York, 1974,
      and Economic Survey of Latin America, 1973, UN, New York, 1975,
      quoting data from IMF Balance of Payments Yearbooks.

      Note: There are some slight discrepancies with Chilean Central Bank
      figures.

The 1971 current account deficit was very high, more than doubling the 1970
deficit. The value of exports fell, largely due to a sharp decrease in the
copper price. The price of copper on the London Metal Exchange, which
averaged 64.1 US cents per pound in 1970 (and 61.1 US cents per pound in

1965-70) fell to 49.3 US cents in 1971[112]. The current account also deteriorated because of the increase in imports; this was caused in 1971 both by increases in imports of consumer and intermediate goods (resulting from the expansion of aggregate demand and the ensuing increase in production), and by the increase in international prices of Chile's main imports.

As can be seen from Tables 5.XV and 5.II, net remittances of profit and interest abroad fell in 1971 in comparison both with the 1970 level and the 1966-70 average. This was the net result of two opposed tendencies. On the one hand, there was an increase in interest payments due to the growing burden of the external debt; on the other hand, as an effect of the nationalization of copper, there was a sharp fall in the remittances of profit to foreign capital.

The net external non-compensatory capital account also had a very important negative effect on the 1971 balance of payments. As can be seen from Tables 5.V and 5.II, this item passed from an average of + US $ 227 million in the period 1966-70 to - US $ 31.0 million in 1971. This variation occurred to a great extent as a consequence of the political goals of the Allende government and of the changes in property relations which this goal implied. As can be seen in Table 5.XV, the flow of foreign direct investment became negative in 1971. Short-term liabilities, mainly representing short-term banking credit, crucial for foreign trade, also fell sharply in 1971. Long and medium-term loans fell - in relation both to 1970 and to the 1966-70 average.

A further factor which explained the decline in the non-compensatory capital account during 1971 was the sharp increase in amortization payments - an effect of the inherited high burden of the external debt, and the high proportion of it due that year.

In 1972, and even more in 1973, increasingly serious problems, such as inflation and scarcity, manifested themselves in the economy. These resulted mainly from the accumulated and growing pressures of excessive demand in an economy whose level of production could not expand much further. The balance of payments deficit continued, only partly as a result of the short-term economic policies pursued.

As can be seen in Table 5.XIII, Gross Domestic Product grew by a mere 2.1 per cent in 1972 (that is, a rate lower than the average growth rate in 1965-70); in 1973, Gross Domestic Product fell by 4.1 per cent. Industrial output grew by a mere 3.5 per cent in 1972 and fell by 5.1 per cent in 1973. Construction and agriculture both fell in 1972; their decline became sharper in 1973.

The poor performance of both industry and construction can be explained principally by restrictions in the availability of inputs, both of national and imported origin. Bottlenecks became widespread, and one of the worst problems seems to have been the limitations of the transport system. Political elements made the problems even more acute. The prolonged transport (bosses') strike worsened the situation both in these sectors and in agriculture; the strike in the copper mines organized by the opposition in 1972 naturally harmed production in that vital sector; militant strikes and occupations on the part of the workers also affected production levels, especially after October 1972[113]. As production could hardly expand any more, the gap between aggregate demand and supply was increasingly bridged by inflation, scarcity and imports.

Following the fall in the rate of inflation in 1971, it grew at an accelerating rate - till it reached hyper-inflationary dimensions. Furthermore, as can be seen in Table 5.XIV, by 1972, and even more by 1973, prices were growing at a much faster rate than money in the hands of the private sector. Several elements explain this. One important factor was the existence of lags. As was pointed out, most of the monetary expansion during 1971 did not manifest itself in price increases during that year. These accumulated inflationary pressures, however, influenced the evolution of prices during 1972 and 1973.

Furthermore, during 1972 and 1973, the demand for money fell as the 'once-for-all' factors which had acted during 1971 were exhausted. One such factor was the contraction of private credit; another was the increase in aggregate supply not resulting from a growth in output, such as a fall in industrial stocks.

Perhaps of greater importance in provoking a fall in the demand for money was the sharp increase in inflation expectations[114]. Gradually, inflationary expectations stopped being a function of past inflation and started being a function of expectations about the future.

Expectations of higher inflation and the growing cost of holding money affected the way in which the public wished to maintain its liquid assets. On the one hand, demand for national currency was transferred to demand for foreign exchange. This explains the sharp rise in the 'black price' for foreign exchange. On the other hand, demand for money was transformed into demand for goods, providing a base for speculative activities.

Furthermore, in 1972 and even more in 1973, the government was increasingly unable to impose its administrative price controls effectively, due both to its decreasing authority and, even more, to the high level of excessive demand which could not be satisfied by an increase in supply.

After 1971, rising inflation was accompanied by increasing scarcity and black markets, with very adverse effects for the Popular Unity government (see also section 4.I.b.ii). The effects on distribution of goods and services amongst the population will be stressed here.

As price controls still had some limited effectiveness, scarcity and therefore informal rationing took place; goods and services were erratically distributed, tending to favour those more influential in the society and/or able to pay higher prices on the black market. For certain regions and sectors of the population, it seems to have become true at the time, as Griffin and James[115] say, that 'price controls on final goods unaccompanied by formal rationing may be as injurious to the poor as the market solution of allowing prices to rise to equate demand and supply'.

Scarcities and queuing were time-wasting and provoked widespread irritation; scarcities were artificially exacerbated by hoarding. As was mentioned, the appearance of black markets generated an atmosphere of corruption and speculation, particularly undesirable in an experience of transition to socialism. News of shortages — both real or exaggerated — were very effectively exploited by the opposition's propaganda.

As a result of increasing inflation and scarcity, there was wide discussion within the government about the need, scope and form of introducing a relatively comprehensive rationing system. As on other issues, there were many disagreements on the subject.

Particularly after the October 1972 'bosses'' strike, the government did take some steps to restrain black markets and assure supplies to the poorer strata of the population; on the whole, these efforts had very partial effects. The JAPs (popular price and supply committees) had some limited success in reducing hoarding and profiteering by merchants. But only a very small part of the population's needs were catered for by the efforts of

direct distribution at official prices of essential goods carried out by
DINAC (the state wholesale distribution company), mainly to the JAPs, and by
the creation of state-owned popular super-markets[116]. Distribution not
controlled by the government was carried out at much higher prices.

Even though the government's distribution efforts had relatively limited
scope, they created additional resentment between merchants, consumers and
government officials. As a result of public interference in trade, private
tradesmen and their powerful National Association of Merchants became
increasingly hostile to the Popular Unity government. Their actions
provoked further government interference, which increased the retail
traders' antagonism further. This hostility to the government (together
with that of the lorry-owners) played a relatively important role in the
government's overthrow. Middle and upper class consumers also resented the
government's attempts to divert some of their regular supplies to the poor.

The problems caused by scarcity and black markets could have been eliminated
to a large extent had an efficient and more comprehensive rationing system
been introduced. However, it seems clear that such a rationing system was
not feasible during Popular Unity's first years in power, given prevailing
political and economic conditions. First, the country was divided between a
virulent opposition and Popular Unity supporters. Therefore, while one
section of the population could be expected to accept and support the
government's rationing schemes, another could be expected openly to boycott
it. In fact, when the government tried to establish very partial rationing
schemes and distribution organizations, the opposition not only boycotted
them but even established parallel distribution organizations.

Second, the Chilean government had very little direct control over the
distribution sector; roughly 80 per cent of agricultural production in Chile
was privately marketed during the Allende period[117]. The government's
efforts to compete with the private sector had only very partial success.
In fact, the black market already prevalent at the time was one of the main
factors which undermined the efforts of new state-controlled enterprises to
distribute foodstuffs; private merchants were able to outbid the state
agents trying to purchase foodstuffs at official prices, and the latter's
share of the market remained low.

Political factors were obviously also involved. There was no clear decision
on the part of the government to control wholesale trade. Transport and
retailing were almost completely privately owned, mainly by small
proprietors. The magnitude and effectiveness of their opposition to the
Popular Unity government (as a response to very limited state action in the
distribution sphere) were an indicator of the gigantic opposition which
would have arisen had the state attempted to control retailing and transport
effectively.

Third, even if Popular Unity had had the political will and strength to
achieve state control over distribution of goods and services very rapidly,
it seems extremely doubtful that the government, during its first years in
power, would have had enough administrative expertize to establish and run a
comprehensive rationing system efficiently. As we saw, the Popular Unity
government was already facing great difficulties in managing and planning
the newly nationalized sector in industry, agriculture, mining and finance.
It is interesting that some of the worst management and financial problems
arose in those new state enterprises attempting the wholesale distribution
of foodstuffs[118]: the particular difficulty of the task, under the
circumstances, was probably the main reason.

As regards the evolution of income distribution in 1972 and 1973, any
measurement not based on physical indicators has serious limitations given
the increasingly widespread scarcities and black markets. According to

figures produced by the present government [119], the share of payments to
labour grew from 61.7 per cent of national income in 1971 to 62.8 per cent
in 1972; according to these figures, income distribution became much more
regressive in 1973, the share of payments to labour falling to only 45.7 per
cent of national income. Only a part of the 1973 change can be attributed
to the evolution of incomes and prices during Popular Unity (due mainly to
rapid inflation during those eight months); the other part is due to the
very rapid fall of real payments to labour, in the months immediately
following the coup.

In 1972 there was again a huge balance of payments deficit, which reduced
the net international reserves of the monetary system to below zero. As can
be seen in Table 5.XV in 1972, the positive result in the net external
non-compensatory capital flows was able to compensate only partly for the
very high current account deficit, which was more than five times the 1970
level (see Table 5.XV). The value of exports - both of copper and of other
goods - continued to fall. In 1972, the average international price of
copper fell below even its 1971 level, to 24.5 per cent below the 1970
average. Even though copper production increased, it was still well below
maximum potential output[120]. Exports of other goods fell, partly as a
result of the low exchange rate. The value of imports rose quite sharply;
this was due both to an increase in imports in real terms and to the rise in
international prices for the goods imported by Chile[121]. Thus, the
deterioration of Chile's terms of trade in 1971 and 1972 due both to lower
export prices and higher import prices had a particularly adverse effect on
the trade balance.

The increase in the level of imports in 1971 and 1972 was accompanied by a
sharp change in their composition. Imports of foodstuffs and inputs for the
food industry increased sharply, while imports of capital goods fell; the
former's participation in total imports increased from 14.1 per cent in 1970
to 30.7 per cent in 1972, while the latter's fell from 29 per cent in 1970
to 15 per cent in 1972[122]. In 1973 total imports were still growing in
real terms; imports of foodstuffs and raw materials for the food industry
increased quite substantially. Imports of all other items, including
non-food raw materials, fuels and lubricants, consumer goods, spare parts
and capital goods, fell in real terms during 1973.

In 1972, the net external non-compensatory capital account again became
positive, surpassing, in fact the average 1960-70 level. This was due
mainly to a sharp fall in amortization payments, resulting from a
renegotiation of the debt. Due to the critical balance of payments and
foreign exchange reserves situation, the Chilean government had decided to
renegotiate with its main foreign debtors. Chile managed to reduce its
payments to public foreign debtors by US $ 165 million for the period
November 1971 - December 1972; relatively favourable arrangements were also
reached with private banks[123].

Another factor which improved the net external non-compensatory account was
an increase in the level of long and medium-term loans (which in 1972
surpassed even the 1966-70 average).

Just as in 1971, loans from US public agencies and from the international
credit institutions - to a great extent controlled by the American
government - were either drastically reduced (i.e. EXIMBANK) or cut to zero
(i.e. World Bank). However, the Chilean government was able to replace
these sources of long and medium-term finance by credits from Western
Europe, Latin America, Japan and the socialist countries; a similar
evolution occurred with short-term credit[124]. Thus the effect of the
'invisible blockade' launched by the US Government against Chile was
particularly damaging in 1971; however, by 1972 its impact was neutralized
by alternative credit sources. This was the result both of a very effective

policy pursued in this field by the Popular Unity government, and of the
political and economic international context. Within the latter, a factor
not mentioned in the literature on the Chilean experience is the excessive
liquidity prevalent during 1972 and 1973 in international private capital
markets, which was increasingly being channelled to the developing
countries. (For an analysis of this trend, see, for example, S.
Griffith-Jones, 'The Growth of Multi-National Banking, the Euro-currency
Market and their effects on developing countries', Journal of Development
Studies, January, 1980.)

We have analyzed the different factors which caused Chile's net reserves of
foreign reserves to fall so rapidly during the Popular Unity government.
During this period, the country maintained a level of imports - in real
terms - higher than that of 1970[125]. However, once the numerous
bottlenecks and scarcities had begun to spread, due to the generalized
excesive demand in the economy, the foreign trade situation became very
crucial; it often looked as if the limited supply of imported goods was the
economy's main constraint. Shortages of imported spare parts, equipment and
imports gave rise to bottlenecks which rapidly spread to other sectors.

It seems an impossible task to prove conclusively the exact extent of
influence of economic developments during the Allende government on the
final political outcome. However, as was pointed out in Chapter 1 and in
this chapter, the 'Chilean road' (as defined by President Allende and the
majority in Popular Unity) implied an alliance with the 'middle groups', as
well as ensuring that the Armed Forces maintained their traditional respect
for the Constitution (the latter being of fundamental importance).

Undoubtedly, there was an important link between the real and perceived
'economic chaos', rapidly growing inflation, increasing scarcities, critical
foreign exchange situation and growing opposition to the Popular Unity
government by the middle classes and the Armed Forces, particularly after
late 1972. We shall illustrate briefly how some of the most senior members
in Popular Unity perceived this link. President Allende himself is reported
to have said at a Cabinet meeting on July 2nd 1973 (a few days after the
failed coup of a section of the Army) 'I have searched for a political
solution. The Armed Forces see mainly the economic crisis and
sectarianism.' (this quote is from notes taken at the meeting by Bitar, and
reproduced in his book, op.cit.). Clodomiro Almeyda, former Minister of
Foreign Affairs and of Defence in the Allende government writes in his
ex-post analysis:

> It is well worthwhile pausing to think about the
> factors which made it possible for the armed forces to
> intervene successfully in the political arena and to
> transform themselves into self-confessed and efficient
> agents of counter-revolution. There is no doubt that,
> among those factors, the country's worsening economic
> situation was of great influence. This predisposed
> significant middle sectors against the government, and
> decisively shaped the alignment of social forces in
> the conflict which the armed forces could foresee when
> they decided to take power by force.

('The reasons for self-criticism of the Unidad Popular Government', in
Sideri, op.cit.). Bitar in his book (op.cit. above) particularly stresses
the influence of the disruption of the market, of scarcities and high
inflation on the political behaviour of the 'middle strata'. One of the
senior participants to take a different view is Vuskovic, particularly in
his most recent book on the subject. In Una sola lucha, (op.cit. page 85)
he categorically says: 'the Popular Government did not fail on the economic
level, as others pretend, but on the political level.' From the analysis

made in this chapter, it can be concluded that Vuskovic is correct in stressing political factors (although many may not agree with his particular political perception), but incorrect in denying the important role of economic factors as well as Popular Unity's mistakes in this area.

V   Evaluation of short-term and financial policies - some
     alternative proposals

In this section we shall first summarize our critique of Popular Unity's short-term and financial policies. Alternative financial policies - more conducive to the achievement of Popular Unity's aims - are then examined. It should be stressed that these alternative policies are of a tentative character only. The calculations made are very simple; an accurate estimate would probably require a much more sophisticated model (even though the large parametric changes during this period might pose serious problems). Obviously, the sociological and political factors are not - and cannot be within the scope of this work - fully examined. However, even at the cost of sacrificing rigour, it seems useful to examine these alternative policies and their possible effects.

As was discussed above, the political stratregy implicitly adopted by Popular Unity was a gradual one. Given this gradual political strategy, a gradual economic policy would have been most conducive towards achieving its goals. This would have implied that when the crucial moments of confrontation came, popular support for the government would be increased by the continuous positive effects of demand expansion still prevailing in the economy. Within this framework, a key policy objective should have been to limit the growth of aggregate demand and to time this growth adequately. However, the economic policy in fact followed, implied a very strong expansion of aggregate demand both during the first and second year of the Popular Unity government, which was clearly working against the political strategy de facto chosen. This policy exhausted the positive effects during the first year, when there were no important elections. When the more crucial electoral and other power confrontations occurred, the economy was clearly within the Kaldorian range; all the negative effects of excessive demand growth had manifested themselves (see section 5.IV).

Within this context, we shall evaluate specific financial policies, examining possible alternative policies which could have allowed a smaller and more gradual growth of aggregate demand. We shall examine wages, taxation and public enterprises' prices, as well as the level of inflation.

One of the key reasons for the financial disequilibria in the public sector was the excessive level of wage and salary increases (see section 5.II). Given the gradual political strategy pursued, a strategy of lower and more gradual wage and salaries increase should have been attempted. Thus, in the crucial moments of power confrontation, payments to labour could still have been rising.

Popular Unity initially hardly attempted to control wage increases; the emphasis was always on income increases for the workers, hardly ever on their limits. For reasons already discussed, the effectiveness of an attempt to control wage increases was not clear. However, strong representation of the Left amongst the Councillors of the Central Única de Trabajadores and the non-economic advantages granted to workers in nationalized enterprises - i.e. participation in decision-making - should have made some degree of wage control feasible.

Within this context, Popular Unity should have attempted at least to obtain a commitment from the Central Unica de Trabajadores that the high initial margins of readjustment would be respected. The government could have tried to include such a clause in its agreement with the Central Workers' Union.

We shall attempt to quantify the effect of such a clause being successfully implemented. We shall assume that for the whole public sector, just as in the fiscal sector (see section II), 25 per cent of the increase in incomes of public employees was higher than that initially agreed upon. The increase in total incomes of public employees during 1971 was equal to E 9,900 million[126,127]. Had the government been able to limit payments to public employees to the levels initially agreed upon, then it would have saved approximately E 2,500 million during 1971.

In relation to taxation, as we saw in section II, during 1971 no significant increase in revenues could be obtained within the existing legislation. Practically the only way to obtain higher taxation was to alter existing legislation. The Executive did not - in 1971 - display great initiative in presenting bills to Congress (as it did in 1972) nor did it use political mobilization to force the Congress to approve those initiatives which it did present. Given the degree of popular support which the government had at the time and the weakness and divisions within the opposition, such an attempt at mass mobilization could have had some success. We shall here assume tentatively that through political pressure the Executive did manage to force Congress to approve half the sum rejected by it during 1971. This would have implied an increase of tax revenue equal to approximately E 1,300 million.

The possibility of imposing the wages and tax measures proposed above would not have depended on the Executive's willingness to implement them, but to a great extent on its power within society to impose these measures. Naturally the Executive should have attempted the measures just discussed; however the greatest efforts should have been concentrated on measures where the Executive's efforts to diminish financial disequilibria could have been easily implemented, as the Executive had discretionary power over them.

We shall refer here to the policies of prices in state and nationalized enterprises and interest rates in nationalized banks. (Prices - both for the public and private sector - were fixed by the Ministry of Economic Affairs and the interest rate was fixed by the Central Bank. Therefore, the Executive had complete discretionary power over these policies.)

The policy pursued in the case of prices of nationalized enterprises was clearly disfunctional to the political strategy followed. One of the aims of nationalization had been to capture for the state the surplus obtained by the monopoly enterprises; it was hoped that this would in fact improve public finance. As a result mainly of the financial policies pursued (particularly of prices and wages) the opposite occurred; the potential surplus was transferred partly to the workers in this sector via increases in their incomes, and partly to the private sector through low prices. The resulting deficit in state and nationalized enterprises in fact contributed strongly to increasing the public sector deficit, leading to excessive aggregate demand.

Furthermore the state and nationalized enterprises did not achieve the aim of strengthening the state sector nor its role in the accumulation process (see again the discussion of Preobrazhensky's work in chapter 1). On the contrary, the nationalized sector transferred surplus to the private sector, thus strengthening the latter. It seems important to note that those who benefited most from this policy were mainly the small and middle entrepreneurs - in both the productive and distributive sphere - whose enterprises were not nationalized. In fact, these groups were important in contributing to the government's downfall. As we saw, Popular Unity had hoped that economic concessions and transfer of incomes to certain groups would mechanically increase the degree of support which they would give the government and its policies. However, the relation may in fact have been inverse. The transfer of income to these groups accentuated the financial

disequilibria, and their negative effects, such as scarcities and black
markets; as discussed above, this was eventually very influential in turning
these groups against the government[128].

The second problem which arose from the transfer of the potential surplus by
the state and nationalized enterprises to the private sector and to its own
workers concerns capital accumulation.   As was to be expected, private
capitalists were too fearful of Popular Unity's political project to
re-invest their profits.   As the government did not invest sufficiently to
compensate for this fall of private accumulation, the rate of Gross
Geographical Investment as percentage of Gross National Product dropped well
below the already insufficient level of the 1960s[129], thus restricting the
potential for future growth.   Given the transfer of financial surplus and
the balance of payments situation, in 1971 and 1972, an attempt by the state
to invest more would only have exacerbated the monetary disequilibria and
reduced further the very scarce foreign exchange.   In fact, larger state
investment was clearly not compatible with the level of income increase and
redistribution[130].

As was described, prices of nationalized and state enterprises were
increased very slightly during 1971 and the first half of 1972.

We shall propose here an alternative price policy which would have implied:
a) a weighted average increase of 30 per cent for 1971 above the level
effectively applied, and b) differential increases with high rates for
non-essential goods and resources, smaller rates for exports and low - or
perhaps even zero - increases for basic consumer goods. This policy would
have increased the surplus captured by the state sector and thus diminished
the financial disequilibria generated in it.   It would not have affected so
much the redistributive aims of the government: in fact, it could have
allowed the government to regulate better the extent to which it wished to
redistribute income.

The problem with this alternative policy was its effect on the retail price
index and therefore on the next year's (1972) readjustment of wages and
salaries to public employees[131].   However, as the largest price increases
would be in non-basic goods, their impact on the retail price index would be
relatively small[132].   In Chile, the retail price index reflects variations
in the buying power of an average worker, so increases in prices of
non-essential goods affect it only marginally.

In 1971, the level of sales in state and nationalized enterprises was
estimated at E 12,800[133].   An average price increase of 30 per cent would
have implied additional revenue of E 3,800 million.

Our quantitative analysis refers only to 1971.   However, in 1972, had price
increases in state and nationalized enterprises been carried out sooner (see
Section II), the impact would have been even more significant.   The sales
value of state and nationalized enterprises had increased sharply.   Also,
general retail prices were growing at a faster rate during 1972[134]; thus
prices of nationalized enterprises - in real terms - fell quicker, provoking
larger deficits than in 1971.

The interest rate policy followed was both incorrect in terms of
conventional economic analysis and disfunctional to the political strategy
adopted.   Popular Unity economists had in the past correctly criticized
private banks for being instruments used by the private sector - and
particularly by the monopolic groups - to obtain subsidized credit at
negative interest rates. Thus it seems surprising that once the banks had
been nationalized the cost of credit became even lower than it had been
before; the nationalized banks were transferring even more surplus than
before to the private sector.

In fact, during 1971 the real cost of credit was positive - equivalent to nine per cent[135]. However, in 1972 the cost of credit in real terms became strongly negative at -122 per cent[136].

During 1972 the level of credit granted to the private sector was on average E 15,000 million[137]. This implied that during that year the state banking system transferred E 18,300 to the private sector, a sum equivalent to 44 per cent of the 1972 public sector deficit and to 48 per cent in 1972 total tax revenue; these percentages are far higher than in former years[138]. Had the real cost of credit been zero, this enormous transfer of real suplus would have been avoided. Had the real cost of credit been ten per cent, the state banking sector would have captured an additional E 1,500 million of revenue. In either case the increase in nominal revenues of the state banking system could have been used during 1972 to improve public finances considerably.

There is no justification for the Popular Unity government not following a more correct policy in this field. The explanation seems to lie in Popular Unity's fear than an increase in interest rates would increase inflationary cost pressures; however, by 1972 inflation was basically demand-generated and the negative cost of credit was feeding this inflation, via larger state sector deficit.

We shall now attempt to estimate the impact which alternative policies would have had on the 1971 monetary situation[139]. The methodology used here is very similar to that used in the Central Bank of Chile for projections. Though based on simple assumptions, it usually yielded quite accurate projections.

First, we shall estimate the effect of an alternative policy only for prices of state and nationalized enterprises, that is, the policy over which the Executive had complete discretionary power. If, on average, these prices had been 30 per cent higher, this would have implied a revenue increase of E 3,800 million. We shall assume that would have implied a reduction in their deficit, which would have caused an equivalent reduction of the adjusted money issue. This assumed: 1) that higher revenues of state and nationalized enterprises would not have been accompanied by higher expenditures, and 2) that other sources and credit from the banking system were used up already as alternative sources of financing the deficit; as this reduction in the public deficit is relatively marginal, it is assumed to affect just the financing by money issue. When larger reductions of the public deficit are discussed below, this assumption will be modified. Under these assumptions, the increase in the adjusted money issue would have been 33 per cent less, which would have implied that the money in the hands of the private sector would have increased during 1971 by 79 per cent instead of by 119 per cent.

We shall examine now the effect if all the financial policies proposed above had been successfully implemented; this would have required not only the willingness of the Executive but also a certain degree of political control, which it is not quite clear that the Executive had. However, the modifications in wages and taxation policies proposed are relatively small; given the extent of popular support enjoyed by the government in 1971, the relative weakness and division within the opposition ranks, and the general atmosphere of enthusiasm and success which at the time surrounded the government's actions, it is fair to assume that the Executive could have imposed such measures.

We shall maintain the assumption of an increase of 30 per cent in the prices of state and nationalized enterprises; we shall assume that the government was able to impose some wage restraint, and that public employees' unions did not surpass those initially agreed upon; finally, we shall assume that

the Executive managed to force the Congress to approve taxation equal to
half the sum which had been rejected during 1971. The total reduction in
the public deficit would be equal to approximately E 7,600 million.

As these alternative measures would have implied a significant reduction in
the public deficit, we shall assume that only a part of this deficit was
financed by money issue, while the rest was financed by credit from the
banking system and by other sources. We shall assume that the proportions
in which this occurred were the same as those in which the total public
deficit was financed that year[140].

Given these assumptions, the increase in the adjusted money issue would have
been 48 per cent smaller, which would have implied that the increase in the
money in the hands of the private sector during 1971 would have been
approximately 61 per cent instead of 119 per cent. An increase of 61 per
cent in the amount of money in the hands of the private sector was not
extraordinarily high, in terms of past Chilean economic history; during 1965
– the first year of the previous government – this variable grew by 51.5 per
cent. Due to increases in the demand for money, prices grew by only 25.9
per cent during that year.

Given that there were several special elements which increased the demand
for money considerably during 1971 (for details see section III), an
increase in the money supply of 61 per cent could have been easily absorbed
without creating any large financial disequilibria during 1971 and without
leaving much excessive supply of money to provoke financial disequilibria
for 1972. Furthermore, if – as shall be discussed below – the level of 1971
inflation had been somewhat higher, hardly any financial disequilibria would
have been generated. Again, in 1972 alternative financial policies would
have been followed which would have implied smaller growth in the money
issue and more limited financial disequilibria.

We shall now evaluate the policy followed in relation to inflation[141].
First, it seems that politically, it was not necessary for the Popular Unity
government to fix such ambitious targets for inflation control during its
first year. In 1971, the government had important achievements in other
fields (such as the advance of structural reforms and the recovery of the
economy), which would have assured increased support from large sectors of
the population. Given the high level of nominal wage increases,
considerable income redistribution could have been achieved, even with
higher levels of inflation. Furthermore, given the probable evolution of
financial variables as well as the situation inherited from 1970, it was not
feasible to achieve very low rates of inflation in 1971 without generating
important disequilibria for 1972 and 1973.

An alternative policy for 1971 could have included maintaining the 1970
inflation rate – that is, around 35 per cent. This would have had little or
no political cost; it would have diminished the excessive supply of money
transferred for future years and the problems this created. A higher rate
of inflation would have made the discussed increases in prices of state and
nationalized enterprises feasible. It would have implied lower increases of
workers' and employees' real incomes, probably far nearer to those initially
projected by the government.

The proposed alternative policies are compared with those actually pursued
during 1971 in Table 5.XVI.

Even though there may be errors of estimate in these figures, the orders of
magnitude are such that it seems clear that less financial disequilibria
would have resulted from alternative policies.

TABLE 5.XVI

ALTERNATIVE FINANCIAL POLICIES FOR 1971

	Increase in money supply (a)	Rate of increase of retail prices
Effective	119%	22.1%
Alternative 1 (b)	79%	c.35%
Alternative 2 (c)	61%	c.35%

(a)   For Alternatives 1 and 2, the increases in money supply are estimates, based on a methodology very similar to that applied in the Studies Department of the Central Bank of Chile at the time.

(b)   Assumes that prices of state and nationalized enterprises were on average 30% higher than the effective 1971 ones.

(c)   Assumes same as Alternative 1 and also supposes alternative wage and taxation policies described above.

VI   Concluding observations

Study of the Chilean Popular Unity experience shows that an adequate financial short-term policy in situations of transition to socialism is both very important and very difficult to achieve. Naturally, these difficulties are greater in a small, underdeveloped, dependent country with a relatively complex social and political structure, such as Chile. Financial policies in Chile had a far smaller range of manoeuvre than was initially perceived. This margin for action diminished rapidly in the Chilean case, as after mid-1972, the financial disequilibria and their effects became extremely important and difficult to manage; nor was there any coherent programme with sufficient political backing to overcome them. For this reason, we have centred our analysis on the first two years (and particularly on 1971) when there was much greater margin for alternative action.

The crucial importance of adequate financial policies in the Chilean case was not clearly perceived by most Popular Unity economists or politicians; an important reason for this seemed to be the implicit belief that structural changes (in particular changes in property relations) would mechanically ease economic problems in the short-term; thus financial policies were believed to become far less important. As we have seen in the Chilean case, structural reforms in fact often initially exacerbate short-term economic problems.   Thus, in such situations, correct short-term economic management is more essential than in a capitalist economy.

Furthermore, at the beginning of a process of transition, the apparatus for administering production and distribution in a planned way is only just beginning to develop and is still very fragmented. At this stage, even if there has been a large nationalization programme, there is still an essential role for market relations in performing the functions of production and distribution, as there is, in practice, no alternative mechanism.   In the Chilean experience under Popular Unity, there was practically no effective planning, nor even a clear idea about how to plan, given the existing possibilities and constraints. It would seem that the speed with which market relations are eliminated should not exceed the speed at which it is feasible to replace them by planning mechanisms.   For the functioning of these market relations, a minimum of monetary stability is essential, as has been shown in the Chilean and other cases (for example, the Soviet Union during NEP).

The vital task of creating an effective system of planned management of the
economy as rapidly as possible is very complex in itself. It should not be
made even more difficult by the serious disruptions provoked by large
financial disequilibria which distract precious time and effort from
creating and running this new system. In Chile the high rates of inflation
made effective planning and control of the state sector extremely difficult.
For example, by 1972, it became unrealistic to discuss annual budgets and
credits for state enterprises, as the main variables could not be predicted
with any reasonable degree of accuracy. Budgets and credit grants had to be
revised and discussed on a monthly or bi-monthly basis; this created a vast
amount of additional work for the planning and financial institutions, as
well as for the enterprises themselves[142]. At the same time, scarcities
of inputs and spare parts made the management of the state enterprises a
much more difficult task. We can see that at all levels, by mid-1972,
considerable effort was put into solving very short-term problems, either
caused or accentuated by financial disequilibria. Little time and energy
was left for discussing longer-term plans, or for the development of a
complete planning and management apparatus. This may help to explain the
fact that so little attempt was made at effective planning.

As we saw, similar problems arose in the sphere of distribution.
Distribution via the market suffered serious disruptions, mainly as an
effect of financial disequilibria, at a time when it was not feasible either
technically or politically to implement a comprehensive rationing scheme to
replace market distribution. Again, considerable effort was channelled into
attenuating these disruptions in the short-term.

We can see from the Chilean experience under Popular Unity that great
concern with financial and short-term policies was not 'a monetarist
deviation' or 'essentially conservative' as many believed at the time. The
design and evaluation of both general and specific financial policies
appropriate to the achievement of the basic political and economic goals of
the transition to socialism was an essential task, not fully carried out by
economists in the Chilean case. It is true that this task was made much
more difficult by serious political disagreements within Popular Unity at
different levels, as well as by the sectarianism resulting from rivalries
between the different political parties.

Even given these limitations, economists should have spelled out much more
clearly to the political leadership the incompatibility between their
economic and political strategies - as well as the negative medium-term
effects of the economic policy pursued.

Although financial policies were very useful in revealing the limitations of
available resources, deeper issues could have been posed, starting from the
financial perspective. An obvious point was the extent to which the level
of income redistribution (as well as the absolute level of its increase) was
consistent both with efficient management of the transition economy in the
short-term, and with growth in the medium and long-term. This could have
focused the attention of the political leadership on key economic issues,
and the need to take decisions on them. By not drawing sufficient attention
soon enough to some of these key issues, and the alternatives available,
economists were partly responsible for the fact that often explicit
decisions were not taken at all. Last but certainly not least, the
clarification of economic issues and alternatives could have led to some
concrete discussions at mass level. The maturity and organization of the
Chilean working class would have probably made such an initiative extremely
fruitful; it could also, perhaps, have led to greater mass support for the
government and its policies.

A final comment seems necessary. This study may seem too critical of
Popular Unity's management of the economy. The mistakes are stressed here

more than the achievements, in the hope that were a similar opportunity to
be repeated, in Chile or elsewhere, this type of evaluation might prevent,
if only partially, similar mistakes being made.

Notes

1   There is a vast literature available on the political aspects. For a
    very complete survey, see Jirina Rybacek, 'Chile under Allende: a
    bibliographical survey', Discussion Paper No. 63, March 1976, Woodrow
    Wilson School, Princeton University, New Jersey. An interesting work
    in Spanish on the political problems faced can be found in J.E.
    Garcés, Allende y la experiencia chilena, Editorial Ariel, Barcelona,
    1976 (J. Garcés was President Allende's political adviser). A good
    article in English is that by A. Valenzuela, 'Political constraints to
    the establishment of socialism', in Chile: Politics and Society,
    edited by A. Valenzuela and J.S. Valenzuela, Transaction Books, New
    Brunswick, New Jersey, 1976.   In the same book, the article 'The
    Invisible Blockade: the United States reacts', by E. Farnsworth, R.
    Feinberg and E. Leensom, deals clearly with the actions taken by the
    United States. A very good account of US intervention, particularly
    that of the CIA, can be found in US Senate, Hearings before the Select
    Committee to Study Governmental Operations with Respect to
    Intelligence Activities' Covert Action in Chile, Washington DC,
    Government Printing Office, 1976.

2   Economic Commission for Latin America, Economic Survey of Latin
    America, 1970, United Nations, New York, 1972, p.10.

3   Economic Commission for Latin America, Economic Survey of Latin
    America, 1973, United Nations, New York, 1975.

4   Same source as 3.

5   Same source as 2, page 43. In the period 1960-65, the index grew at a
    similar average rate (27.0%).

6   For good descriptions of the economic policies pursued in this period,
    see R. Ffrench-Davies, Políticas económicas en Chile, 1952-70,
    Ediciones Nueva Universidad, Universidad Catolica, Santiago, Chile,
    1973, and E. Sierra, Tres ensayso de estabilización en Chile,
    Editorial Universitaria, Santiago, Chile, 1970.

7   Source: Departamento de Economía, Universidad de Chile.

8   This expression was coined by Popular Unity.   It described and
    denounced the image, created by the right, of the disastrous effects
    which Popular Unity's triumph would have on the economy.

9   These actions were taken by the Christian Democrat Administration,
    with the collaboration of Popular Unity experts.

10 By then, pre-September levels for banking and saving deposits had been
    recovered.

11 Money held by the private sector is defined here as notes and coins
    plus bank deposits.

12 The increase during 1970 of money held by the private sector was
    larger than that during any other year in that decade.

13 This is particularly so in the case of the Soviet Union (see Chapter
    II on War Communism).   However, it is also true for East European
    countries after World War II.

14 Source of data: Banco Central de Chile, Boletín Mensual No. 599 –
    Enero 1978, Santiago, Chile.

15   Id. as note (14).

16   The 'structuralist' school of thought arose in the mid 1950s in Latin
      America; it was basically created by progressive Chilean economists
      working in ECLA (Economic Commission for Latin America, belonging to
      the United Nations) operating in Santiago. The link between the
      'structuralist' school and Popular Unity was close, as several of the
      architects of Popular Unity's policy had worked in ECLA, and had
      either contributed to or been influenced by what is somewhat loosely
      known as 'structuralist' thinking.   For a brief discussion and
      bibliography on the 'structuralist' school, see Chapter I of this
      study, as well as 'Introduction' in R. Thorpe and L. Whitehead (eds),
      Inflation and Stabilization in Latin America, Macmillan, London, 1979.

17   A relevant aspect was emphasized by Brian Pollitt, in his Seminar
      'Some Problems of Agriculture in the Early Stages of Socialism', given
      at the Centre of Latin American Studies, Cambridge, in February, 1975.
      He pointed out how often the Left (not only in Chile, but also in
      other countries such as Cuba) designs its economic policy, mainly
      based on a diagnosis of the malfunctioning of the capitalist system,
      tending to ignore those elements within the existing system which can
      be both positive and useful in situations of transition to socialism.
      As these positive elements - such as market links between economic
      units - are ignored, their destruction is carried out quite
      unconsciously, without considering its harmful effects on the
      transition.

18   Pedro Vuskovic 'The Economic Policy of the Popular Unity Government',
      in The Chilean Road to Socialism. Proceedings of an ODEPLAN - IDS
      Round Table, March, 1972, edited by Ann Zammitt, with cooperation from
      Gabriel Palma, 1973, Institute of Development Studies, Sussex.

19   Correct is defined as 'functional to the political and economic goals
      of Popular Unity'.

20   Sergio Ramos, Chile: Una Economía en Transición?, La Habana, 1972,
      Premio Casa de las Americas. Sergio Ramos was personal adviser to the
      Minister of Finance, member of the Executive Committee of Odeplan
      (National Planning Office) and Secretary of the Economic Committee of
      Ministers.

21   A relatively similar diagnosis from the Popular Unity perspective can
      be found for example in CESO (several authors) Chile Hoy, Siglo XXI,
      Mexico, 1970, and Pedro Vuskovic, 'Distribución del ingreso y opciones
      de desarrollo' in Cuadernos de la Realidad Nacional, Septiembre de
      1970, Santiago, Chile. An English version can be found in A. Guardia,
      A. Martinez and S. Ramos, 'General Considerations on the Chilean
      Economic Structure' in S. Sideri (ed) Chile 1970-73: Economic
      Development and Its International Setting, 1979, Nijhoff, The Hague.

22   Exposición sobre la política económica del gobierno y del estado de la
      hacienda pública, Presentado por el Ministro de Hacienda, don Américo
      Zorrilla a la Comisión Mixta de Presupuestos el 27 de Noviembre de
      1970, published by the Ministerio de Hacienda, Santiago de Chile,
      1970.

      Exposición del Ministro de Economía, Pedro Vuskovic, ante el Comité
      Interamericano de la Alianza para el Progreso, Washington, 22 de
      Febrero de 1970, reproduced in El pensamiento económico del Gobierno
      de Allende, Editorial Universitaria, Santiago de Chile, 1971.

23   The subject of dependence had been an important concern of Latin

American social scientists during the last decade. The main works
from the dependency perspective seem to be O. Sunkel and P. Paz, El
Subdesarrollo Latinoamericano y la Teoria del Desarrollo, Mexico,
1970, Siglo XXI, and F. Cardoso and E. Faletto, Dependencia y
Desarrollo en América Latina, Mexico 1969, Siglo XXI. For a recent
very complete and critical evaluation of the development of dependency
theory, see G. Palma, 'Dependency: A Formal Theory of
Under-development or a Methodology for the Analysis of Concrete
Situations of Under-Development?' World Development, Vol. 6, number
7/8, July/August 1978.

24   The penetration of foreign capital into Chilean industry during the
1960s has been studied in some detail. An important contribution was
L. Pacheco, La inversión extranjera en la industria chilena, Tesis,
Facultad de Ciencias Físicas y Matemáticas, Universidad de Chile,
1970. A good summary and interesting analysis of studies on the
subject can be found in S. Bitar, 'La presencia de la empresa
extranjera en la industria chilena', Desarrollo Económico No. 50, vol.
13, July-Sept. 1973, Buenos Aires, Argentina. For an analysis in
English, see S. Griffith-Jones, Foreign Investment in Chile, 1950-70,
a quantitative evaluation,' Mimeo, IDS, 1977.

25   Source: Exposición sobre la política económica...presentada por el
Ministro de Hacienda, op.cit. note (22).

26   Gross surplus is defined as aggregate value less wages and salaries.
Source: Sergio Ramos, op.cit.

27   Source: Sergio Ramos, op.cit.

28   Source: Sergio Ramos, op.cit. As Bitar, op.cit. points out (based on
ECLA data), the proportion of public investment in total fixed
investment in 1969 Chile was the highest in Latin America (with the
exception of Cuba).

29   This illustrates the point that Popular Unity did not learn from its
own diagnosis. While Sergio Ramos, op.cit. correctly criticized this
pricing policy as one of the manifestations of state monopoly
capitalism, in another chapter he praises as positive the Popular
Unity measure to eliminate already approved electricity tariff
increases; this had the above-mentioned effect of decreasing the state
enterprise's profits, and transferring them to the private enterprise.

30   The policies through which it did this - i.e. price and interest rate
policies - will be discussed in detail below.

31   For an excellent example of this kind of analysis, see Pedro
Vuskovic's article, 'Distribución del ingreso y opciones de
desarrollo', op.cit. above.

32   Source: Exposición sobre la política económica....presentada por el
Ministro de Hacienda, op.cit. note 22.

33   Source: ODEPLAN, Plan Anual 1971, Santiago, March, 1971.

34   Source: ODEPLAN, Antecedentes sobre el desarrollo chileno 1960-70.
Plan de la Economía Nacional, 1971-76, Santiago, 1971.

35   'Reformist' economists did not stress - or not enough - the basic need
to carry out structural reforms so as to achieve an improvement in the
future functioning of the economy, and to eliminate the contradictions
and distortions existing in it.

36   This comment is based on personal observation. Often meetings with
      top officials to discuss credit and monetary policies or decisions
      were postponed or cancelled; they were very often replaced by
      discussions on structural reforms in the banking system.

37   Similarly, the Ministry of Economic Affairs concentrated its attention
      on the complex problems of nationalization of industry.   More
      short-term policies, such as price policy, sometimes suffered from
      insufficient attention.

38   'Chile: Toward the Building of Socialism', pre-election report by
      Pedro Vuskovic, The Chilean Road to Socialism, ed. Dale Johnson
      Anchor Books, New York, 1973.

39   Article in El Siglo, December, 1970.

40   For example, in his Exposición sobre la política económica.....op.cit.
      above, the Minister said: 'The orientation for the long-term solution
      against inflation is to begin the structural transformations of the
      Chilean economy'.

41   Popular Unity had a minority in Congress, which implied that it could
      not modify existing laws or pass new ones, unless agreement was
      reached with some or all of the opposition parties. Congressional
      elections did not coincide with Presidential elections. Furthermore
      the Judiciary - traditionally controlled by very conservative elements
      - was completely independent of the Executive (see, also, Chapter I of
      this study).

42   It seems that there was too mechanistic a link in Popular Unity's
      analysis betwen structural reforms and the political weakening of
      these groups.   Even though most of the structural reforms were
      successfully carried out, these groups kept an important part of their
      economic power, received external support and controlled most of the
      key press media.   Their attack on the government was basically
      ideological. It is interesting that Vuskovic in his ex-post analysis
      (Una sola lucha, op.cit. p.52) makes this same point, stressing that
      it is erroneous to believe that economic transformations will by
      themselves create greater political power.

43   See Vuskovic's article, 'Política económica y poder político', op.cit.
      for a discussion of these two alternatives.   For a perceptive
      discussion of Popular Unity's alliance with the "middle classes", see
      S. Bitar, 'Interacción entre economía y política', in F. Gil, R. Lagos
      and H. Landsberger (Eds.), Chile, 1970-73, Editorial Tecnos, Madrid,
      1977, and S. Bitar, Transición, Socialismo y democracia, op.cit.
      particularly Chapter XI.

44   Many other discrepancies arose. For an interesting discussion of some
      of them, see for example, Barbara Stallings and Andy Zimballist, 'The
      Political Economy of the Unidad Popular', Latin American Perspectives,
      Issue 4, Vol. II, No. 1, California, Spring 1975. Also see literature
      mentioned in 43 and others on alliance with the "middle classes".

45   Even this 'rapid institutional change' could not have been pursued
      immediately.   According to the rules established by the Chilean
      Constitution, it would have taken at least eight months for the
      Executive's decision to call a plebiscite to be approved by Congress
      and implemented. (In any case, this could have allowed popular voting
      long before scheduled elections, and with greater potential for power
      changes.)   Furthermore, Congress might have defeated the Executive's
      proposal.   However, this negative attitude would have probably

increased support for Popular Unity, as well as polarizing more the
positions of government and opposition. I wish to thank Carlos Fortin
for clarifying this point.

46   Popular Unity was very successful in carrying out structural reforms,
in spite of strong opposition actions. A description of these
structural changes is outside the scope of this study; a detailed
description of this process, as well as its magnitude can be found,
for example, in Stefan de Vylder, Allende's Chile, the political
economy of the rise and fall of the Unidad Popular, Cambridge
University Press, 1976.

47   Source: 'Orientaciones básicas del programa economica de corto plazo',
October 1970, mimeographed document with restricted circulation. This
document gave the initial general orientation for the government's
economic policy. It summarized the work of the Technical Commission
of Popular Unity; amongst its members were most of the future
ministers or officials of the Popular Government in charge of
implementing this policy.

48   The existence of sectoral limits to idle capacity can be illustrated
by the fact that while industrial capacity utilization in 1970
averaged only 63% in the consumer durables sector, it reached 85.5% in
the intermediate goods industry. Source: Norberto Garcia, 'Algunos
aspectos de la política de corto plazo de 1971,' La Economía chilena
en 1971, Instituto de Economía, Universidad de Chile, Santiago, 1972.
There were also general bottlenecks (i.e. transport, skilled manpower)
which impeded full use of industrial capacity.

49   Source: Exposición sobre la Política Económica del Gobierno y del
Estado de la Hacienda Publica, presentado por el Ministro de Hacienda,
don Américo Zorrilla a la Comision Mixta de Presupuestos el
16.11.1971. Ministerio de Hacienda. Santiago de Chile, and Stephen
de Vylder op.cit.

50   See section 4.II below.

51   See Table 4.III below.

52   Source: Norberto Garcia's article, op.cit. in La economía chilena en
1971, op.cit.

53   Source: 'Situación actual y perspectivas de la política financiera'
internal document of the government's Financial Committee, (with
representatives from the Finance Ministry, Central Bank and Banco del
Estado), Mimeo, Santiago de Chile, April 1971.

54   Julio Lopez, 'La estrategia económica del Gobierno de la Unidad
Popular', Cuadernos de la Realidad Nacional, September 1971.
Universidad Católica de Chile, Santiago de Chile. His economic
analysis, as the author points out, is based on Kalecki's work,
particularly on the articles 'A theory of commodity, income and
capital taxation', 'Determinants of profits' and 'Class struggle and
distribution of national income' in Michael Kalecki, Selected Essays
on the Dynamics of the Capitalist Economy, 1933-1970, Cambridge
University Press, op.cit.

55   It would increase the share of wages - and decrease that of profits -
in the National Income.

56   Here it is assumed that there is neither public sector nor foreign
trade.

57 This assumes that the higher wages bill will be financed by dissaving or by credit, and not by a reduction of capitalists' expenditure.

58 Kaldor's theoretical analysis is basically taken from his article 'Alternative Theories of Distribution', Review of Economic Studies, Vol. 23, No. 2, 1956.

59 In the Chilean case, a combination of the three occurred.

60 See also Chapters 2 and 3.

61 If import controls were established, once the economy was in the Kaldorian range, this would throw the burden back on inflation and/or scarcity.

62 In the Chilean context, the private sector was quite unwilling to invest; neither did the public sector invest much. The expansion of imports was basically in consumption goods (see below).

63 Measures such as import controls and/or subsidies to exports and/or devaluation would be necessary if increased internal production created balance of payments problems.

64 It is more correct to include the government budget deficit plus the deficit of nationalized enterprises plus the expansion of banking credits to private business. Once monetary savings are subtracted, this equals the increase in the money supply.

65 During the first year, other elements contributed to increase mass support for the government. The opposition was divided, and failed to present any viable political alternative. Popular Unity was full of initial enthusiasm.   There was substantial mass support for the structural changes carried out, such as copper nationalization and workers' participation.

66 Therefore, if the electoral way were followed, the first crucial power confrontation would occur two and a half years after Popular Unity took over the Executive.

67 In 1971, Gross Domestic Product grew by 8.3% (more than double the average of the 1960s).   National unemployment fell from 7.2% in December 1970 to 3.9% in December 1971.   The share of workers' and employees' earnings in National Income rose sharply in 1971 (for more details see section IV).

68 This refers for example to the Minister of Economic Affairs, Pedro Vuskovic, and his group of advisers. Another important member in the Cabinet, the Under-Secretary of Economic Affairs, Oscar Garretón, also shared Vuskovic's view.   In 'Política económica y poder político', op.cit. Vuskovic clearly describes his political perceptions and the link with the short-term economic strategy he implemented during 1971.

69 These problems seem to have been basically caused by the lack of unity within the Popular Unity leadership. This was also reflected at all levels within the state administration, due to the 'quota' system of allocating jobs to different parties within the coalition.

70 An exception were memoranda, written in the Central Bank, which pointed out the inevitable negative effects - on income distribution and centralized management of the economy - of the growing financial disequilibria.   For example, 'La situación monetaria, sus efectos y posibles medidas de corto plazo', Stephany Novy and Enrique Goldfarb,

Santiago de Chile, October 1971.

71   It is my personal impression, confirmed by interviews with high-ranking officials, that the political leadership was not fully aware of the limits of the economic policy, nor how dangerous politically its medium-term negative effects could be.

72   At the beginning of 1971, the two main Marxist parties in the Popular Unity coalition (Socialists and Communists) controlled 75% of the Councillors of the CUT.   Source: Alan Angell, Politics and the Labour Movement in Chile, Oxford University Press, London, 1972.

73   Particularly during 1971, Popular Unity parties made insufficient efforts to impress upon their trade union leaders the vital need of restraining wage demands. This is discussed in more detail in Section 4,II.

74   Source: Estimates based on Comentarios sobre la situacion económica 1er semestre, 1973, Universidad de Chile, Taller de Coyuntura, Santiago de Chile, 1973.

75   The companies claimed that they could not repatriate profits, which they owed their foreign share-holders both for 1971 and 1972.   The reason they gave was lack of cash, mainly due to the fall in the international price of copper and the fixed exchange rate. (It was impossible to verify exactly whether this claim was completely true.) The companies offered the government the possibility of obtaining a medium-term foreign bank credit, guaranteed by the Chilean government. This would be used for: (a) repatriation of profits to the foreign shareholders, (b) payment of profits to the Chilean part of the companies (the companies were half nationalized at the time) and (c) tax payments. This mechanism had the disadvantage of increasing both the country's medium-term debt, and the profits repatriated by the foreign companies, just before nationalization. It had the advantage of increasing fiscal income, which was badly needed to reduce financial disequilibria. After internal discussion, the government decided against accepting the companies' proposal. (Information based on interview material.)

76   Other measures were introduced which favoured the less wealthy tax payers; this reduced tax revenue.

77   Source: Exposición sobre la política económica del Gobierno y del Estado de la Hacienda Pública, Presentada por el Ministro de Hacienda don Américo Zorrilla a la Comision Mixta de Presupuestos el 16 de Noviembre de 1971.

78   For example, Ernesto Miranda, La política monetaria del Gobierno de la Unidad Popular. Marco de referencia, objetivos y resultados, Tesis de grado para Magister en Ciencias Economicas, Santiago, 1974.

79   Based on interview material.

80   It seems surprising that the programmed tax revenues for 1972 appear to be lower than those in 1971 (see Table 5.IV).   However, what occurred was that programmed revenue was far higher in 1972 in nominal terms (and it could have been higher in real terms, had the rate of inflation been lower).

81   Source: Exposición sobre la política económica del Gobierno y del Estado de la Hacienda Pública, Presentada por el Ministro de Hacienda don Americo Zorrilla a la Comision Mixta de Presupuestos el 16 de

Noviembre de 1971.

82   Source: Ernesto Miranda, La política monetaria....op.cit.

83   This explains why in 1972 Effective Expenditure is so much larger than
      Budgeted Expenditure.

84   Source: Ernesto Miranda, La política monetaria....op.cit.

85   To calculate the part of Transfers going to labour payments, we have
      taken in each year the percentage of Total Expenditure in the
      Decentralized Enteprises and State Entities spent on payments to
      labour and multiplied it by the value of the Transfers.   Source for
      the data: Balance Consolidado del Sector Público de Chile....op.cit.

86   The same method of calculation is used as for 1971.

87   The levels of re-adjustment were much higher for those public
      employees who had lower incomes. Details of the progressive nature of
      the 1972 re-adjustment can be found in Instituto de Economia y
      Planificacion, La economía Chilena en 1972, op.cit.

88   These data are based on Norberto Garcia's article, op.cit. and on
      Table No. 5.VI.

89   It is assumed here that Social Security and Family Allowances increase
      proportionally to the growth of wages and salaries, both in the Fiscal
      and in the Decentralized Sector.   These assumptions seem quite
      realistic, given the characteristics of the Chilean wage system.
      There may be a slight over-estimation of the relation between wage and
      family allowance increases, which may imply an over-estimation of the
      non-agreed upon part of the wage increase.   However, the effect is
      quite marginal, as family allowances are a low proportion of total
      incomes of public employees.

90   More than 60% of the workers were affiliated to this Central Union.
      One of its most striking features was the co-operation between
      supporters of different parties on the same executive.   Attempts by
      the Christian Democrats to form 'parallel' trade union organizations
      had failed.

91   Data taken from Alan Angell, Politics and the Labour Movement in
      Chile, Oxford University Press, London, 1972.

92   See for example interview with President Allende in The Guardian,
      London, March 29, 1972.

93   As Alan Angell, op.cit. points out, the government authorized wage
      increases of 38% in 1965, 26% in 1966 and 17% in 1967; however,
      Central Government wages went up by 50%, 33% and 32%.   Therefore, the
      extent to which during those three years government wage increases
      surpassed the levels determined by government policy was similar to
      what occurred in 1971.   The difference was that the increases
      authorized by the government in 1971 already implied much higher
      increases than had been granted in former years.

94   Source: Instituto de Economía: La economía chilena en 1971, op.cit.

      This growth rate refers both to nationalized and state industries.
      From the data disaggregated by sector, it seems that output grew at an
      even higher rate if one considers only the state enterprises.

95   Source: Instituto de Economía y Planificación, La economía chilena en
      1972, op.cit.

96   Sources: Same as for Table 5.III.

97   Perhaps the most spectacular case was the prolonged conflict in the
      large El Teniente copper mine, when not only rightist trade union
      leaders but also opposition senators and journalists rallied to the
      support of the miners' stiff demands. This two month strike had
      damaging effect on the economy, particularly on exports.

98   Information based on interview material.

99   Information based on personal experience, internal memoranda of the
      Central Bank and on Ernesto Miranda, La política monetaria....op.cit.

100   For a brief but good account of these inter-institutional
      co-ordination problems, see A. Martinez, 'The Industrial Sector: Areas
      of Social and Mixed Property in Chile', in S. Sideri (ed.), Chile
      1970-73: Economic Development and its International Setting, 1979,
      Martinus Nijhoff, The Hague.

101   The 1970 growth rate was already the second highest during the last 18
      years. The former highest rate was 62% during 1955. Source: Ricardo
      Ffrench-Davies, Las políticas...op.cit.

102   There are two methods of determining the growth of money in the hands
      of the private sector. One, which will be examined here, determined
      this variable as the product of the 'Adjusted Money Issue' times the
      'Banking Multiplier'. The 'Adjusted Money Issue' refers to the net
      effect of the Central Bank's operations. This method has the
      advantage of greater simplicity for calculations and projections.

103   The expansion of money issue by the Central Bank to finance Internal
      Credit was oriented during 1971 and 1972 nearly completely towards
      State and Nationalized Enterprises.

104   As will be seen below, in 1972 the situation changed.

105   The public's preferred cash/deposit ratio is defined as the ratio
      between notes and coins and total money in the hands of the private
      sector.

106   As will be discussed below, these phenomena are themselves effects
      mainly of the large expansion in the money supply.

107   Source: ODEPLAN, Cuentas Nacionales de Chile 1960-75, Santiago, Chile.

108   The payments to labour include the employers' contribution to Social
      Security.

109   Source: same as note 107.

110   Detailed information can be found in internal memoranda of the Central
      Bank.

111   This uncertainty was exacerbated by the opposition's 'campaign of
      terror' described above.

112   Source: Banco Central de Chile, Boletín Mensual No. 599, Enero 1978.
      The average price of copper fell 23.2% between 1970 and 1971.

113   For more detailed accounts, see for example S. de Vylder, Chile
      1970-73, op.cit. and Instituto de Economia La economía chilena en
      1972, op.cit. and I. Roxborough, P. O'Brien and J. Roddick, Chile: The
      State and Revolution, Macmillan, 1977.

114   The crucial role of the anticipated rate of increase of prices in
      determining the demand for money in situations of hyper-inflation is
      clearly brought out in M. Kalecki, 'A model of hyper-inflation', The
      Manchester School of Economic and Social Studies, Vol. 130, 1962.

115   For an interesting discussion (both theoretical and empirical, with
      case studies including the Chilean one) of supply policy and
      rationing, see K. Griffin and J. James, Supply Management Problems in
      the Context of a Basic Needs Strategy, A Report prepared for the World
      Bank, Queen Elizabeth House, Oxford, February 1978.

116   According to de Vylder, op.cit. in 1973 the number of families in
      Gran Santiago (where the system was most developed) receiving
      commodity baskets from DINAC once a week or once every two weeks never
      exceeded 100,000 to 130,000 (c. 10% of families in Gran Santiago); the
      baskets containing only a limited selection of groceries. The public
      serviced by the state supermarkets was also very limited.

117   According to Griffin and James's analysis, op.cit., nearly complete
      state control over distribution is a necessary, though not sufficient
      condition, for underdeveloped countries to successfully redistribute
      goods via some scheme of comprehensive rationing.

118   Based on personal experience and visits to these enterprises.

119   Source: ODEPLAN, Cuentas Nacionales 1960-75, op.cit. This estimate
      incorporates revised price indexes for 1973, which may underestimate
      1973 inflation.

120   For a good discussion of Popular Unity's problems in the copper
      sector, as well as for the external sector in general, see A. Guardia
      Basso, 'Structural Transformations in Chile's Economy and in its
      System of External Relations', and F. Faynzylber, 'The External Sector
      and the Policies of the Unidad Popular Government', in S. Sideri
      (ed.), op.cit.

121   According to Guardia Basso, the index price for Chilean imports (base
      1970 = 100) was 105 in 1971 and 109 in 1972.

122   Source: Boletín del Banco Central, Octubre 1975.

123   In the case of all creditor nations (except the USA) and of private
      American and European banks, bilateral agreements were reached after a
      general re-negotiation. With the US government no agreement was
      reached. After the conversations had broken down completely, Chile
      decided to suspend unilaterally all debt servicing to American public
      institutions. For details of the re-negotiation, as well as
      evaluations of it, see Exposición sobre la política económica del
      Gobierno y del Estado de la Hacienda Pública, 16.11.1972, Ministerio
      de Hacienda, Santiago, 1972. Also see among others Guardia Basso,
      op.cit.

124   More details can be found for example in Exposición sobre la política
      económica del Gobierno y del Estado de la Hacienda Pública; op.cit.
      and in F. Faynzylber, op.cit.

125   Based on Central Bank data, Guardia Basso estimates that in real

terms, imports increased by 1.1% in 1971 and by 4.5% in 1972. ECLA estimates that in 1973, imports in real terms grew by slightly over 3 per cent.   Source: ECLA, Economic Survey of Latin America, 1973, op.cit.

126 Source: Balance Consolidado del Sector Público de Chile. Años 71 - 72 - Enero - Sept. 1973 y Período 1970-Sept. 1973, op.cit. Increases include wages and salaries, social recruiting payments and family allowances.

127 We are not including workers' incomes in the newly nationalized enterprises here, due to their relatively small importance within the total in 1971 and due to lack of precise data. This would increase our figure.

128 As was seen above ideological and political elements as well as mistakes by the government in those areas also played an important role in alienating the small and medium entrepreneurs. On this subject, see for example the article by S. Bitar, 'Interaccion entre economia y politica'; also see some of the ex-post critical evaluations made by Popular Unity parties; for example, J. Gazmuri, Aprender las lecciones del Pasado para construir el Futuro. Ediciones Barco de Papel, Rome, 1977.

129 See data in Odeplan, Cuentas Nacionales de Chile, 1960 - 75, op.cit.

130 A good numerical discussion of the incompatibilities between income redistribution and growth targets in the period can be found in A. Foxley and O. Munoz, 'Income redistribution, economic growth and social structure: the case of Chile', Income Distribution in Latin America, (ed.) A. Foxley. Cambridge University Press, 1976.

131 In Chile, re-adjustment of wages and salaries, both for the private and public sector, were by law at least equal to the former year's inflation - as measured by the retail price index.

132 A simulation model made in the Ministry of Finance attempted to measure the impact on inflation of such a weighted increase in prices of state and nationalized enterprises for 1973. The model concluded that with higher prices in these enterprises, inflation in 1973 would be slightly lower than with alternative lower prices; furthermore, inflation would decrease by 1974, whereas with lower prices in nationalized enterprises inflation would increase in 1974.

Source: Ministerio de Hacienda. Perspectivas del APS y el resto de la economía en 1973 y algunas proposiciones generales de política, Mimeo, 1973.

133 Source: Claes Croner and Oriana Lazo, 'El Area de propiedad Social en la Industria', La Economía Chilena en 1971, op.cit. above.

134 Between January and July 1972, retail prices grew by 33.2%; during the same period in 1971, retail prices had grown by a mere 11.5%.

135 Source: Diego Fleischmann, 'El costo nominal del credito bancario 1952-71', Mimeo, Ceplan, Santiago de Chile, 1972. The nominal cost of credit includes the maximum interest rate charged by the banks plus tax surcharges on it. The retail price index is used as a deflator to obtain the real cost of credit.

136 The interest rate considered here is the maximum one. Some special credits were granted at lower rates.

137   Source: <u>Boletín Mensual</u>, Banco Central, October 1975.

138   Data for previous years: R. Ffrench-Davies, <u>Políticas económicas en Chile</u>...., op.cit. above.

139   Due to problems of lags, it would be very difficult to make a similar estimate for 1972.   However, from the above discussion it can be concluded that in 1972, large changes, particularly in those policies over which the Executive had a discretionary effect, were feasible and could have greatly diminished the financial disequilibria.

140   Data based on Table 5.XI.

141   I wish to thank Ricardo Ffrench-Davies for a useful discussion and suggestions on the subject.

142   Based on personal experience and interview material.

6

CONCLUSIONS

In the experiences studied above, the view that short-term economic and financial policies have little importance during the preliminary transition to socialism was very influential. This is related to the fact that socialists base their economic policy on a diagnosis of the malfunctioning of the capitalist economy, tending to ignore those elements within the existing system, such as market links between economic units, which can be both positive and useful during the transition to socialism[1]. However, market links are necessary in this phase to continue the functions of both production and distribution, particularly while there is no alternative mechanism. For the market links to perform these functions, and for the rapid construction of an effective system of planning and management, a certain degree of stability in the value of money is required; this implies limits for financial policies. As they underestimate the role which market links can play in the pre-transition, socialist policy-makers undervalue the role of money and finance in this phase. Furthermore, as discussed in Chapter I, most Marxist discussions on the role of money in the transition have been so abstract that they have obscured rather than illuminated the concrete issues faced by countries beginning the transition to socialism.

Social scientists and politicians on the Left tend to concentrate their efforts and expertize — both in theoretical work and during policy making — on structural reforms. Such large emphasis on structural reforms diverts theoretical attention and operative capacity from short-term and financial issues, where a serious gap is left. This is often linked to the belief that structural reforms, (i.e. nationalization and land reform) will by themselves, lead to or contribute substantially to the solution of short-term problems. A good example of simplistic views on the link between structural reforms and short-term solutions to financial disequilibria can be found in views on inflation. In Czechoslovakia in 1946, the Communist representative of the State Planning Office said: 'in the People's Democracy, because it is a planned economy, there can be no inflation unless the authorities wish it'; (for source, see Chapter IV, footnote 27); in 1970 Chile, the Popular Unity programme stated: 'The struggle against inflation is basically resolved by structural changes' and promised: 'We will control prices and stop inflation by immediately setting up the new economic structure'. The similarity of the views is noteworthy! Furthermore, in both cases, (as at the beginning of the Soviet Revolution, see Chapter 2, Section II.2) the Left believed that nationalization of large enterprises would allow the state to capture a large financial surplus, helping it finance the Budget deficit and control inflation. In fact, in the three cases, nationalized industry initially suffered important losses, and required additional working capital; this implied an initial additional burden on the Budget, leading to increased inflationary pressures. The Left seems reluctant to accept that however essential and positive structural reforms may be for the long-term evolution of the economy under socialism, they may often accentuate rather than solve short-term problems, especially in the financial sphere. In particular, as the three case studies show, often during the preliminary transition to socialism, an increase in the size of the state sector though implying an increase in the potential financial surplus the state could capture, may in fact coincide with a decline of the financial surplus controlled by the state.

Furthermore, both in the Czechoslovak and the Chilean case, when growing financial disequilibria developed in state and nationalized enterprises, the Left-wing parties proposed to control them mainly by further structural changes, such as bank re-organization (transformation strongly opposed in both cases by the opposition). Particularly given these political circumstances, insufficient attention and support was given - both by the government authorities and the political leadership - to the imposition of global limits on credit to state-owned enterprises; these could have been exercised given existing attributions of the National (Central) Bank and national banks. Bank re-organization, although helpful for implementing such macro-economic controls, was far from indispensable for such controls[2].

In Chapter 1 we discussed the main reasons why appropriate financial policies have a particularly important role to play in the preliminary transition to socialism. During this phase the most crucial task for the Left is to gain and consolidate political power; it is therefore essential to pursue financial and economic policies functional to the achievement of the particular political strategy defined by the revolutionary forces to gain and maintain power. An example of such functional links can be found in the economic and financial policies pursued during the early stage of NEP; as we discussed in Chapter 3, the Soviet State could only extract the agricultural surplus crucial for it to maintain power by obtaining the peasantry's support. To obtain this support, it was necessary to ensure the restoration of market links between agriculture and industry. Although often criticized for being conservative, the stabilization policy pursued at the beginning of Nep in fact contributed towards the viability of the market, the economic mechanism chosen by the political leadership at that stage to achieve its political strategy[3]).

An important distinction must be made between cases when there was a possibility of alternative policies to those pursued and cases where options did not exist. As we discussed in Chapter 2, there was very little scope for alternative financial policies to those followed by the Bolsheviks during 1917-21; the main elements determining large financial disequilibria escaped the Bolsheviks' control; they had their origin in the fact that the Bolshevik Revolution - with its socialist aims - had taken place in the Soviet Union, at that particular historical moment. Similar situations may arise - or have already arisen - in cases when a Socialist revolution is carried out or defended by widespread use of violence; the resulting disruption in production, destruction of assets, high military expenditure and difficulties for taxation may make large financial disequilibria unavoidable. (Even though it should be noted that the Soviet Revolution faced particularly adverse circumstances such as no external allies and a very difficult economic and financial situation inherited from World War I.)

When exogenous circumstances exist which make large financial disequilibria inevitable, a passive financial policy is the only alternative. In such cases however, it is essential to be aware of the severe disruptive effects which such large disequilibria will have, and to attempt to minimize them by rapidly developing emergency mechanisms to replace market links in production and distribution, i.e. physical planning and rationing. Furthermore, large financial disequilibria - and emergency measures of administrative management of the economy - should not be justified ideologically as correct per se; such an attitude might risk delaying the introduction of different policies, more functional if new circumstances and a new political strategy arose.

In cases of a non-violent road to socialism, there will in several aspects usually be a larger range of options for financial and short-term economic policy, as production will probably not be greatly disrupted; however, the pursuit of correct financial policies is much more crucial in such cases. In a parliamentary transition, the government may not have sufficient power over the state and society to implement mechanisms - such as rationing or a Monetary Reform - which could control or reduce the negative effects of large financial disequilibria. Furthermore, these negative effects, i.e. very high levels of inflation and widespread scarcities, may easily increase the opposition to the government of important social groups and/or weaken the support of others. The political capital which the opposition and its media can extract from these problems will be particularly harmful to a

government attempting a parliamentary road to Socialism and particularly
dangerous within a context where the socialist forces have a very incomplete
control of the state and face strong potential opposition from the Armed
Forces (which includes the possibility of a coup!).

The Chilean experience illustrates well the difficulties faced by a small,
dependent economy when it attempts a parliamentary road to socialism; this
reinforces the need in such cases to pursue carefully designed financial and
short-term economic policies functional to the political strategy adopted.
As we discussed in Chapter 5, the short-term economic and financial policies
pursued (leading to very rapid and large expansion of aggregate demand) was
clearly out of line with the gradual political strategy de facto chosen by
Popular Unity. It has been correctly argued that the Allende Government was
unlucky because of exogenous factors, such as an unexpected sharp
deterioration of its terms of trade which coincided with the 'invisible
blockade' (the curtailment of foreign official and private credit,
particularly from the United States); these factors obviously made
short-term economic management more difficult. However, such negative
changes in the international economic environment are not unusual, and any
small, underdeveloped dependent economy beginning a transition to socialism
will be particularly vulnerable to them. In designing its economic
policies, it must therefore consider and plan for such unfavourable
elements; this should be easier in cases like the Chilean one, where there
were no inherited large financial disequilibria and the economy initially
had relatively high foreign exchange reserves, industrial stocks and
industrial idle capacity.

As we discussed in the Introduction and have illustrated in the experiences
studied, large financial disequilibria have particularly negative effects
for the preliminary transition to socialism. As we saw in more detail in
Chapter 5, growth in aggregate demand, via wage or government deficit
increases will have positive effects for a government attempting a
transition to socialism while the economy can respond by increasing output
and employment (this has been called the Kaleckian range). Once idle
resources are completely used up or limits arise to further expansion of
output, additional increases of aggregate demand will lead to a growing gap
between total demand and supply.

The size of the resulting gap between supply and demand (both aggregate and
in specific sectors) will depend not only on the magnitude of the expansion
and change in the composition of total demand, but also on the extent to
which supply can expand. Existing constraints to a short-term expansion of
output will probably become more serious as a result of the changes in
property and management that occur during the preliminary transition to
socialism. In the cases studied here (as well as in other cases of
pre-transition) the gap was particularly serious in agricultural foods,
because demand for them tended to grow rapidly largely as a result of
increased incomes of urban workers while food supply (particularly to the
cities) tended to grow little or even decline as a result of agrarian
reform.

The gap between demand and supply will have to be bridged by inflation
and/or scarcities and/or imports.

As we have seen, very high levels of inflation disrupt the operation of the
market essential in the initial phases of the transition, as well as making
planning much more difficult; such levels may also worsen income
distribution unless a comprehensive system of rationing can be established.
Scarcities, queueing and black markets have equally negative consequences
for a process of transition to socialism; they are time-consuming and
provoke widespread irritation; they lead to an erratic (and often unfair)
distribution of goods and services, as well as to an atmosphere of

speculation and corruption. Large increases in imports - if unaccompanied by corresponding export growth and/or net inflow of foreign credit - may exhaust foreign exchange reserves; this would increase future scarcities by reducing the supply of imported goods. As foreign exchange reserves reach low levels, the government becomes increasingly vulnerable to pressures from foreign governments and international financial institutions.

Large financial disequilibria will allow the country to live above its means for a time, thus obscuring the urgent need for the political leadership to make explicit choices on the investment and consumption levels of different groups.

If financial disequilibria become very large, they may challenge the viability of the economy and of the socialist government. In such cases, they may be one of the important factors leading to the socialist government's downfall, either through elections or, more probably, through violent counter-revolution (see Chapter 5); recent historical experiences suggest that very large financial disequilibria will strengthen those social forces most strongly opposed to socialism and more committed to strict economic orthodoxy and 'free-market' economics[4].

As we have seen in the case studies, financial disequilibria are specially disruptive to the main aims of a pre-transition to socialism under particular conditions. First, financial disequilibria will have very harmful effects when they are very large, thus implying large growth in aggregate demand. Thus, in the Czechoslovak case, although financial disequilibria were significant, they were not so large as to threaten complete disruption of the economy. Second, financial disequilibria are more harmful when supply (particularly of necessities) cannot expand much - or even declines - in the short-term. Third, financial disequilibria can be much more harmful in parliamentary pre-transition to socialism, especially if the question of power has not been resolved, cannot be decided quickly and when an extra-parliamentary power confrontation will probably not favour the Left; this is well illustrated by the Chilean case. The Czechoslovak experience is in this respect very a typical of a parliamentary road to socialism, as special political elements favouring the Communist Party had an overwhelming importance in Czechoslovak developments; particularly significant was the international context (the fact that it was accepted by the Allies that C.S.S.R. would be in the Soviet sphere of influence), as well as the Communists' influence over the army and police and their large, organized, and closely controlled working class support. Fourth, financial disequilibria are less important if comprehensive alternative mechanisms can be rapidly and efficiently developed so that resources are physically allocated. Again there is a strong contrast between the Czechoslovak and the Chilean experiences; in Czechoslovakia, a system of rationing was inherited from the War; in Chile, as we discussed in Chapter 5, there were serious political and technical difficulties for implementing a comprehensive rationing system.

Finally, financial disequilibria are less harmful in the short-term if the country has sufficient access to <u>net</u> inflows of credit and aid from abroad. This will depend on the willingness of socialist countries to supply sufficient external finance, particularly before and during the crucial moments of struggle for power (as occurred in the Czechoslovak case); it will also depend on the extent to which different capitalist governments and financial institutions will curtail new credits, possibly causing an important net outflow of funds, (particularly if the country is already heavily indebted and has high short-term debt service commitments[5]). Recently, the diversity of positions assumed by capitalist governments and the rapid development of private capital markets seems to open up some new possibilities of finance from the capitalist world. In any case, large reliance on foreign finance from any source to sustain a balance of trade

disequilibrium for a long period may be particularly hard to obtain for a
country attempting to begin its transition to socialism, as the Chilean case
illustrates. Even if it were feasible, a large level of external financial
inflows may be undesirable to a government beginning the transition to
socialism, as it may make it too vulnerable to foreign pressures.

Given the particularly harmful effects which large financial disequilibria
have on economies attempting the preliminary transition to socialism, it
seems important to implement policies at this stage which control the growth
of aggregate demand. As we have seen in the case studies, in situations of
struggle for power and preliminary transition to socialism, there is a
tendency towards large increases in government expenditures, difficulties
for increasing taxation and therefore growing fiscal deficits; it is
therefore essential for the government to deliberately pursue policies which
will allow the state to capture larger financial surplus from the private
sector; this will allow it to rely less on a large state deficit financed by
money issue as a tax, which leads to financial disequilibria and which after
a time will necessarily exhaust itself[6]. We shall discuss specific
policies for reducing the government's budget deficit, which were
insufficiently or incorrectly used in some or all of the cases studied; we
will refer particularly to prices of state and nationalized enterprises,
interest rates in nationalized banks and taxation policy; finally, we shall
examine incomes policy, with particular reference to wages and salaries in
the state sector.

It is interesting that in the three cases studied a common pattern emerges
of price increases in state-owned enterprises which were well below the
average for private enterprises. Similar policies were pursued, for
example, in Great Britain after the Second World War during the Labour
Government! The governments may have hoped to help reduce inflation by
controlling prices of state-owned enterprises; however, given the conditions
of excessive aggregate demand prevalent in the three cases and the
importance of private enterprise, particularly in retail trade, the main
effect was the transfer of financial surplus from state-owned to private
enterprises. This had several undesirable implications for the socialist
governments, including an additional unnecessary burden on public finance
and the economic strengthening of the private sector (the latter point
should have been clear to anyone who studied Preobrazhensky's works!).

More appropriate price policies for state-owned enterprises would, in the
cases studied above, have helped reduce the public sector deficit; it would
have strengthened the state sector and also perhaps financed larger
investment in state-owned enterprises. Such measures could have been easily
implemented, not only in the Soviet and Czechoslovak case, but also in
Chile, as price policy was controlled exclusively by the Executive.
Undesired effects on income distribution could have been avoided or limited
to a great extent by discriminatory price increases, with large increases in
non-essential consumer goods.

A particular case of incorrect 'pricing' policy in nationalized enterprises
was the very negative real interest rate charged by recently nationalized
banks to the private sector in Chile. This policy was both incorrect in
terms of conventional economic analysis and disfunctional to the political
strategy adopted. Popular Unity economists had in the past correctly
criticized private banks for being instruments used by the private sector to
obtain subsidized credit at negative interest rates. It seems surprising
that once the banks had been nationalized by the Allende Government, the
cost of credit became even more negative than before; thus, the nationalized
banks transferred more surplus than before to the remaining private sector.
The explanation seems to lie in Popular Unity's fear that increases in
interest rates would generate inflationary cost pressures; however, by 1972,
inflation was basically demand-generated, and the negative cost of credit

was feeding inflation via a larger state sector deficit.

Another area of financial policy whose importance is often under-estimated
or overlooked in preliminary transition to socialism - both as a means of
obtaining larger state revenue and for political use - is taxation. In the
Soviet Union, mainly during the first year after the Revolution, indirect
taxation could have raised higher revenue, had the traditional ideological
opposition to it been overcome. Through attaching greater importance to
taxation, under NEP, higher direct taxes could have been extracted,
particularly from well-to-do-peasants. The taxation policy pursued in the
countryside was justified by the political leadership as part of necessary
concessions to maintain the peasants' political support and willingness to
market their surplus. As we discussed in detail in Chapter 3, the
exaggeration of tax concessions to the richer peasants was in fact
disfunctional to the Bolsheviks economic and political aims, as it seems to
have decreased their need to market their produce and strengthened their
power and influence. Similarly, in Chile, it was wrongly believed that the
tax concessions granted to small and medium private entrepreneurs would be
an important element in obtaining their economic and political support. As
discussed above, this social group's behaviour seemed determined more by
factors such as lack of future security for their property; it was
negatively influenced by the effects of large financial disequilibria, which
concessions to them had helped increase.

On the whole, in Chile insufficient technical and political effort was put
into taxation initiatives. During 1971, the Executive did not display
sufficient technical initiative in presenting taxation bills to Congress;
neither did it make sufficient political issue of the opposition's rejection
or delay in approving these bills in Congress. When in 1972 and 1973,
Popular Unity presented important taxation initiatives, (which were both
progressive and could have represented a high revenue yield), they were
rejected with increasing zeal by the opposition, as a result of growing
political tension in the country. Particularly at that time, Popular Unity
should have reacted more strongly; it should have shown - by campaigns in
the media and in discussions within the trade union movement - the class
content of the opposition's attitudes. Even if Congress' attitude had
remained unchanged, important political capital could have been extracted
from the fact that in a time of economic difficulties (fall in the price of
Chile's main export, 'invisible blockade' by the United States, etc.) the
opposition refused to 'let the wealthy pay', thus contributing to financial
disequilibria and its negative effects. Very useful lessons could have been
learned here from the Czechoslovak Communists' initiative on the
millionaire's tax discussed in detail above. Such a simple issue, with a
clear class content, might have helped Popular Unity regain the initiative
on mass mobilization. Had Popular Unity been able to modify Congress'
attitude, a relatively significant decrease in the state deficit might have
been achieved, as well as a political triumph.

In each case of pre-transition, there naturally are different political
limits to increases in taxation (which may vary in time, if the socialist
government's power over the state or the class alliance on which it is based
change). However, from the cases studied, it seems clear that correct
taxation policy can have a far more important potential role for extracting
surplus from the private sector during preliminary transition to socialism
than most economists on the left believe. There is also important political
potential in the use of taxation issues, which show the inherent
contradictions between the interests of the majority of the people and the
very wealthy; this is well illustrated by the example of the millionaire's
tax in Czechoslovakia. Former experience, including that of the
millionaire's tax, seems to show however that the resources available for
potential taxation and redistribution from the 'very rich' are relatively
limited. Therefore, it may become necessary also to increase taxation of

the richer sectors amongst the middle groups.

One of the main factors leading to an excessively large and rapid expansion of aggregate demand in any attempt at parliamentary pre-transition to socialism will almost inevitably be the pressure for higher wages and salaries, particularly in the rapidly growing state sector. As we saw in Chapter 5, Chile certainly provides a good example.

Undoubtedly, the political leadership's lack of clarity on this issue (both before and after the Left had begun to govern) carries an important part of the responsibility for excessive wage increases; thus Popular Unity hardly attempted to control wage increases initially. It was not made sufficiently clear to workers and state employees that the future long-term benefits of socialist construction could not be granted them during the first year of the transition. Popular Unity did not make enough effort to impose limits on incomes increases, particularly through the influential CUT (trade unions council) where the Left was so strongly represented and through unions controlled by the Left. Neither were financial institutions (i.e. Central Bank and Ministry of Finance) given enough power and leverage to refuse financing excessive income increases in the state sector.

However, the possibility of regulating wage increases in experiences such as the Chilean one does not depend only on the political leadership's willingness to implement them, but to a great extent on its power within the society to impose these measures of restraint. In Chile, the trade unions and employees' associations were powerful; they were backed by different political parties (within and outside Popular Unity) competing for their support both in union and national elections; the trade unions council had important - but seriously limited - influence on individual unions. This contrasts sharply with the situation in the Soviet Union under NEP, where the only existing Party - the Communist one - exerted important political control over the workers via the trade unions. As we saw, on the occasions when workers resisted government wage policy, the trade union leaders followed the party line, opposing both the workers' demands and their strikes.

An intermediate situation arose in Czechoslovakia, where workers' incomes grew more than the government had planned, but there was no incomes explosion. Undoubtedly, the workers were more willing to exercize restraint, wishing to contribute to post-war reconstruction; there was much less political challenge than in Chile to official policy, as all legal parties formed part of the government. Finally, Czechoslovak post-war trade union structure was highly centralized, allowing great concentration of power in the central organ, URO, which was controlled by the Communist Party. The inability of the public employees in 1948 to obtain larger incomes increases than the Communist Party wished to grant - even though they had the support of all the other parties - illustrates well the powerful Communist influence in Czechoslovakia at the time on incomes policy, achieved largely by their control over the centralized trade union movement.

We can conclude that in parliamentary pre-transitions to socialism, avoidance of an incomes explosion will require not only great skill and clarity from the political and government leadership, but also a high level of political education and conscience of workers and state employees. As policies cannot be imposed from above by administrative methods or by coercion, persuasion must play an important role. Political backing for financial institutions so as to avoid financing incomes increases which surpass officially agreed guidelines between the government and the central trade union council would also be useful. The design of policies which link real wage increases to approval of larger taxation by Congress (such as was achieved in the Price Intervention Fund in Czechoslovakia) may also be helpful in such circumstances, as the government would grant higher wages only if the opposition approved higher taxation. That type of measure should probably have been explored far more in the Chilean case. In such situations, greater technical effort on measures should be placed where the Executive's attempts to decrease financial disequilibria and increase the surplus captured by the state can be easily implemented, as it has discretionary power over them. Adequate price policies for state-owned enterprises are perhaps the best example, at least for the Chilean case.

Incomes policy is one area of economic policy where there is a particularly sharp difference between cases where the socialist party or parties has practically complete control over the state and society and cases where much control is very partial. The feasibility of particular financial policies (whether they be in the field of incomes, taxation, prices or others) will depend not only on the particular institutional arrangements of a country, but also on the control over the state apparatus which the socialist government has, at a particular period. The challenges tend to be greater in a parliamentary transition, as the technical options are more often restricted by political constraints and mistakes tend to be more costly in their economic and political effects. However, a successful transition to socialism which would preserve somewhat more pluralism in society during the transition (as well as afterwards) than existing state socialist societies have done would imply a great political achievement.

As we saw, in 1919, the Soviet Comissar for Finance, Kristinskii, apologized for speaking on finance, as it should not exist in a socialist community. One hopes that in future experiences of pre-transitions to socialism, economists in Ministries of Finance, Central Banks and trade union organizations, will be too busy with the complex and important task of designing imaginative financial policies - functional to the achievement of the goals of that particular stage, given the economic and political constraints - to have the time or the willingness to apologize for their work.

In fact, a recent very encouraging attitude in this field is provided by the Sandinista Revolution in Nicaragua. Concern with the relevance of financial equilibria, as well as awareness of the existing resource constraints and the harmful effects of surpassing these constraints in a preliminary transition to socialism is clearly and repeatedly expressed in their first Plan, Plan de Reactivación Económica en Beneficio del Pueblo, Managua, 1980. The first task defined for the defence, consolidation and defence of the Nicaraguan revolution is that of reactivating the economy so as to benefit the people, (increase production, while income is being re-distributed). The Plan emphasizes (Page 12) that:

> ...To achieve the former, it is essential to maintain the process of economic recovery within the limits imposed by these fundamental balances: the macro-economic balance, the external balance and the fiscal-financial balance. That is, it is necessary to increase the levels of popular consumption and of state accumulation within the limits of national and international markets, without excessively increasing the country's foreign debt and without causing an inflationary process that would harm precisely the main beneficiary of the Programme, 'the Working People'

The existence of limits to the expansion of supply is clearly perceived. On p.22, it is stressed that: '...The aim is to expand, restructuring social demand, but realising that there are short-term and structural limits to the internal supply of goods...' On page 24, the point is very clearly made that: 'Economic policy will be flexible, but it will be inflexible in the maintenance of external and fiscal-financial balances. The presence of the world economy and of the laws of the market which prevail in our economy, create a general situation characterized by tensions and instability between aggregate supply and demand; between financial sources and uses; between fiscal income and revenues; between recovery of production and consumption; between inflows and outflows of foreign exchange. These tensions are caused by the conjunctural and structural limits to the expansion of production, as well as by the unequal, spatial, sectoral and temporal distribution of the recovery.'

The Sandinista plan stresses not only their need for respecting financial balances, but also the specific characteristics which these balances have in a popular planned economy. Thus, in p.117, the point is made that:

> the recovery of the economy based on a new pattern of consumption runs the risk of breaking the internal and external balances, due to excessive aggregate demand, creating inflation and a foreign exchange imbalance...The fiscal-financial balance is therefore central in this programme...Specifically, the pressure of public expenditure generates excessive monetary issue, or alternatively, larger external debt. The solution of this problem in the reformist capitalist economies is usually inflation for wage goods, import of non-essential consumer goods and curtailment of public expenditure; in the popular planned economy it must be the import of basic consumer goods, higher prices for conspicuous goods and an increase in the taxation pressure. The difference between these two styles of controlling aggregate demand depends on what groups or social classes will pay for stabilization. In our case, the cost of stabilization will not fall exclusively in the popular strata, as has traditionally happened...

On page 126, the Plan explains that:

> within a programmed economy, the 'monetary discipline' has a completely different character than in a market economy, as it serves to adjust private consumption, adapting it to the necessary level of public expenditure and popular consumption, instead of reducing the real salary so as to increase capitalist consumption and investment.

Finally, the Plan stresses clearly the potential dangers of large disequilibria. On p.129, it concludes that: 'Any deviation which is not rapidly compensated with an appropriate adjustment may convert itself rapidly into a serious disequilibrium, which may not only inhibit the recovery but the transition itself.'

Clarity on financial and economic matters, such as the Sandinistas have shown till now, will hopefully contribute both to the success of their own revolution, as well as to an understanding of these important issues by socialists in other countries.

Notes

1   This seems true for socialist policy-makers, not only in the cases
      studied above, but also in other experiences, such as the Cuban one
      (see B. Pollitt's comments, quoted in Chapter 5, footnote 17).

2   The possibility in preliminary transition to socialism of effective
      macro-economic controls of credit to state-owned enterprises without
      bank re-organization is illustrated by the 1947 Polish experience (see
      Chapter 4, section II, 2.b.iii).

3   As we discussed in Chapter 3, the character of the stabilization
      programme under NEP implied certain decisions about the high level of
      unemployment and limited subsidies to the unemployed which seem
      contradictory with Marxist principles.   It was argued above that
      stabilization might have been achieved by other measures, more
      compatible with socialist principles.

4   Chile in 1973 illustrates this well; so did Indonesia in the mid
      1960s. For a discussion of these issues, see S. Griffith-Jones, 'The
      Evolution of External Finance, Economic Policy and Development in
      Chile, 1973-78'. Discussion Paper, IDS, Sussex. Thorpe and Whitehead
      eds., op.cit. seem also to take a similar position. Thus, on p.265,
      they conclude that 'It is almost certainly no accident that the three
      countries out of their six case studies which reverted most fully to
      liberal economic policies were those which experienced annual
      inflation rates of more than 100 per cent - Chile (over 500 per cent
      in 1974), Argentina (over 400 per cent in 1976) and Uruguay (107 per
      cent in 1974).'

5   The alternative of repudiating all foreign loans to capitalist
      governments and financial institutions may have too high a cost in an
      increasingly interdependent world. This important and complex subject
      is outside the scope of this study.

6   See Chapters 2 and 3 for an illustration of the limits of money issue
      as a tax; also see J.M. Keynes, A Tract on Monetary Reform, op.cit.
      for a simple and perceptive treatment of the subject.